THE EVOLUTION OF CLOUD COMPUTING

BCS, THE CHARTERED INSTITUTE FOR IT

BCS, The Chartered Institute for IT, is committed to making IT good for society. We use the power of our network to bring about positive, tangible change. We champion the global IT profession and the interests of individuals engaged in that profession, for the benefit of all.

Exchanging IT expertise and knowledge

The Institute fosters links between experts from industry, academia and business to promote new thinking, education and knowledge sharing.

Supporting practitioners

Through continuing professional development and a series of respected IT qualifications, the Institute seeks to promote professional practice tuned to the demands of business. It provides practical support and information services to its members and volunteer communities around the world.

Setting standards and frameworks

The Institute collaborates with government, industry and relevant bodies to establish good working practices, codes of conduct, skills frameworks and common standards. It also offers a range of consultancy services to employers to help them adopt best practice.

Become a member

Over 70,000 people including students, teachers, professionals and practitioners enjoy the benefits of BCS membership. These include access to an international community, invitations to a roster of local and national events, career development tools and a quarterly thought-leadership magazine. Visit www.bcs.org/membership to find out more.

Further Information
BCS, The Chartered Institute for IT,
First Floor, Block D,
North Star House, North Star Avenue,
Swindon, SN2 1FA, United Kingdom.
T +44 (0) 1793 417 424
F +44 (0) 1793 417 444
www.bcs.org/contact

http://shop.bcs.org/

THE EVOLUTION OF CLOUD COMPUTING
How to plan for change

Clive Longbottom

Published by BCS Learning & Development Ltd, a wholly owned subsidiary of BCS, The Chartered Institute for IT, First Floor, Block D, North Star House, North Star Avenue, Swindon, SN2 1FA, UK.
www.bcs.org

Paperback ISBN: 978-1-78017-358-0
PDF ISBN: 978-1-78017-359-7
ePUB ISBN: 978-1-78017-360-3
Kindle ISBN: 978-1-78017-361-0

British Cataloguing in Publication Data.
A CIP catalogue record for this book is available at the British Library.

Disclaimer:
The views expressed in this book are those of the authors and do not necessarily reflect the views of the Institute or BCS Learning & Development Ltd except where explicitly stated as such. Although every care has been taken by the authors and BCS Learning & Development Ltd in the preparation of the publication, no warranty is given by the authors or BCS Learning & Development Ltd as publisher as to the accuracy or completeness of the information contained within it and neither the authors nor BCS Learning & Development Ltd shall be responsible or liable for any loss or damage whatsoever arising by virtue of such information or any instructions or advice contained within this publication or by any of the aforementioned.

Publisher's acknowledgements
Reviewers: Andy Wilton and Matthew McGrory
Publisher: Ian Borthwick
Commissioning Editor: Rebecca Youé
Production Manager: Florence Leroy
Project Manager: Anke Ueberberg
Copy-editor: Hazel Bird
Proofreader: David Palser
Indexer: Jonathan Burd
Cover design: Alex Wright
Cover image: Friedrich Böhringer

Typeset by Lapiz Digital Services, Chennai, India.

CONTENTS

List of figures   ix
About the Author   x
Foreword   xi
Acknowledgements   xii
Abbreviations   xiii
Glossary   xvii
Preface   xxiii

PART 1 LOOKING BACK: CLOUD COMPUTING IN CONTEXT   **1**

1.   BACKGROUND   **3**
         Looking backward to look forward   3
         The price war   4
         The rise of the PC   5
         Changing to a distributed model   6
         Web computing to the fore   7
         The rise of the age of chaos   8
         Virtualisation, service-oriented architecture and grid computing   8
         The role of standards   10
         Summary   11

**PART 2 THE CLOUD NOW: CLOUD AT ITS SIMPLEST, AS IT SHOULD BE
        IMPLEMENTED**   **13**

2.   THE CLOUD   **15**
         Back to the future   15
         Summary   21

3.   WHY CLOUD?   **23**
         Resource utilisation   23
         Cost   26
         Meeting future needs   28
         Workload portability   29
         High availability   31
         Summary   31

4.   BASIC CLOUD PLATFORMS   **32**
         Popular cloud platforms   32
         The architecture of a cloud   36

	Open compute project	39
	Summary	40
5.	**ALTERNATIVE CLOUD PLATFORMS**	**41**
	Private and public cloud offerings	41
	Container platforms	45
	The current chaos of cloud	47
	Summary	52
6.	**ALTERNATIVE CLOUD MODELS**	**54**
	Cloud broker	54
	Cloud aggregator	55
	Summary	56
7.	**MAIN TYPES OF SaaS CLOUD SERVICES**	**58**
	SaaS cloud services	58
	File share and sync	59
	Shadow IT	61
	Summary	64
8.	**WHERE SHOULD A CLOUD PLATFORM RESIDE?**	**65**
	Private clouds	65
	Where should private clouds be based?	65
	Hybrid clouds	66
	The organisational value chain	68
	The use of colocation facilities	69
	Data centre and cloud tiering	70
	Summary	73
9.	**PAYING FOR CLOUD SERVICES**	**74**
	The battle between cost levels and their predictability, and business flexibility	74
	Basic cost models	75
	Increasing cost model complexity	76
	Cost tiering	77
	Summary	80
PART 3	**THE VERY NEAR FUTURE: CLOUD AT A MORE COMPLEX LEVEL, AS YOU SHOULD BE IMPLEMENTING IT**	**81**
10.	**BUILDING THE RIGHT CLOUD**	**83**
	Mixing clouds	83
	Planning for workload migrations	84
	It's all about the process	85
	Summary	88
11.	**ISSUES WITH CLOUD COMPUTING**	**89**
	System availability	89
	Data security	91
	Performance	92

The need for standards and APIs   94
'Noisy neighbours'   95
The business issues of highly dynamic cloud-based systems   97
Software and usage licensing issues   99
The mirage of self-service   101
The cessation of service by a provider   102
Maintaining governance in a hybrid cloud   105
Summary   106

12. CLOUD AND THE 'CDs'   **107**
Why use CD?   107
DevOps flows   108
Summary   109

13. CREATING THE BUSINESS CASE FOR THE CLOUD   **111**
Total value proposition   111
Summary   118

14. SCALE OUT, SCALE UP AND SCALE THROUGH   **119**
Building the right cloud platform   119
The cloud and 'software defined'   121
The power of idempotency   122
Converged and hyperconverged systems   123
Summary   125

15. CLOUD AND DATA   **127**
Data sovereignty   127
Data flows   128
Database issues   129
Distance and latency   130
High availability   130
Summary   131

16. CLOUD SECURITY   **133**
The myth of data security in private data centres   133
Assume that security is breached   135
Data classification   136
The badly protected walled garden   138
The importance of multi-factor single sign-on   140
Edge security   142
Physical security   143
Summary   144

17. VIRTUALISATION, SHARABLE RESOURCES AND ELASTICITY   **145**
The lure of virtualisation   145
The move to cloud   146
Scaling for massive use: G-Cloud   148
Summary   149

18. THE CHANGE IN APPLICATIONS   151
     The death of the monolith   151
     The need for technical contracts   152
     Summary   155

19. APPLICATIONS, VIRTUAL MACHINES AND CONTAINERS   156
     The differences between virtual machines and containers   156
     The future for containers   160
     Summary   161

20. FULL AUDIT IS REQUIRED   162
     The importance of a full audit   162
     Summary   166

21. MONITORING, MEASURING AND MANAGING THE CLOUD   167
     Modern levels of standardisation and abstraction   167
     Choosing an over-arching system to manage chaos   168
     Automate for effectiveness and efficiency   169
     Summary   169

PART 4 THE FUTURE OF CLOUD: CLOUD AS YOU SHOULD BE PLANNING
        FOR IT IN THE FURTHER-OUT FUTURE   171

22. THE ULTIMATE FUTURE   173
     The evolution of the cloud   173
     Summary   174

23. IN CONCLUSION   175

     Index   176

LIST OF FIGURES

Figure 2.1	The sliding scale of ownership in different IT platform models	17
Figure 2.2	BS ISO/IEC 17788:2014 cloud service categories and cloud capability types	20
Figure 3.1	Variable workload model	24
Figure 4.1	Main AWS functional architecture	37
Figure 4.2	Main Microsoft Azure functional architecture	37
Figure 4.3	Main Google Cloud Platform functional architecture	38
Figure 4.4	Basic OpenStack functional architecture	39
Figure 6.1	Cloud broker	55
Figure 6.2	Cloud aggregator	56
Figure 8.1	Disconnected hybrid platform	67
Figure 8.2	Integrated hybrid platform	67
Figure 8.3	Simple value chain	68
Figure 9.1	Tiered costing	77
Figure 10.1	Bridging the capability gap	85
Figure 10.2	The process pyramid	87
Figure 11.1	The impact of data latency in different architectures	93
Figure 12.1	Conceptual flow chart of the DevOps process	109
Figure 13.1	Total value proposition: scope, resources and time	112
Figure 13.2	Total value proposition: value, risk and cost	113
Figure 13.3	Total value proposition: game theory	114
Figure 13.4	Total value proposition: game theory graphs	115
Figure 13.5	Calculator for total value proposition, total cost of ownership and return on investment	117
Figure 17.1	Aggregated virtualised workloads	146
Figure 17.2	Averaging out workloads in a private cloud	147
Figure 17.3	Averaging out workloads in a public cloud	148
Figure 19.1	Virtual machines and hypervisors	157
Figure 19.2	Containers	158
Figure 19.3	System containerisation	159
Figure 19.4	Microservice metadata containers	161
Figure 20.1	Microsoft Word metadata	165

ABOUT THE AUTHOR

Clive Longbottom is the founder of Quocirca Ltd, a group of industry analysts following the information technology and communication markets.

Clive trained as a chemical engineer and began his career in chemical research, working on diverse areas including anti-cancer drugs, car catalysts, low-NOx burners and hydrogen/oxygen fuel cells.

He moved into a range of technical roles, first implementing office-automation systems and writing applications for a global technology company before moving to a power-generation company, where he ran a team implementing office-automation systems for 17,500 people.

For a period of time, Clive was a consultant, running projects in the secure data transfer and messaging areas, before becoming an industry analyst for the US company META Group (now part of Gartner Inc).

Upon leaving META Group, Clive set up Quocirca to operate as a small group of like-minded analysts focusing on how technology can help an organisation from a business point of view, rather than focusing purely on the technology.

To Clive, everything is a process, and the technology chosen by an organisation should be there to optimise the manner in which its processes operate.

In the late 1990s, Clive wrote a report on the burgeoning application service provider market. The report predicted that the vast majority of these companies would fail, as they did not have sufficiently robust business models and were not adopting any level of standardisation. In the 2000s, Clive worked on many reports looking at the usage of grid computing and came up with a set of definitions as to the various possible grid models that could be adopted; these reflect the current models generally used around cloud computing today.

As cloud computing has become more widespread, Clive has continued to look at what has been happening and has worked with many technology companies in helping them to understand cloud computing and what it means to them.

In this book, Clive distils his views to explain not just what cloud computing is but what it can (and should) be, along with how it can be best implemented and how the business case for cloud can be best discussed with the business in terms that it can understand.

FOREWORD

Cloud has quickly become a prevalent and ubiquitous term in both the IT and business sectors, delivering affordable computing power to the masses and disrupting many companies and industry sectors. We are now experiencing velocity and acceleration of technology, with a breadth of it being empowered by cloud under the covers. The internet of things (IoT), mobile apps and Big Data, for example, are inherently cloud driven.

It is becoming increasingly important to understand cloud, not only as a technologist but also as a business analyst and leader, as this empowering technology medium changes our lives both in work and at home.

Cloud has been, and is, changing our consumer lives: who does not know of or use Amazon, Netflix, Ebay, Uber, Airbnb, Shazam, and the plethora of new world options presented to us? Of course, cloud also changes how we operate and engage in business. Vendors are fast migrating their own offerings to be cloud-focused; take Microsoft, Oracle and SAP as prime examples. Not to understand this, why it is happening and where we are going will increasingly reduce your value to any organisation as they look for more cloud-experienced and skilled staff.

A top ten topic on all CIO agendas is digital transformation, moving from the shackles of legacy technologies to adapt and adopt the new available and affordable, more flexible and agile offerings now presented. This change, whilst important and high on agendas, is not an easy one, and many directing and implementing the path are pioneering for themselves and their organisation.

Any guidance and context that can reduce risk and accelerate digitisation is a must-read, and here Clive provides real world experience and valuable information to empower you to better serve in this new cloud world and ensure you remain relevant to employment demands over the coming years.

Clive has provided a very readable foundation to fill those gaps that many have missed along their cloud journeys. This book gives us a better understanding of the why, how and what of the cloud world, so important to us all today. Notably, he explains in a digestible format some of the key cloud areas that I have seen others make complex and difficult to get to grips with.

A recommended read for all and anyone involved in the cloud sector, from beginner to expert, there is much to gain from Clive's contribution.

Ian Moyse, November 2017
Industry Cloud Influencer, Board Member Cloud Industry Forum & Eurocloud and recognised as #1 Global Cloud Social Influencer 2015–2017 (Onalytica)

ACKNOWLEDGEMENTS

All company and product names used throughout this document are acknowledged, where applicable, as trademarks of their respective owners.

Permission to reproduce extracts from BS ISO/IEC 17788:2014 is granted by BSI. British Standards can be obtained in PDF or hard copy formats from the BSI online shop (https://shop.bsigroup.com) or by contacting BSI Customer Services for hardcopies only: Tel: +44 (0)20 8996 9001, email: cservices@bsigroup.com.

ABBREVIATIONS

2FA	two-factor authentication
ACI	application-centric infrastructure
ACID	atomicity, consistency, isolation and durability
API	application programming interface
ARPANET	Advanced Research Projects Agency Network
ASP	application service provider
BASE	basically available soft-state with eventual consistency
BLOb	binary large object
BOINC	Berkeley Open Infrastructure for Network Computing
BYOD	bring your own device
CaaS	communications as a service
CD	continuous development/delivery/deployment
CDN	content delivery/distribution network
CIF	Cloud Industry Forum
CISC/RISC	complex and reduced instruction set computing
CompaaS	compute as a service
CP/M	Control Program/Monitor, or latterly Control Program for Microcomputers
CPU	central processing unit
CRC	cyclic redundancy check
CRM	customer relationship management
DCSA	Datacenter Star Audit
DDoS	distributed denial of service (attack)
DevOps	development and operations
DIMM	dual in-line memory module
DLP	data leak/loss prevention

DMTF	Distributed Management Task Force
DNS	domain name system
DRM	digital rights management
DSaaS	Data storage as a service
EC2	Elastic Compute Cloud
EFSS	enterprise file share and synchronisation
ENIAC	Electronic Numerical Integrator And Computer
ERP	enterprise resource planning
ETSI	European Telecommunications Standards Institute
FaaS	function as a service
FCA	Financial Conduct Authority
FSS	file share and synchronisation
GPL	General Public License
GPU	graphics processing unit
GRC	governance, risk (management) and compliance
HCI	hyperconverged infrastructure
IaaS	infrastructure as a service
IAM	identity access management (system)
IDS	intrusion detection system
IETF	Internet Engineering Task Force
I/PaaS	infrastructure and platform as a service
IPS	intrusion prevention/protection system
LAN	local area network
LEED	Leadership in Energy and Environmental Design
MDM	mobile device management
NaaS	network as a Service
NAS	network attached storage
NFV	network function virtualisation
NIST	National Institute of Standards and Technology
NVMe	non-volatile memory express
OASIS	Organization for the Advancement of Structured Information Standards
OCP	Open Compute Project

OLTP	online transaction processing
ONF	Open Networking Foundation
PaaS	platform as a service
PC	personal computer
PCIe	peripheral component interface express
PCI-DSS	Payment Card Industry Data Security Standard
PID	personally identifiable data
PoP	point of presence
PPI	payment protection insurance
PUE	power usage effectiveness
RAID	redundant array of independent/inexpensive disks
RoI	return on investment
RPO	recovery point objective
RTO	recovery time objective
SaaS	software as a service
SAM	software asset management
SAML	Security Assertion Markup Language
SAN	storage area network
SDC	software-defined compute
SDDC	software-defined data centre
SDN	software-defined network(ing)
SDS	software-defined storage
SLA	service level agreement
SALM	software asset lifecycle management (system)
SOA	service-oriented architecture
SSO	single sign-on (system)
TCO	total cost of ownership
TIA	Telecommunications Industry Association
TVP	total value proposition
VM	virtual machine
VoIP	voice over internet protocol
VPN	virtual private network

W3C	World Wide Web Consortium
WAN	wide area network
WIMP	windows, icons, mouse and pointer
XACML	eXtensible Access Control Markup Language

GLOSSARY

Abstracting   The act of creating a more logical view of available physical systems so that users can access and utilise these resources in a more logical manner.

API   Application programming interface. A means for developers to access the functionality of an application (or service) in a common and standardised manner.

Automation   The use of systems to ensure that any bottlenecks in a process are minimised by ensuring that data flows and hand-offs can be carried out without the need for human intervention.

Bring your own device (BYOD)   Individuals sourcing and using their own laptop, tablet and/or smartphone for work purposes.

Business continuity   The processes by which an organisation attempts to carry on with a level of business capability should a disaster occur that impacts the IT environment.

Cloud aggregator   A third-party provider that facilitates the use of multiple cloud services, enabling integration of these services through its own cloud.

Cloud broker   A third party that facilitates access to multiple cloud services without providing integration services.

Cloud computing   Running workloads on a platform where server, storage and networking resources are all pooled and can be shared across multiple workloads in a highly dynamic manner.

Cold image   An image that is stored and then subsequently provisioned on a secondary live platform to create a viable running application as a failover system for business continuity or disaster recovery.

Colocation   The use of a third party's data centre facility to house an organisation's own IT equipment. Colocation providers generally offer connectivity, power distribution, physical security and other services as a core part of their portfolio.

Composite application   A form of application that is built from a collection of loosely coupled components in order to provide a flexible means of ensuring that the IT service better meets the organisation's needs.

Compute   In the context of compute, storage and network systems, the provision of raw CPU power, excluding any storage or network resources.

Container   A means of wrapping code up in a manner that enables the code to be implemented into the operational environment rapidly in a consistent, controlled and manageable manner. Containers generally share a large part of the underlying stack, particularly at the operating system level.

Continuous delivery   Often used synonymously with 'continuous deployment', this can be seen as the capacity for operations to move functional code into the operational environment, or can be seen as an intermediate step where the development team delivers code to testing and production on a continuous basis.

Continuous deployment   The capacity for an organisation's operations team to move small, incremental, functional code from development and test environments to the operational environment on a highly regular basis, rather than in large packaged amounts, as seen in waterfall or cascade projects.

Continuous development   The capacity for an organisation's development team to develop new code on a continuous basis, rather than in discrete 'chunks', as generally found in waterfall or cascade project approaches.

Data centre   A facility used to house server, storage and networking equipment, along with all the peripheral services (such as power distribution, cooling, emergency power and physical security) required to run these systems.

Data classification   The application of different classifications to different types of data so as to enable different actions to be taken on them by systems.

Data leak prevention   The use of a system to prevent certain types of data crossing over into defined environments.

Data sovereignty   Where data is stored and managed within specified physical geographic or regional locations. With the increasing focus on where data resides, the issue of data sovereignty is growing.

DevOps   A shortened form of Development/Operations. Used as an extension of Agile project methodologies to speed up the movement of code from development to testing and then operations.

Digital rights management (DRM)   The use of systems that manage the movement and actions that can be taken against information assets no matter where they reside – even outside an organisation's own environment.

Disaster recovery   The processes by which an organisation attempts to recover from an event to a point of normalcy as to application and data availability.

Elasticity   The capability for a cloud platform to share resources on a dynamic basis between different workloads.

(Enterprise) file share and sync   The provision of a capability for documents to be copied and stored in a common environment (generally a cloud) such that users can access the documents no matter where they are or what device they are using to access the documents.

Game theory   A branch of theory where logic is used to try to second-guess how one or more parties will respond to any action taken by another party.

Governance, risk (management) and compliance   A corporate need to ensure that company, vertical trade body and legal needs are fully managed.

High availability   The architecting of an IT environment to ensure that it will have minimum downtime when any foreseeable event arises.

Hot image   An image that is held already provisioned on a secondary live platform as a failover system for business continuity or disaster recovery.

Hybrid cloud   The use of a mixture of private and public cloud in a manner where workloads can be moved between the two environments in a simple and logical manner.

Hyperconverged systems   Engineered systems consisting of all server, storage and networking components required to create a self-contained operational environment. Generally provided with operating system and management software already installed.

Hyperscale   A term used for the largest public clouds, which use millions of servers, storage systems and network devices.

Hypervisor   A layer between the physical hardware and the software stack that enables virtualisation to be created, allowing the abstraction of the logical systems from the underpinning physical resources.

IaaS   Generally refers to a version of public cloud, as infrastructure as a service. The provision of a basic environment where the user does not need to worry about the server, storage or network hardware, as this is managed by a third party. The provider layers a cloud environment on top of this to separate the hardware from the user, so that the user only has to deal with logical blocks of resources as abstract concepts rather than understanding how those blocks are specified and built. The user can then install their software (operating system, application stack, database etc.) as they see fit. IaaS can also be used in reference to private cloud, but this use is less valid.

Idempotency   The capability for a system to ensure that a desired outcome is attained time after time.

Internet of things (IoT)   Where a collection of devices, ranging from small embedded systems sending a large number of small packets of data at regular intervals up to large systems used to analyse and make decisions on the data, is used to enhance the operations of an environment.

Keeping the lights on   A colloquial but much used term that covers the costs to an organisation at the IT level for just maintaining a system as it is. As such, this cost is faced by the organisation before any investment in new functionality is made.

Kernel   The basic core of an operating system. Other functions may be created as callable libraries that are associated with the kernel. For community operating systems such as Linux, the kernel of a distribution should only be changed by agreement across the community to maintain upgrade and patch consistency. Additional functionality can always be added as libraries.

Latency   The time taken for an action to complete after it has been begun. Generally applied to networks, where the laws of physics can create blocks to overall system performance.

Local area network (LAN)   Those parts of the network that are fully under the control of an entity, connecting (for example) servers to servers, servers to storage or dedicated user devices to the data centre. A LAN can generally operate at higher speeds than a wide area network.

Metadata   Data that is held to describe other data, used by systems to make decisions on how the original data should be managed, analysed and used.

Microservice   A functional stub of capability, rather than a full application. The idea with microservices is that they can be chained together to create a composite application that is more flexible and responsive to the business's needs.

Mixed cloud   The use of two or more different cloud platforms (private and/or public) where workloads are dedicated to one part of the platform, making data integration and the overall value of a hybrid cloud platform more difficult to achieve.

Noisy neighbour   Where a workload within a shared environment is taking so much of one or more resources that it impacts other workloads operating around it.

Open source software   Software that is made available for users to download and implement without financial cost. Often also provided with support that is charged for but where the software provides a more enterprise level of overall capability.

Orchestration   The use of systems to ensure that various actions are brought together and operated in a manner that results in a desired outcome.

PaaS   Generally refers to a version of public cloud, as platform as a service. The provision of a platform where the provider offers the server, storage and network, along with the cloud platform and parts of the overall software stack required by the user, generally including the operating system plus other aspects of the software stack required to offer the overall base-level service. The user can then install their applications in a manner where they know that the operating system will be looked after by the third party.

Power utilisation effectiveness   A measure of how energy effective a data centre is, calculated by dividing the amount of energy used by the entire data centre facility by the amount of energy used directly by the dedicated IT equipment.

Private cloud   The implementation of a cloud platform on an organisation's own equipment, whether this is in a privately owned or colocation data centre.

Public cloud   The provision of a cloud platform on equipment owned and managed by a third party within a facility owned and operated by that or another third party.

Recovery point objective   The point at which a set of data can be guaranteed to be valid, as used within disaster recovery.

Recovery time objective   The point in future time at which the data set defined by the recovery point objective can be recovered to a live environment.

Resource pooling   The aggregation of similar resources in a manner that then allows the resources to be farmed out as required to different workloads.

Return on investment   A calculation of how much an organisation will receive in business value against the cost of implementing a chosen system.

SaaS   A version of public cloud where all hardware, the cloud platform and the full application stack are provided, operated and managed by a third party. Often pronounced as 'sars'.

Scale   The approach of applying extra resources in order to meet the needs of a workload. Used as scale out (the capability to add elements of resources independently of each other), scale up (the capability to add extra units of overall power to the system in blocks that include server, storage and network) and scale through (the option to do both scale out and scale up with the same system). Scale can also be used within a logical cloud to increase or reduce resources dynamically as required for individual workloads (elastic resourcing).

Self-service   In the context of cloud computing, where a user uses a portal to identify and request access to software, which is then automatically provisioned and made available to them.

Serverless computing   The provision of a consumable model of resources where the user does not have to worry very much about resource sizing.

Service level agreement (SLA)   A contractual agreement between two entities that defines areas such as agreed performance envelopes and speed of response to issues.

Shadow IT   Where staff outside the formal IT function buy, operate and manage IT equipment, software or functions outside of normal IT purchasing processes, often without the formal IT function being aware.

Single sign on   Systems that allow users to use a single username and password (generally combined with some form of two-factor authentication) to gain access to all their systems.

Software asset lifecycle management   A system that details and manages the presence and licensing of software across a platform and also provides services to add additional business value to that provided by basic software asset management across the entire life of the software.

Software asset management   A system that details and manages the presence and licensing of software across a platform.

Software defined   Used in conjunction with compute, network or storage as well as data centre. 'Software defined' describes an approach where functions are pulled away from being fulfilled at a proprietary, hardware or firmware level and are instead fulfilled through software running at a more commoditised level.

Total cost of ownership   A calculation of the expected lifetime cost of any system. Often erroneously used to try to validate a chosen direction by going for the system with the lowest total cost of ownership.

Two-factor authentication   The use of a secondary security level before a user can gain access to a system. For example, the use of a one-time PIN provided by an authentication system used in combination with a username and password pair.

Value chain   The extended chain of suppliers and their suppliers, and customers and their customers, that a modern organisation has to deal with.

Virtualisation   The means of abstracting an environment such that the logical (virtual) environment has less dependence on the actual physical resources underpinning it.

Virtual machine   A means of wrapping code up in a manner that enables the code to be implemented in the operational environment rapidly in a controlled and manageable manner. Unlike containers, virtual machines tend not to share aspects of the underlying stack, being completely self-contained.

Waterfall or cascade project methodology   A project approach where, after an initial implementation of major functionality, extra functionality (and minor patches) are grouped together so as to create controlled new versions over defined periods of time, generally per quarter or per half year.

Wide area network   The connectivity between an organisation's dedicated environment and the rest of the world. Generally provided and managed by a third party and generally of a lower speed than that seen in a local area network.

Workload   A load placed on an IT resource, whether this be a server, storage or network environment, or a combination of all three.

PREFACE

I never read prefaces, and it is not much good writing things just for people to skip. I wonder other authors have never thought of this.

E. Nesbit in *The Story of the Treasure Seekers*, 1899

Attempting to write a book on a subject that is in a period of rapid change and maturation is no easy thing. As you're reading this book, please bear in mind that it does not aim to be all-encompassing, as the services being offered by the cloud service providers mentioned are constantly evolving to react to the dynamics of the market.

The purpose of this book, therefore, is to provide a picture of how we got to the position of cloud being a valid platform, a snapshot of where we are with cloud now, and a look out towards the hypothetical event horizon as to how cloud is likely to evolve over time.

It also includes guidelines and ideas as to how to approach the provisioning of a technical platform for the future: one that is independent of the changes that have plagued IT planning in the past. The idea is to look beyond cloud, to enable the embracing of whatever comes next, and to ensure that IT does what it is meant to do: enable the business rather than constrain it.

Sections on how to approach the business to gain the necessary investments for a move to cloud – by talking to the business in its own language – are also included.

It is hoped that by reading this book you will be better positioned to create and finance a cloud computing strategy for your organisation that not only serves the organisation now but is also capable of embracing the inevitable changes that will come through as the platform matures.

Throughout the book, I use named vendors as examples of certain functions. These names have been used as they are known by me; however, such naming is not intended to infer that the vendor is as fit or more fit for purpose than any other vendor. Any due diligence as to which vendor is best suited to an individual organisation's needs is still down to you.

As an aside, it is important to recognise that no technology is ever the complete silver bullet. Alongside continuous change, there are always problems with any technology that is proposed as the 'next great thing'. Indeed, in the preparation of this book I used cloud-based document storage and versioning. On opening the document to continue working on it one day, I noticed that several thousand words had disappeared. No problem – off to the cloud to retrieve a previous version. Unfortunately not: all versions previous to that point in time had also been deleted. It appears that the provider somehow reverted to an earlier storage position and so lost everything that had been created beyond that point.

Again – no problem: I believed that I would be able to return to my own backups and restore the document. Yet again, no use: the cloud had synchronised the deletions back onto my machine, which had then backed up the deletions. As it had been over a week since the document had last been opened, my chosen backup model had removed all later versions of the document.

I managed to recover the graphics I had spent a long time creating by accessing a separate laptop machine. However, by the time I tried to recover the actual document from that machine, the cloud had synchronised and deleted that version too. If only, on opening the laptop, Wi-Fi had been turned off to prevent the machine connecting to the cloud. If only I had used the time-honoured and trusted way of backing up an important document by emailing it to myself...

It just goes to show that even with all the capabilities of modern technology available, sometimes it is still necessary to have multiple contingency plans in place.

PART 1
LOOKING BACK
Cloud computing in context

1   BACKGROUND

On two occasions I have been asked, 'Pray, Mr. Babbage, if you put into the machine wrong figures, will the right answers come out?' In one case a member of the Upper, and in the other a member of the Lower, House put this question. I am not able rightly to apprehend the kind of confusion of ideas that could provoke such a question.

Charles Babbage ('the Father of Computing') in *Passages from the Life of a Philosopher*, 1864

It is interesting to see how far we have come in such a short time. Before we discuss where we are now, it can be instructive to see the weird but wonderful path that has been taken to get us to our current position. The history of electronic computing is not that long: indeed, much of it has occurred over just three or four human generations. By all means, miss out this chapter and move directly to where cloud computing really starts, in Chapter 2. However, reading this chapter will help to place into perspective how we have got here – and why that is important.

LOOKING BACKWARD TO LOOK FORWARD

That men do not learn very much from the lessons of history is the most important of all the lessons that history has to teach.

Aldous Huxley in *Collected Essays*, 1958

Excluding specialised electromechanical computational systems such as the German Zuse Z3, the British Enigma code-breaking Bombes and the Colossus of the Second World War, the first real fully electronic general-purpose computer is generally considered to be the US's Electronic Numerical Integrator And Computer (ENIAC). First operated in 1946, by the time it was retired in 1955 it had grown to use 17,500 vacuum tubes, 7,200 crystal diodes, 1,500 relays, 70,000 resistors, 10,000 capacitors and around 5,000,000 hand-soldered joints, all in a space measuring 168 m^2. Compare this with Intel's 2016 Broadwell-EP Xeon chip, which contains 7.2 billion transistors in a chip of 456 mm^2.

Weighing in at around 27 tonnes and needing 150kW of electricity, ENIAC could compute a military projectile's trajectory around 2,400 times faster than a human. Its longest continuous operating period without breaking down was less than five days.[1] It has to be noted, though, that a 1973 legal case found that the designers of ENIAC had seen a previous Atanasoff-Berry Computer and that ENIAC shared certain design and functional approaches.

Meanwhile, in Manchester, UK, the first stored program computer was developed and ran its first program in 1948. The Small Scale Experimental Machine 1, developed at the Victoria University, was the first such machine and led to the development of the

---

[1] Weik, Martin H. (1961) The ENIAC story. *Ordnance: The journal of the American Ordnance Association*, January/February. Available from www.uwgb.edu/breznayp/cs353/eniac.html.

first commercially available stored program computer, the Ferranti Mark 1, launched in 1951.

In the 70 years since ENIAC, the use of computers has exploded. The development and wide availability of transistors drove the digital computer market strongly in the 1950s, leading to IBM's development of its original series 700 and 7000 machines. These were soon replaced by its first 'true' mainframe computer, the System/360. This then created a group of mainframe competitors that, as the market stabilised, became known as 'IBM and the BUNCH' (IBM along with Burroughs, UNIVAC, NCR, Control Data Corporation and Honeywell). A major plus-point for mainframes was that everything was in one place – and through the use of virtualisation, as launched in 1966 on the IBM System/360-67, multiple workloads could be run on the same platform, keeping resource utilisation at 80% or higher.

However, mainframes were not suitable for all workloads, or for all budgets, and a new set of competitors began to grow up around smaller, cheaper systems that were within the reach of smaller organisations. These midicomputer vendors included companies such as DEC (Digital Equipment Corporation), Texas Instruments, Hewlett Packard (HP) and Data General, along with many others. These systems were good for single work-loads: they could be tuned individually to carry a single workload, or, in many cases, sev-eral similar workloads. Utilisation levels were still reasonable but tended to be around half, or less, of those of mainframes.

The battle was on. New mass-production integrated chip architectures, where the use of transistors is embedded into a single central processing unit (CPU), were built around CISC/RISC (complex and reduced instruction set computing) systems. Each of these systems used different operating systems, and system compatibility was completely disregarded.

Up until this point, computers were generally accessed through either completely dumb or semi-dumb terminals. These were screen-based, textually focused devices, such as IBM's 3270 and DEC's VT100/200, which were the prime means of interfacing with the actual program and data that were permanently tied to the mainframe or midicomputer. Although prices were falling, these machines were still not within the reach of the mass of small and medium enterprises around the globe.

THE PRICE WAR

Technological innovation has dramatically lowered the cost of computing, making it possible for large numbers of consumers to own powerful new technologies at reasonably low prices.
James Surowiecki (author of *The Wisdom of Crowds*) in *The New Yorker*, 2012

The vendors continued to try to drive computing down to a price point where they could penetrate even more of the market. It was apparent that hobbyists and techno-geeks were already embracing computing in the home. Led by expensive and complex build-your-own kits such as the Altair 8800 and Apple I, Commodore launched its PET (Personal Electronic Transactor) in mid-1977 but suffered from production issues, which then allowed Apple to offer a pre-built computer for home use, the Apple II. This had colour graphics and expansion slots, but cost was an issue at £765/$1,300 (over £3,300/$5,000 now). However, costs were driven down until computers such as the Radio Shack TRS-80 came through a couple of months after the Apple II, managing to provide a complete system for under £350/$600. Then, Clive Sinclair launched the Sinclair ZX80 in 1980 at a cost of £99.95/$230, ready built. Although the machine was low-powered, it drove the emergence of a raft of low-cost home computers, including the highly popular BBC Micro, which launched in 1981, the same year as the IBM Personal Computer, or PC.

Suddenly, computing power was outside the complete control of large organisations, and individuals had a means of writing, using and passing on programs. Although Olivetti had brought out a stand-alone desktop computer in 1965 called the Programma 101, it was not a big commercial success, and other attempts also failed due to the lack of standardisation that could be built into the machines. The fragility of the hardware and poor operating systems led to a lack of customers, who at this stage still did not fully understand the promise of computing for the masses. Companies had also attempted to bring out desktop machines, such as IBM's SCAMP and Xerox's Alto machine, the latter of which introduced the concept of the graphical user interface using windows, icons and a mouse with a screen pointer (which became known as the WIMP system, now commonly adopted by all major desktop operating systems). But heterogeneity was still holding everybody back; the lack of a standard to which developers could write applications meant that there was little opportunity to build and sell sufficient copies of any software to make back the time and investment in the development and associated costs. Unlike on the mainframe, where software licence costs could be in the millions of dollars, personal computer software had to be in the tens or hundreds of dollars, with a few programs possibly going into the thousands.

THE RISE OF THE PC

Computers in the future may ... weigh only 1.5 tons.

Popular Mechanics magazine, 1949

It all changed with the IBM PC. After a set of serendipitous events, Microsoft's founder, Bill Gates, found himself with an opportunity. IBM had been wanting to go with the existing CP/M (Control Program/Monitor, or latterly Control Program for Microcomputers) operating system for its new range of personal computers but had come up against various problems in gaining a licence to use it. Gates had been a key part of trying to broker a deal between IBM and CP/M's owner, Digital Research, and he did not want IBM to go elsewhere. At this time, Microsoft was a vendor of programming language software, including BASIC, COBOL, FORTRAN and Pascal. Gates therefore needed a platform on which these could easily run, and CP/M was his operating system of choice. Seeing that the problems with Digital Research were threatening the deal between IBM and Microsoft, Gates took a friend's home-built operating system (then known as QDOS – a quick and dirty operating system), combined it with work done by Seattle Computer Products on a fledgling operating system known as SCP-DOS (or 8-DOS) and took it to IBM. As part of this, Gates also got Tim Paterson to work for Microsoft; Paterson would become the prime mover behind the operating system that became widespread across personal computers.

So was born MS-DOS (used originally by IBM as PC-DOS), and the age of the standardised personal computer (PC) came about. Once PC vendors started to settle on standardised hardware, such that any software that needed to make a call to the hardware could do so across a range of different PC manufacturers' systems, software development took off in a major way. Hardware companies such as Compaq, Dell, Eagle and Osbourne brought out 'IBM-compatible' systems, and existing companies such as HP and Olivetti followed suit.

The impact of the PC was rapid. With software being made available to emulate the dumb terminals, users could both run programs natively on a PC and access programs being run on mainframe and midicomputers. This seemed like nirvana, until organisations began to realise that data was now being spread across multiple storage systems, some directly attached to mainframes, some loosely attached to midicomputers and some inaccessible to the central IT function, as the data was tied to the individual's PC.

Another problem related to the fact that PCs have always been massively inefficient when it comes to resource use. The CPU is only stressed when its single workload is being run heavily. Most of the time, the CPU is running at around 5% or less utilisation. Hard disk drives have to be big enough to carry the operating system – the same operating system that every other PC in a company is probably running. Memory has to be provided to keep the user experience smooth and effective, yet most of this memory is rarely used.

CHANGING TO A DISTRIBUTED MODEL

The future is already here – it's just not very evenly distributed.
William Gibson (author of *Neuromancer*) on *Talk of the Nation*, NPR, 1999

Then the idea of distributed computing came about. As networking technology had improved, moving from IBM's Token Ring configurations (or even the use of low-speed modems over twisted copper pairs) and DEC's DECnet to fully standardised Ethernet connections, the possibility had arisen of different computers carrying out compute actions on different parts or types of data. This opened up the possibility of optimising the use of available resources across a whole network. Companies began to realise: with all of this underutilised computer and storage resources around an organisation, why not try and pull it all together in a manner that allowed greater efficiency?

In came client–server computing. The main business logic would be run on the larger servers in the data centre (whether these were mainframes, midicomputers or the new generation of Intel-based minicomputer servers) while the PC acted as the client, running the visual front end and any data processing that it made sense to keep on the local machine.

Whereas this seemed logical and worked to a degree, it did bring its own problems. Now, the client software was distributed across tens, hundreds or thousands of different machines, many of which used different versions of operating system, device driver or even motherboard and BIOS (Basic Input/Output System). Over time, maintaining this overall estate of PCs has led to the need for complex management tools that can carry out tasks such as asset discovery, lifecycle management, firmware and software upgrade management (including remediation actions and roll-back as required) and has also resulted in a major market for third-party support.

WEB COMPUTING TO THE FORE

I just had to take the hypertext idea and connect it to the Transmission Control Protocol and domain name system ideas and – ta-da! – the World Wide Web ... Creating the web was really an act of desperation, because the situation without it was very difficult when I was working at CERN later. Most of the technology involved in the web, like the hypertext, like the Internet, multifont text objects, had all been designed already. I just had to put them together. It was a step of generalising, going to a higher level of abstraction, thinking about all the documentation systems out there as being possibly part of a larger imaginary documentation system.

Tim Berners-Lee, 2007

While client–server computing had been growing in strength, so had commercial use of the internet. The internet had grown out of the Advanced Research Projects Agency Network (ARPANET) project, funded by the US Department of Defense in the late 1960s. As more nodes started to be connected together using the standardised networking technologies defined by ARPANET, the internet itself was born, being used primarily for machine-to-machine data transfers. However, there were some proprietary bulletin board systems layered over the internet, enabling individuals to post messages to each other with the messages being held in a central place. Likewise, email (based on the X.400 and X.500 protocols) started to grow in use.

In 1980, UK engineer Tim Berners-Lee proposed a means of layering a visual interface over the internet using hypertext links to enable better sharing of information between project workers around the globe. Berners-Lee's proposal was accepted by CERN in 1989, he carried out work at CERN over the next couple of years and the first website (http://info.cern.ch) went live on 6 August 1991. Berners-Lee founded the World Wide Web Consortium (W3C) in 1994, bringing together interested parties to drive standards that could be used to make the web more accessible and usable. The W3C made all its standards available royalty free, making it cheap and easy for any individual or company to adopt the technology. This was followed by rapid growth in the adoption of both internet and web technologies; as this growth became apparent, software vendors realised that using web-based approaches made sense for them as well.

The web was built on standards – it had to be. The very idea of connecting dissimilar organisations together using the internet meant that there had to be a set of underlying capabilities that abstracted each organisation's own systems from the way the organisations interacted with each other. The web could then be built on top of the internet standards, leading to the widescale adoption of browsers.

As browsers were (generally) standardised, the intention was that applications that ran from a central location could be accessed by any device that could run a browser. The idea was that web-based standards would be used as the means of passing graphical output from the central location to the device.

THE RISE OF THE AGE OF CHAOS

> Change always involves a dark night when everything falls apart. Yet if this period of dissolution is used to create new meaning, then chaos ends and new order emerges.
> Margaret Wheatley (author of *Leadership and the New Science: Discovering Order in a Chaotic World*) in *Leader to Leader* magazine, 2006

The big problem with such a pace of change is that any single change rarely replaces what has gone before. Each new technological change was touted as the only real way forward for the future, but what actually resulted was a mix of mainframe, midicomputer, PC client–server and web-based systems with poor ability to easily exchange information between different enterprise systems. The growth in integration approaches, such as enterprise application integration and enterprise service buses (ESBs), showed how organisations were increasingly reliant on their IT platforms – and how badly these platforms were supporting the businesses.

It was still a world of 'one application per physical server': a research project conducted in 2008 showed that resource utilisation rates were poor, often as low as 5% and certainly generally lower than 50%.[2] Indeed, the same research project indicated that the spread of distributed computing had led to 28% of organisations being unable to state how many servers they had, with 42% saying that it would take a day or longer to find a server that had crashed.

IT was moving away from being a facilitator for the business and was rapidly becoming an expensive barrier to how organisations needed to operate.

VIRTUALISATION, SERVICE-ORIENTED ARCHITECTURE AND GRID COMPUTING

> To understand why virtualisation has had such a profound effect on today's computing environment, you need to have a better understanding of what has gone on in the past.
> Matthew Portnoy in *Virtualization Essentials*, 2012

Something had to be done to try to pull IT back into a position of supporting the business. What happened was a confluence of several different technologies that came together – unfortunately, not quite in a 'perfect storm'.

---

[2] Longbottom, Clive. (17 March 2008) Data centre asset. Quocirca. Available from http://quocirca.com/content/data-centre-asset-planning.

As mentioned earlier, IBM had been using virtualisation for many years. However, the technology had not been used in any widespread manner in the distributed computing world (which was based on Intel architectures). However, in 2001, VMware released GSX (discontinued as of 2011) and ESX (now commercially available as vSphere or ESXi) as virtualisation hypervisors, which enabled multiple instantiations of operating systems to be run on top of a single piece of server hardware.

In 2008, Microsoft launched its own virtualisation hypervisor, Hyper-V. As of 2007, the Kernel-based Virtual Machine (KVM) was merged into the main Linux 2.6.20 kernel.

Virtualisation in the distributed world laid the groundwork for greater utilisation of resources and for greater flexibility in how resources were used. However, on its own, it did not provide the much-needed flexibility to provide resources elastically to the workloads placed on the virtualised servers.

Alongside the development of virtualisation came the concept of service-oriented architecture (SOA). First mentioned in the early 2000s, SOA opened up the concept of a less monolithic application world; it would now be possible to construct composite applications across a distributed environment using loosely coupled services. SOA laid the groundwork for a new form of application: one where discrete packages of workload could be dealt with across a distributed platform, as part of a set of serial and parallel tasks in an overall process. These tasks needed to be orchestrated, with the results from each task or set of tasks brought together in a meaningful manner to maintain process integrity.

SOA fitted in well with another concept that had become popular in the late 1990s: the idea of a 'compute grid'. Here, small workload tasks could be packaged up and distributed to discrete systems that would work on these small tasks, sending their results back to a central environment. The data could then be aggregated and further analysed to come to an end result.

In the public sector, grid computing has continued. The World Community Grid is (as of April 2017) operating with over 3.4 million connected and shared machines, running the open source Berkeley Open Infrastructure for Network Computing (BOINC) platform supporting over 500,000 active academic and scientific users. Several BOINC projects gained a high degree of public notice in the late 1990s and early 2000s, and one of these was SETI@home, focused on the search for extraterrestrial intelligence. This project scavenged underutilised CPU cycles on home computers to analyse packets of data from radio telescopes to try to see whether messages were being transmitted from elsewhere in the universe. Similar community grids were used to analyse data to plan for the eradication of smallpox. Indeed, when IBM set up the computing grid that ran the Australian Olympics in 2000, an agreement was reached such that when the Olympic grid was being underutilised, the smallpox grid could use its resources. The other side of the coin was that when the Olympics was particularly busy, the Olympic grid could use some of the smallpox grid's resources.

In 1999, Ian Foster, widely regarded as one of the 'Fathers of the Grid' (along with Carl Kesselman and Steve Tuecke) released a paper titled 'The Anatomy of the Grid: Enabling

Scalable Virtual Organizations'.[3] This, along with interest from companies such as IBM and Oracle, drove the founding of the Global Grid Forum and Globus. These groups started to develop solid standards that could be used across a complex environment.

Grid computing met with a modicum of success. Companies such as Wachovia Bank, Bownes & Co and Butterfly.net used grid architectures from companies such as DataSynapse (now part of IBM), Platform Computing (now part of IBM) and IBM itself to create commercial grids that solved business problems. The EU has continued with a grid project called the European Grid Infrastructure (which includes sites in Asia and the US), based on a previous project called the Enabling Grids for E-science project, which was itself a follow-up project to the European DataGrid.

However, grid computing did not gain the favour that many expected. The lack of standards at the hardware and software level and the need for highly proprietary platforms meant that few workloads could be suitably supported in a grid environment.

THE ROLE OF STANDARDS

> The nice thing about standards is that you have so many to choose from.
> Andrew S. Tanenbaum (creator of Minix) in *Computer Networks*, 1994

What all of the above had demonstrated was that IT had developed in the midst of two main problems. One was that there was not enough basic standardisation to create a solid platform that could be easily worked across. The second was that there were far too many standards.

In the early days of computing, the Institute of Electrical and Electronics Engineers and the International Telecommunications Union (ITU) set the majority of the standards. These standards were used through a complex *de jure* method of gaining agreement through processes of proposing, discussing and modifying ideas. However, as time went on, vendors developed their own groups to create *de facto* standards that applied more directly to their products. Not only did the number of standards explode but there were also often many competing standards for each area.

When the internet and web usage emerged, the need for basic standards became an imperative. As mentioned, the W3C was founded by Tim Berners-Lee in 1994, and the Organization for the Advancement of Structured Information Standards (OASIS) was founded in 1993. The idea was that *de jure* and *de facto* standards would come from these two organisations. Another central organisation has been the Internet Engineering Task Force (IETF).

For the most part, these organisations have overseen the standards as intended. The overlying data and visualisation capabilities now being used across the internet and the

---

[3] Foster, Ian. (2001) The anatomy of the grid: Enabling scalable virtual organizations. In: *Proceedings of the first IEEE/ACM International Symposium on Cluster Computing and the Grid*. Brisbane, Queensland, Australia, 15–18 May 2001. IEEE. Available from http://ieeexplore.ieee.org/document/923162.

web are based on standards agreed and developed by them. Yes, there are other groups working in specific areas (such as the SNIA (Storage Networking Industry Association) and the DMTF (Distributed Management Task Force)), but the web is predicated on there being a solid, underlying set of standardised capabilities that work for everyone.

In the late 1990s, the concept of an application service provider (ASP) was born. These service providers would take steps beyond simple hosting to provide multi-tenanted platforms where users could share resources in order to gain access to software services at a lower cost than by operating them in-house.

Unfortunately, due to a lack of suitable standards combined with poor business models, a lack of acceptance by users and major issues caused by the dot com crash of the early 2000s, the ASP model died a rather spectacular death. With ASP, SOA and grid computing all perceived to be failing, vendors and organisations were looking for the next big thing: something that could provide the big leap in platform terms that would help IT deal with the business needs of the 2000s.

After 70 years, we have come conceptually full circle. What is now being sought is a single logical platform that makes the most of available resources through the elastic sharing of these resources, while providing a centralised means of provisioning, monitoring and managing multiple workloads in a logical manner: in other words, a modern take on the mainframe.

And so, enter the cloud.

SUMMARY

What have we learned?

- Cloud is not a brand new approach to computing.
- Getting to cloud has involved multiple evolutions of previous models.
- Such a shared environment has become more workable due to evolution at the hardware and software levels.

What does this mean?

- Cloud will, by no means, be the final answer.
- Further evolution is inevitable.
- It will be necessary to create a platform that is not just optimised for the short term but can embrace technological changes in the longer term.

PART 2
THE CLOUD NOW
Cloud at its simplest, as it should be implemented

2   THE CLOUD

If you think you've seen this movie before, you are right. Cloud computing is based on the time-sharing model we leveraged years ago before we could afford our own computers. The idea is to share computing power among many companies and people, thereby reducing the cost of that computing power to those who leverage it. The value of time share and the core value of cloud computing are pretty much the same, only the resources these days are much better and more cost effective.

David Linthicum in *Cloud Computing and SOA Convergence in Your Enterprise: A Step-by-Step Guide*, 2009

In its essential form, cloud computing is nothing new. The idea of providing resource pools that can be shared across multiple workloads is the same approach that mainframes have been taking for decades. However, the modern take on this basic principle goes a lot further: the capability to not only have a single platform but also have shared platforms that span self-owned platforms and those owned by other parties. Such an approach holds much promise, but it also comes with lots of problems.

In this chapter, we will consider what constitutes a cloud and why it matters in how users begin to sketch out an overall architecture.

BACK TO THE FUTURE

The interesting thing about cloud computing is that we've redefined cloud computing to include everything that we already do. I can't think of anything that isn't cloud computing with all of these announcements.

Larry Ellison (chairman of Oracle) in an interview in *The Wall Street Journal*, 2009

As cloud started to be touted as a concept, many existing service providers attempted to force their portfolios into using the cloud message. Many simple hosting companies therefore started to advertise themselves as cloud providers. For many, this was pushing the truth somewhat: what they were offering were dedicated servers that customers could rent and on to which customers could then load their own software and applications. This was not, and is not, a cloud platform.

Nor is cloud a virtualised hosting model. Even though a virtualised model provides an underlying shared hardware platform, there is no elasticity in how resources are provided.

In both these cases, hosting is being provided. These models had, and still do have, a part to play in some organisations' overall platform needs. But neither case is cloud.

Such problems necessitated a basic set of definitions of what cloud really was. In 2011, the National Institute of Standards and Technology (NIST) issued its *Special Publication*

800-145.[4] This document set out a simple definition of what cloud computing was. It defined three cloud models and five service-provision characteristics alongside four deployment models that are required for something to be deemed to be cloud.

NIST's base definition of a cloud system is as follows:

> Cloud computing is a model for enabling ubiquitous, convenient, on-demand network access to a shared pool of configurable computing resources (e.g. networks, servers, storage, applications and services) that can be rapidly provisioned and released with minimal management effort or service provider interaction.[5]

To put it more simply, cloud computing is a means to enable a group of different workloads to have better access to the resources they require in an automated manner.

Paraphrasing NIST's definitions, the three cloud models are deemed to be:

- **Infrastructure as a service (IaaS):** The provision of a base layer of elastic, shared compute, storage and network resources. The user then applies and manages all the software above this, from operating system all the way through to the applications themselves.

- **Platform as a service (PaaS):** The provision of an IaaS infrastructure layer along with components of the software (generally, the operating system, database and so on). The user then applies and manages the rest of the software stack to meet their needs.

- **Software as a service (SaaS):** The provision of a total service: a shared-resource platform along with a total software stack. The end user uses the system but has few capabilities around managing it.

Alongside these three models, of course, is the traditional on-premises model, where the user builds up the entire stack (cloud-based, virtual, clustered, physical) in their own data centre or using a colocation facility.

This is best shown in Figure 2.1 The sliding scale of ownership in different IT platform models, where the various aspects of the cloud models are depicted according to who has responsibility for the provision and management of which components of the overall stack.

Again, paraphrasing NIST, the five service-provision characteristics are:

- **Broadly accessible across a network:** This kind of network can be private (it does not have to be publicly available across the general internet) but it should be available by dispersed and mobile users who require access to the service.

---

[4] Mell P., Grance T. (2011) *The NIST definition of cloud computing.* Special Publication 800-145. National Institute of Standards and Technology. Available from http://nvlpubs.nist.gov/nistpubs/Legacy/SP/nistspecialpublication800-145.pdf.
[5] Ibid., p. 4.

Figure 2.1 The sliding scale of ownership in different IT platform models

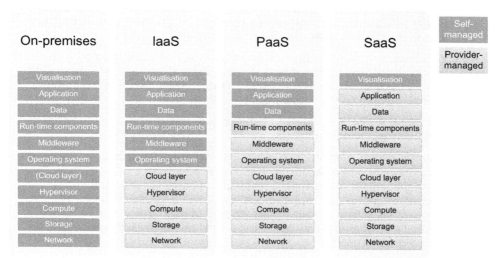

* **Resource pooling:** There should be an abstraction between the physical resources themselves (such as compute, storage and network capabilities) and how they are used and allocated via virtual pools of resources.

* **Rapid elasticity or expansion:** When an application or functional service requires additional resources, those resources should be capable of being automatically and rapidly provided from the resource pools.

* **On-demand self-service:** Applications, functional services and aspects of management of the platform should be made available for each user to access directly. For example, users should have access to a portal where they can see which applications or services are available to them and should then be able to select what they need and have it automatically provisioned for their use. For reasons that will be covered in Chapter 11, this has proven the most contentious of the traits.

* **A measured service:** Each application or functional service should be fully measured and reported through to users and providers alike. Potential reasons for this include the need to monitor who is using which applications and functional services and to what extent; the need to charge at a granular level for the use of each application or functional service; and the need to monitor for the effective (or otherwise) running of the whole platform.

The four deployment models are:

* **Private cloud:** The cloud implementation is owned, operated and used by one organisation alone. That being said, some public cloud providers offer a pseudo-private cloud service where a part of their overall cloud is partitioned off for use by a single organisation only. Other providers do offer purely dedicated

private clouds where they provision either just the dedicated hardware (IaaS) or the dedicated hardware and the cloud stack (PaaS) to the customer. For the purposes of this book, only platforms where the hardware and software are dedicated to a single customer will be regarded as private cloud. Note that a colocation model can still be seen as private cloud.

- **Public cloud:** The cloud implementation is owned and operated by a third-party organisation, with a range of customers sharing the underlying hardware platform. Customers may also share all (SaaS) or part (PaaS) of the software stack implemented on the hardware.

- **Hybrid cloud:** A mix of private and public cloud. This is where the majority of organisations will find themselves.

- **Community cloud:** A collaborative platform where infrastructure is shared across a group of organisations (or even individuals) with a common aim. The overall management of the shared resources is normally allocated to a single member of the group. Community cloud is mainly being used in academia and social research, where resources are shared in such a manner as to allow either dedicated shared resources or excess resources in existing clouds to be used for a 'greater good'.

The Need for 'Hybrid Multi-cloud'

Further granularity is needed alongside the definition of 'hybrid cloud'. To date, many hybrid cloud implementations have essentially involved having some workloads running on a private cloud with other workloads running on a public cloud. While this is a hybrid cloud usage model, it leads to islands of data being created across those different clouds and takes organisations back to the need to integrate the data stores through alternative means. It also leads to one of the greatest values of cloud – the capability to share resources elastically – becoming constrained, as the resources underpinning one cloud have no links to the resources underpinning the other.

This means we need a definition of a 'hybrid multi-cloud'. Here, multiple clouds are used by the customer, but the aim is to run them as a single logical platform. Workloads on one platform can be moved as required to another platform to make use of cheaper resources or to manage spikes in resource needs. This requires not only advanced orchestration of how workloads are provisioned onto the platform but also a full understanding of all the contextual links between the workload and its needs. At this stage, the capacity to embrace a full hybrid multi-cloud model is limited, but it should be borne in mind as a possibility for the future.

For most, this set of basic definitions and criteria remains adequate for their needs. However, in the complex and dynamic world of cloud computing, there has been scope for a more granular level of detail to be agreed around aspects of cloud.

In 2014, the ISO standards group created the two-part BS ISO/IEC 17788:2014 and BS ISO/IEC 17789:2014 standards around cloud computing.[6] BS ISO/IEC 17788:2014 sets out the overview and vocabulary for cloud computing. BS ISO/IEC 17789:2014 provides details of a reference architecture for cloud.

In BS ISO/IEC 17788:2014, several more cloud 'models' are defined, although these are now designated as 'categories'. These are:

- **Communications as a service (CaaS):** The provision of voice and collaboration services via a cloud-based platform. The main example here is the growing use of hosted VoIP (voice over internet protocol) systems, where on-premises hardware (such as key systems) is removed, with such functions being provided and managed by a third party. This has then grown into the provision of instant messaging, videoconferencing and collaboration services, as seen in services such as Microsoft's Office 365 and Skype for Business.

- **Compute as a service (CompaaS):** This is a somewhat misleading model, as it is really just a subset of PaaS, although the concept is predicated on being priced on a resource-consumption basis only. It is meant to be the provision of compute (server) resources that are required to run an application or analyse data, but this cannot really be done in isolation. Network and storage resources are still required, and so CompaaS is just a slightly nuanced version of IaaS. Currently, the model that comes closest to CompaaS is 'serverless' compute.

- **Data storage as a service (DSaaS):** There has been a growth in cloud storage providers. Some (such as Rackspace[7] and Storagepipe[8]) provide backup and restore services whereas others (such as AWS Glacier[9] and Google Cloud Storage Nearline[10]) provide archive capabilities. Others provide 'live' storage for use in production environments. However, if the business logic is held too far away from the storage capability, data latency can become a major issue. Therefore, the general usage is for live storage to be held in the same environment as the compute and network resources.

- **Network as a service (NaaS):** Another strange model, NaaS is essentially the provision of connectivity. To fit in with the traits of cloud, this must be elastic (which few network providers offer) and must be self-service (which is difficult if a customer wants an end-to-end solution). Those service providers offering NaaS tend to focus on discrete value-added services, such as the provision and management of virtual private network (VPN) connections, domain name system (DNS) management, interconnects and connection peering, content delivery network (CDN) services, and dynamic management of bandwidth on demand alongside priority and quality of service.

---

[6] *ISO/IEC 17788:2014: Information technology – Cloud computing – Overview and vocabulary.* Geneva, Switzerland: International Organization for Standardization. Available from www.iso.org/iso/catalogue_detail?csnumber=60544.
[7] www.rackspace.com/en-gb/cloud/backup
[8] www.storagepipe.com
[9] https://aws.amazon.com/glacier
[10] https://cloud.google.com/storage-nearline

The ISO standard also introduced 'emerging cloud service categories', such as email as a service, identity as a service and security as a service.

Each of these operates within one or more of three types of cloud service 'capabilities':

- application capabilities;
- infrastructure capabilities;
- platform capabilities.

This is shown in Figure 2.2. For the purposes of this book, however, the more accepted terms of IaaS, PaaS and SaaS will be used throughout.

Figure 2.2 BS ISO/IEC 17788:2014 cloud service categories and cloud capability types

Cloud Service Categories	Cloud Capability Types		
	Infrastructure	Platform	Application
Software as a service			✓
Platform as a service		✓	
Infrastructure as a service	✓		
Network as a service	✓	✓	✓
Data storage as a service	✓	✓	✓
Compute as a service	✓		
Communication as a service		✓	✓

The ISO standard also includes one more trait:

- **Multi-tenancy:** The capability for a cloud instance to have more than one set of defined users (for example, customers) using it at the same time. This is problematic for a private cloud instance, as the last thing wanted by most organisations that choose private cloud is for external groups to be using the same hardware platform, even if they are securely partitioned away from the organisation's own users.

The standard then adds three cloud computing roles:

- **Cloud service customer:** Those who are consuming the service provided by the cloud service provider.

- **Cloud service provider:** The entity that is providing the service to the cloud service customer.

- **Cloud service partner:** A third party that is engaged in the support of (or auxiliary to) the activities of the cloud service provider and/or the cloud service customer. An example of a cloud service partner could be an auditor that assesses the effectiveness of an organisation's chosen cloud architecture, or a cloud service broker that takes responsibility for negotiating relationships between cloud service customers and one or more cloud service providers.

The end user can also be added to this list as a cloud service user. The end user is by necessity a subset of the cloud service customer, but it is not necessarily the case that all cloud service users within an organisation will have the same needs or viewpoints as the organisation (the cloud service customer itself). The 'user' also has to include entities operating in the machine-to-machine world as well: in this case, a 'user' could be a machine or device, or it could be an automated task within a broader process. Such a 'user' is becoming increasingly important as the internet of things (IoT) becomes more mainstream.

It is worth comparing these definitions of cloud computing with Quocirca's work on grid computing in 2003.[11] In this report, Quocirca defined the three main types of grid platform (private, public and hybrid, with scope for a community grid) as well as six types of grid assets:

- service assets;
- compute assets;
- network assets;
- functional assets;
- storage assets;
- data assets.

Overall, what has driven the viability and uptake of cloud is an increasing standardisation of hardware and software, along with cheap and broadly available virtualisation technologies that enable a workable cloud platform to be built relatively cheaply. Vendors have increasingly focused on ensuring that cloud platforms are broadly similar (rather than there being a plethora of proprietary platforms), and, as a result, cloud computing has now become a reality.

SUMMARY

What have we learned?

- Cloud is not a single platform.
- Not only are there different physical types of cloud but there are also different delivery models.

---

[11] Longbottom, Clive. (10 September 2003) Business grid computing: The evolution of the infrastructure. Quocirca. Available from http://quocirca.com/content/business-grid-computing-evolution-infrastructure#overlay-context=reports.

- It is unlikely that the majority of organisations will be able to find a single cloud model that suits them for all workloads.

What does this mean?

- A hybrid cloud model will be required.
- That hybrid model must allow for workload portability and real-time movement between the different clouds.
- The cloud models chosen must interoperate as peer services.
- Proprietary clouds have no future in a hybrid cloud model.

3   WHY CLOUD?

Why did you want to climb Mount Everest?
Because it's there.

Reported response of George Mallory (English mountaineer) to
a journalist's question, c.1923

Cloud can be seen as just another platform on which to run workloads. So why has it been positioned as a major disruptor in the markets, and why should an organisation look to move to a cloud-based platform model?

To just decide to use cloud 'because it's there' is not a strategy, unless you want to read it as a strategy for disaster. With any change within a business, the reason to move from something to something else must be based upon a solid foundation: for example, that the existing 'something' is now unfit for purpose and the target 'something else' provides a better way of doing things.

However, in the case of cloud, what does 'better' mean? Let's consider the various areas where cloud promises to provide a different, yet better, approach to the provisioning of an IT platform. These are:

- resource utilisation;

- cost;

- meeting future needs;

- workload portability;

- high availability.

Now, let's consider each one in greater depth.

RESOURCE UTILISATION

The secret of concentration is the secret of self-discovery. You reach inside yourself to discover your personal resources, and what it takes to match them to the challenge.
Arnold Palmer (professional golfer) in *A Life Well Played: My Stories*, 2016

One of the main reasons behind the move to cloud models has been the poor resource utilisation rates that are obtained when using a more physical platform model. Although resource utilisation rates have been improving over time (with a pretty large improvement due to virtualisation), the lack of elasticity in dealing with dynamic resource allocation has still resulted in overall resource utilisation rates languishing in the 30–40% levels, as shown in unpublished research carried out by Quocirca.

Figure 3.1 shows a basic model of a cyclical workload. This could be a workload that is run as a set of analytics and reports after a data collection exercise on a regular basis.

The workload has peaks and troughs in its compute resource needs. However, planning how much basic resources the workload needs is not easy. If the systems architect decides to provide enough resources so that peak loads will always be met (as shown by the dashed line), then for the majority of the time the available resources will be poorly utilised. If the systems architect decides to provide sufficient resources for average workload (as shown by the dotted line), then for periods of time the resources will not be used fully while at peak times the workload will not have enough resources to perform properly.

If the systems architect chooses to go for base load resourcing only (as shown by the solid line), then for most of the time the workload will be struggling to perform. Even if the hardware is architected to deal with average workloads (the dotted line), there will still be large periods of time when the application will be resource constrained.

Figure 3.1 Variable workload model

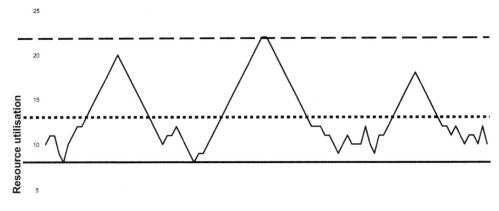

Historically, many systems architects have chosen to go for peak workload provisioning (the dashed line), which has led to average compute resource utilisation rates of around 10% on a one-application-per-physical-server model. As soon as high-availability systems are brought to bear through the use of clustering, then that 10% falls to 5% for a dual-server system – or down to 2.5% for a four-node cluster system, unless full load sharing is also introduced. This is wasteful, not only in terms of the amount of hardware that is being purchased but also n terms of maintenance charges, licences for the operating systems and applications, utility costs (to power and cool the servers) and so on. Whereas this used to be the guilty secret of the IT department, it has become far more visible to the business, which has started to task IT with reducing such waste.

However, the problem with such physical approaches is that workloads have become far less predictable. An example here is in the retail sector, where many retailers have introduced a new campaign and then been surprised at how successful it is. The compute cluster underpinning the retail transactions is sized to meet the expected demand, but the campaign pushes demand well over that threshold. As the platform is physical, there is nowhere for the workload to get extra resources from: it either has to slow down in its response capabilities (to use the resources as they become available) or just crash. Both cases are sub-optimal. Users tend to bail out from a slow system, as evidenced by the 'three-second rule', where if it takes longer than three seconds for an action to complete on a website, the majority of users will go elsewhere.[12]

Many public-sector sites have also suffered from such problems. The UK's public-sector revenue and customs department, HMRC, used to have problems every year when the tax returns deadline occurred.[13] Similarly, when new census details were made available, the Australian census website suffered from an overwhelming demand from the public for information.[14]

The need for better availability of systems while driving higher utilisation levels has therefore been a major force in organisations researching new approaches. Although straightforward virtualisation was seen as a means of solving the resource utilisation problem for a time, it rapidly became apparent that the lack of dynamic resource elasticity in simple virtualisation still meant that virtual workloads had to have virtual resources applied that were pre-sized for peak loads. Moreover, if the workload unexpectedly broke through that expected peak, performance problems would still occur. Virtualisation was a sticking plaster: it made adding new resources easier and less time consuming, but it still tended to require downtime.

Different approaches were needed, such as storage thin provisioning (where a workload is provided with a minimum amount of storage in its initial state with the capability to request and gain more storage volume as the workload requires it) along with other, more flexible means of managing compute, storage and network resources. Cloud computing promised to provide such options.

---

[12] www.hobo-web.co.uk/your-website-design-should-load-in-4-seconds

[13] Taxpayers get an extra 24 hours to file returns after 'overloaded' website crashes in rush to beat deadline. (1 February 2008) *Evening Standard*. Available from www.standard.co.uk/news/taxpayers-get-an-extra-24-hours-to-file-returns-after-overloaded-website-crashes-in-rush-to-beat-6676214.html.

[14] Huffadine, L. (10 August 2016) Does this map shows there was no attack on the Census? IT experts say the ABS website simply wasn't ready for the national survey. *Daily Mail*. Available from www.dailymail.co.uk/news/article-3732538/Census-2016-website-attacked-simply-overloaded-users.html.

COST

He is a man who knows the price of everything and the value of nothing.
Oscar Wilde in *Lady Windemere's Fan*, 1892

Cloud has commonly been regarded as a cheaper means of providing an IT platform than existing approaches. This should be the case as cloud can drive resource utilisation rates up from single-digit percentages to as high as 70–90%. However, Quocirca cautions against moving to cloud just to save money.[15] Creating a cloud that effectively manages resources while still providing high availability and predictable performance is not cheap, no matter whether an organisation opts for a private or a public cloud platform.

The big difference between private and public clouds, however, is that the costs of creating a public cloud can be shared across a multi-customer base, while the private cloud's costs have to be borne by the single organisation using it. Also, as public cloud providers have this multi-customer base, the means through which they share resources is different from the means used by private cloud providers.

In a private cloud environment, the overall platform still has to be architected very carefully. There will only be a certain defined number of possible workloads that can be taken into consideration – those that the organisation itself runs. If just a few of these workloads are co-cyclical (that is, if they reach peak resource requirements at the same time), then the overall platform has to be architected to meet that predicted maximum resource requirement, plus more to cater for the unpredictability of some of the workloads. Therefore, overall utilisation rates on a private cloud may still be low: much higher than on a physical or simple virtualised platform, but likely still lower than 50%.

In contrast, a public cloud has thousands or tens of thousands of workloads running across its entire platform. This means that a very large public cloud provider will have hundreds of thousands to millions of servers, petabytes of storage and terabytes per second of virtualised network bandwidth available to it.

Assume that a single organisation has, say, 100 workloads that it can put on its private cloud. Any spike in the resources needed by just one workload will have an appreciable impact on the resource requirements of the overall cloud platform. When 1% of the total workloads are misbehaving, the impact on the other 99% can be heavy.

Now assume that those same 100 workloads are placed on a public cloud that is shared with 100 other companies each running 100 workloads. Should that one same workload spike, it is now just 1% of 1% of the total workload pressure on the public cloud platform, which the automated elasticity of the cloud can deal with easily.

Quocirca has always stated that if an organisation goes for any solution purely based on price, then it will end up being very expensive. To be the cheapest option, the provider of

---

[15] Longbottom, Clive. (8 January 2008) Prioritise to beat the recession. Quocirca. Available from http://quocirca.com/article/prioritise-beat-recession.

a service will have to cut corners, and that will result in poorer customer service, lower systems availability and reduced technical performance. It could also be that the levels of security applied to the platform are weaker than those of an alternative provider. It is simply not possible for a company to provide a service that meets all the needs of a modern enterprise and charge appreciably lower costs than all of its competitors.

This could have an impact not only on how well an organisation can support its customers but also on brand loyalty if a retail or customer services environment is down for a considerable period of time. Additionally, should customer data be accessed due to poor security, the organisation could well have to disclose the breach in the public arena. Such loyalty and brand costs will wipe out any savings that were expected from using a cheap provider.

There is a truism that is worth mentioning: it is very easy to save your way out of business. However, on the flipside, an investment in the right platform for the right reasons makes a great deal more sense. Moving to a cloud model because a physical model cannot provide the business support that is required is a far better argument than moving to a cloud model to save costs. It also makes sense to move to a public cloud to avoid the need to over-architect a private cloud platform to meet the predicted needs of peak workloads.

What will make the decision easier is to put together a set of business-led arguments as to why workloads should be moved to a cloud platform. This will also help in making the choice of whether the platform should be a private or public cloud, and then which public cloud provider best fits the needs of the business.

Another truism that is worth mentioning is that doing something for all the right reasons is generally cheaper than doing them by any other means. In essence, this means that moving to a cloud platform purely for cost reasons will probably be the most expensive decision that an organisation can make. Investing in what appears at first sight to be a more expensive platform for all the right reasons will probably result in costs savings.

Avoiding the issues of 'keeping the lights on'

There is a basic cost to just keeping things as they are. Within IT, this cost is known as 'keeping the lights on'. It covers such areas as:

- the costs associated with the maintenance of hardware and software (generally anything from 15% to 25% of the original capital or licence costs per annum);
- the cost of electricity to power and cool the systems, which is generally around 50% of the total cost of running an existing private data centre (that is, the overall facility, its IT equipment and its support equipment, such as uninterruptable power supplies, auxiliary generators and all peripheral power, including lighting);
- the cost of the human resources required to patch, monitor and maintain the systems as well as the facility itself.

Within a private data centre environment, these costs are partly predictable (for example, the hardware and software maintenance costs, and most of the power requirements) and partly unpredictable (for example, the cost of responding to an issue that impacts the performance or availability of an application or service). By moving to a private cloud, some of these costs can be brought under greater control: the basic capabilities of a well-architected and well-engineered cloud should mean that there is less need for human resources to take knee-jerk steps to try to fix certain problems (such as the failure of a server or a component within a storage system), as the abstraction of the systems from the hardware should allow for a higher degree of systems availability during the occurrence of such an issue. In other words, a cloud platform is inherently architected to accept failures. The more that this can be built into the complete stack, using abstraction and well-architected software, the less time has to be spent on just keeping a platform operating.

However, although power costs may be lower (because overall resource utilisation rates are driven up), and having less infrastructure means reducing maintenance charges, the cost of keeping the lights on within a private cloud can still be appreciable. By moving through the tiers of public cloud, the costs can be controlled more. For example, with an IaaS platform, all those costs around hardware maintenance (both payments to the vendor and human resources costs relating to patching and managing the platform) are rolled up into a single predictable cost. PaaS takes this further, making the costs of running parts of the software stack predictable. With SaaS, all the costs of keeping the lights on are covered in the one subscription cost. This is best seen by referring back to Figure 2.1.

These higher levels of cost predictability make planning IT's finances far easier. Therefore, the percentage of IT's funds set aside for keeping the lights on can shrink, leaving more of the budget to be allocated to where it should be – investing in the provision of new functionality that better supports the business.

MEETING FUTURE NEEDS

There are no guarantees or crystal balls for the future, and there's no absolute way to know if you are or aren't making the right decision. Give tomorrow the best possible chance that you can.

Kennedth Dino in *The 12 Commandments: A Guide for Entrepreneurs*, 2014

Chapter 19 will take a deep-dive look into the changing face of applications, where a different approach to architecture is required so as to make the most of an overall cloud strategy, using containers and microservices to create composite, dynamic applications. However, it is worth mentioning now that the world of large, multi-function single applications is showing signs of breaking down.

Microservices and APIs

The future of software in the cloud is based around the use of a flexible set of microservices called as required to create a composite application. Organisations are demanding far more flexible IT systems: ones that can respond in near real time to reflect the changes in the markets. By using small functional software components (microservices), pulled together through application programming interfaces (APIs), these new composite applications can be made possible.

Existing large, monolithic applications will struggle with this concept, although it may be possible to identify various functional elements of them that can be used as discrete microservices themselves.

Organisations are requiring far more flexible systems that can respond more dynamically to the business's needs. Business processes are no longer things that are changed once a quarter or less; they are now collections of tasks that must be capable of being changed quickly to meet the changing dynamics of market forces.

Therefore, the concept of a 'composite application', created on the fly from aggregations of microservices, has come to the fore. Cloud makes such an approach far easier – not only can the dynamic and elastic nature of cloud resources provide a far more reactive platform for microservices to be provisioned and run, but the use of a hybrid cloud platform also makes the availability of proven and cost-effective public microservices a usable possibility.

Increasingly, organisations are seeing the future as a place where the business can define exactly what it needs in the way of a collection of tasks that constitute an overall process, and where the IT platform can respond by pulling together the required functional services to make this happen. For such organisations, cloud is the answer.

WORKLOAD PORTABILITY

Whatever people thought the first time they held a portable phone the size of a shoe in their hands, it was nothing like where we are now, accustomed to having all knowledge at our fingertips.

Nancy Gibbs in *Time* magazine, 16 August 2012

As the ubiquity of IT has grown, the need for increased levels of flexibility to better support the dependency of the business on the IT platform has also grown. As organisations have come to make decisions based on desired business outcomes rather than technical capabilities, there has been a need for workloads to become far more 'portable'. A workload that is currently running on the organisation's premises may be better served by running on a public cloud platform next week or next month. As the capabilities of different public clouds evolve, it may make more sense to move a workload onto a different public platform to use that functionality, rather than try to integrate the new functionality into the existing platform from afar.

Should there be a failure of a cloud platform that has an appreciable impact on the performance of a service, it may be required that a workload is moved in full or in part over to another platform away from the issue. For example, a massive distributed denial of service (DDoS) attack may impact the performance of the public internet in a certain geographical area. By having the capability to move the workload (over dedicated links that avoid the DDoS attack) to a different geographical location, the end user experience can be maintained.

Hot, Warm and Cold Images

The increasing availability of pre-configured systems within the cloud has brought the use of various approaches to long-distance high availability into the financial reach of many organisations. In addition, the use of virtual machines or containers as a means of holding an image has allowed for much higher levels of workload portability. The highest level of this is to use a hot image: a complete mirror of a live site that can take over should that site fail for any reason. Indeed, such hot images can also be used for load balancing, with both sites providing live capabilities. However, as both sites are effectively live, the cost of maintaining them is essentially double the cost of maintaining a single live environment.

Warm images are the next level down. Here, the required images are kept running but without any actual live workload being applied against them. They use a minimum amount of resources and cost a lot less to keep running in this close-to-dormant form. Should the live site fail, there will be a break of a short period while the warm images are fully spun up and the live data and user links are pointed at them.

Cold images are the cheapest approach. The images are stored on disk only: they take up no compute or network load at all. When the live site fails, these images are moved into a live environment and data and users are then directed to them. Although this is the slowest of the three approaches, with the increasing speed of provisioning and technical stateful failover (where there is no need for manual intervention in redirecting IP addresses, storage LUNs (logical unit numbers), etc.) now inherent in cloud computing, users can still find themselves back up and running again in short enough timescales to safeguard the longer-term future of the organisation.

In addition, the use of cloud provides various means of dealing with DDoS attacks at a more logical level. Behavioural analytics can be used to identify the DDoS stream, which can then be redirected to a null environment (that is, one where it can have zero impact on the real workload and resources). Streams that are suspect but not proven to be DDoS attacks can be offloaded to lower priority virtual machines (VMs) or containers running on a different part of the cloud, again minimising the impact they have on the overall running of the main systems.

As cloud is an abstracted platform and standards are improving rapidly, such movement of workloads and streams is becoming easier across different clouds. However, real-time movement of workloads across the hybrid multi-cloud platform is still some way off.

HIGH AVAILABILITY

There is no finish line when it comes to system reliability and availability, and our efforts to improve performance never cease.

Marc Benioff (CEO, Salesforce.com), 2006

Just as it manages the allocation of resources to workloads to maintain performance, cloud can also provide much better levels of overall availability to services and applications. As the functionality is effectively abstracted away from the hardware, a well-architected cloud should be capable of surviving the failure of any single piece of hardware. With data mirroring and the use of hot, warm or even cold images across public clouds, organisations that used to consider high availability as being out of their economic reach should now be looking at cloud as a means of gaining high availability in an extremely cost-effective manner.

SUMMARY

What have we learned?

- The promise of cloud is alluring, yet getting cloud wrong can be all too easy.
- Creating a strategy based around cloud being a cheaper platform is the wrong approach: ensure that the right metrics are used.
- IaaS, PaaS and SaaS offer differing models that impact the overall cost–benefit calculation. Make sure that the right platform model is chosen for the right needs.
- Cloud is bringing high availability within reach of most organisations.

What does this mean?

- The provision of a cloud platform is completely different from how previous IT platforms have been provided. IT must change its mindset to meet the challenge of cloud architectures.
- The business will be in far greater control of many decisions, as cloud can offer different levels of service for different risks and costs. Cloud must be able to present the various offers to the business in terms it can understand – and then make sure that the right solution is implemented as the business requires.

4 BASIC CLOUD PLATFORMS

First to mind when asked what 'the cloud' is, a majority respond it's either an actual cloud, the sky, or something related to weather.

Citrix Cloud Survey Guide, August 2012

The market is coalescing around a basic set of core cloud architectures. These may be ones that are owned and run by a single organisation as an IaaS, PaaS or SaaS complete platform (such as Amazon Web Services, Google Cloud Platform, Microsoft Azure or Salesforce.com) or based on a software-only model where the user implements on the cloud their choice of hardware platform (such as CloudStack or OpenStack). It is worth looking at the major platforms currently in use to see the differences between them and what these differences mean for those looking for the right platform or mix of platforms.

POPULAR CLOUD PLATFORMS

In 2000, when my partner Ben Horowitz was CEO of the first cloud computing company, Loudcloud, the cost of a customer running a basic Internet application was approximately $150,000 a month.

Marc Andreessen (co-founder of Netscape and co-founder and general partner at Andreessen Horowitz) in *The Wall Street Journal*, 20 August 2011

As the ASP market died in the early 2000s and was superseded by grid computing, other players were beginning to look at what they needed to power the ever-increasing resource needs of their workloads. A leading light in this space came from a non-IT company. Amazon had built itself up from being a US online-only bookstore that challenged bricks-and-mortar bookshops such as Waterstones and Barnes & Noble to being a global full-service online retail outlet.

Amazon recognised that its current business trajectory would stress pretty much any existing computer architecture. Therefore, in 2003, two of its employees, Chris Pinkham and Benjamin Black, proposed a new scale-out architecture that focused on standardised building blocks that could be heavily automated to remove the costs of maintaining and managing a massive platform. At the end of the proposal, they mentioned that there could be a possibility of renting out any unused resources to third-party entities, much in the same way that commercial distributed grids were then operating.

Amazon built a platform based on Pinkham and Black's proposal, with both its use for Amazon's own workloads and possible public use in mind. The first service that was made available for public consumption was the SQS (Simple Queue Service),[16] in November 2004. This was followed by the Elastic Compute Cloud (EC2),[17] developed by Pinkham and his team in South Africa. The public platform was then named Amazon Web Services (AWS) and became a separate platform from that being used for Amazon itself, which retained its own private platform. However, by 2010, Amazon had ported its own platform over to AWS, demonstrating a belief in the platform as a mission-critical environment.

It took until 2015 for Amazon to state that AWS was profitable. However, by 2016, third-party workloads on AWS were believed to be providing 56% of all of Amazon's profit.[18]

It took a little longer for others in the market to see what Amazon was doing and to respond. Google Cloud Platform was released as a preview platform in April 2008, with the full public release not occurring until October 2011. Microsoft Azure, although announced in October 2008, did not become generally available until February 2010 (under the name Windows Azure, being renamed to Microsoft Azure in 2014).

This allowed AWS to play its first-mover cards. By using a simple pricing model, it made a strong offer to those requiring a development and test environment. Until AWS was launched, the general approach within an organisation, if a new development and test environment needed to be set up, was to identify whether new hardware, operating systems, application servers and so on had to be purchased and provisioned, and then place orders as required, wait for the hardware and software to be delivered, provision and configure it all, and then start on the project work itself. This not only had the potential to be expensive but also took time – many months in some situations.

By providing a ready-built platform that could be up and running in minutes, AWS already had a strong card to play. Backing this up with costs that were low enough to be expensed off a company or personal credit card meant the model was hard to turn down. Developers needing a contained environment could set one up using AWS for a far lower cost than was possible within their own commercial data centre. Moreover, developers didn't have to bother about the technicalities of all the variables that need to be set up during basic provisioning. AWS had tapped into a massive need: its usage grew rapidly.

Although AWS had positioned itself as a full operational environment as well, this was not what organisations wanted from it at first. Workloads that were developed and tested on AWS tended to be pulled back into private data centres for full deployment; the idea of fully commercial workloads being run on someone else's equipment in someone else's facility suffered from poor perceptions around possible security, availability and overall performance. Alongside this, AWS had a pretty basic portfolio, though this was something that it worked to fix, bringing more and more capabilities to the AWS platform, some of which are shown in Figure 4.1 (see page 37).

---

[16] http://docs.aws.amazon.com/AWSSimpleQueueService/latest/SQSDeveloperGuide/Welcome.html
[17] https://aws.amazon.com/ec2
[18] Wingfield, N. (28 April 2016) Amazon's cloud business lifts its profit to a record. *New York Times*. Available from www.nytimes.com/2016/04/29/technology/amazon-q1-earnings.html.

The real breakthrough for AWS came with the companies that found themselves unable to support their business models through the route of a fully owned platform. As more and more transactions moved online, attempting to keep pace with such changes forced some organisations out of business. Others, such as Netflix,[19] knew that to survive they needed to move away from a problematic owned environment to a more predictable and scalable platform. Netflix predicted that its original business model of providing DVD rentals via mail would come under threat as more users took to downloading (at the time, mainly pirated) copies of films. To counter this, Netflix believed that it could instead provide streamed video directly to its customers at a subscription cost over the internet. This would, however, require large storage pools for the video files, massive bandwidth, effective CDN capabilities and a high-availability platform.

Building this as an in-house platform would not be cost-effective. Indeed, in 2008, Netflix had already suffered a large outage on its existing platform that had caused major issues in dealing with its then major DVD rental business.[20] So, rather than build its own data centre facility and its own platform, Netflix went to AWS as a first port of call, using AWS's scale and capabilities to support Netflix's business model from the start. Over time, Netflix has moved more and more of its workloads onto the AWS platform, and the overall project completed in 2016. Using AWS, Netflix has managed to build a platform to enable itself to reach over 80 million customers across most of the globe, bringing in 4K streaming and also creating its own content.

Another major set of customers that helped AWS build momentum were 'born-in-the-cloud' companies. Much like Amazon itself, these companies are predicated on owning as little physical infrastructure as possible. Unlike Amazon, which had to create its own IT platform, this new breed of organisations wants to have access to an easily available and usable IT platform that can flex with their own business models. Organisations such as room-renting business Airbnb[21] and car-ride-share company Lyft[22] use AWS to this end.

Other companies started to see how such a shared infrastructure could benefit them. Many facing a platform review found themselves looking at a choice between building a brand new data centre facility and purchasing and provisioning a complete new plat-form; using a colocation facility for that same new equipment; or looking to the likes of AWS in order to gain a state-of-the-art IT platform rapidly. To this end, AWS has picked up an enviable client list that includes companies such as media software company Adobe,[23] pharmaceutical company Bristol-Myers Squibb,[24] financial provider Capital One[25] and conglomerate General Electric.[26]

As will be covered in Chapters 16, 18 and 19, two major issues that organisations have struggled with have been around the perception of security within the public cloud and

[19] Hunt, N. (2014) Netflix gains new efficiencies using AWS Lambda. AWS. Available from https://aws.amazon.com/solutions/case-studies/netflix-and-aws-lambda

[20] Izrailevsky, Y. (11 February 2016) Completing the Netflix cloud migration. Netflix. Available from https://media.netflix.com/en/company-blog/completing-the-netflix-cloud-migration

[21] https://aws.amazon.com/solutions/case-studies/airbnb

[22] https://aws.amazon.com/solutions/case-studies/lyft

[23] https://aws.amazon.com/solutions/case-studies/adobe

[24] https://aws.amazon.com/solutions/case-studies/bristol-myers-squibb

[25] https://aws.amazon.com/solutions/case-studies/capital-one

[26] https://aws.amazon.com/solutions/case-studies/general-electric

the need for applications to be specifically architected to make the most of a cloud platform. Without the right approach to a new, microservices-based architecture, many 'cloud' projects have resulted in nothing more than a new form of application hosting installed on an IaaS platform.

Whichever way organisations have implemented their workloads on cloud platforms, it is apparent that the main public cloud providers have been successful – particularly in AWS's case. It is believed that by 2015, AWS was hosting workloads on 10 times the amount of infrastructure as the next 14 cloud service providers combined.[27] Measuring such workloads and their actual value is always difficult, but this figure does emphasise how the first-mover advantage of AWS has allowed it to grow to become a considerable player in the market.

Microsoft[28] and Google[29] are by far and away the next largest public cloud providers. Alongside these are a host of other providers, ranging from IBM with its SoftLayer[30] platform through Rackspace[31] to a host of smaller players offering discrete value-added services.

An area that has been a problem for users wanting to create a hybrid environment across multiple private and public platforms has been the speed of interconnects between their own systems and the large public clouds. Historically, such transport has had to be based around either 'best efforts' across the public internet or the use of highly expensive dedicated connections.

In August 2011, AWS introduced Direct Connect,[32] a dedicated link for customers to use into and out of AWS data centre facilities without using existing internet service providers. Direct Connect provides higher data throughputs and more consistent performance at a lower cost than was possible before. Microsoft followed this with its similar approach, Azure ExpressRoute,[33] in February 2014. Both these systems are dependent on third-party cloud service providers or colocation providers (such as NGD[34] in the UK) and are the equivalent of a point of presence (PoP). Therefore, users wanting the best performance should look to a colocation partner for their own systems; alternatively, they will still have to acquire a high-speed initial link from their own facility to one of these PoPs.

Some public cloud platforms can also be marketed as private cloud services through the implementation of a dedicated cloud platform on their systems. However, unless the whole platform is dedicated, then this is really just another instance of a type of public cloud – the underlying hardware is still being pooled and abstracted as resources that are shared across multiple customers. For organisations that have concerns about the sharing of any part of their 'private cloud' platform, this is well worth bearing in mind: make sure you ask prospective service providers what they mean by 'private cloud' before making any decisions.

---

[27] Darrow, B. (19 May 2015) Shocker! Amazon remains the top dog in cloud by far, but Microsoft, Google make strides. *Fortune*. Available from http://fortune.com/2015/05/19/amazon-tops-in-cloud/.
[28] www.microsoft.com/en-gb
[29] https://cloud.google.com
[30] www.softlayer.com
[31] www.rackspace.com/en-gb
[32] https://aws.amazon.com/releasenotes/AWS-Direct-Connect/7982464862957817
[33] https://azure.microsoft.com/en-us/services/expressroute
[34] www.nextgenerationdata.co.uk

THE ARCHITECTURE OF A CLOUD

Never talk to a client about architecture. Talk to him about his children. That is simply good politics. He will not understand what you have to say about architecture most of the time. An architect of ability should be able to tell a client what he wants. Most of the time a client never knows what he wants.

Ludwig Mies van der Rohe (German–American architect) in
Conversations with Mies van der Rohe, 2008

It can be instructive to look at the various platform architectures as put forward by the main players. There are a multitude of such architectural designs available; here, only the basic, general ones will be considered.

The two main public cloud platforms for infrastructure and platform as a service (I/PaaS) are AWS and Microsoft Azure. Both platforms allow users to pick and choose from a selection of functional components to build their own overall system, while providing the capability for users to install their own software as well. Google Cloud Platform tends to be used predominantly as a data manipulation and analysis platform, although it does also act as a general workload platform.

For those wanting to build their own cloud, there are software options, which will be discussed in Chapter 5. However, one platform, OpenStack,[35] is of particular interest, as it is the basis for many of the smaller public cloud choices on the market. It is primarily for those who want to take more of a 'build-your-own' approach to cloud: it comes with fewer functional blocks than AWS, Microsoft Azure or Google Cloud Platform but can be installed on an organisation's or service provider's own hardware. This makes it an ideal platform for third-party public cloud vendors who want to provide their own range of functional services. It also makes it ideal as a private cloud platform and as a hybrid platform with excellent standardisation between the private and public environments.

AWS

At a functional architecture level, AWS (see Figure 4.1) has around 70 basic services[36] with additional subservices under these. The diagram is by no means comprehensive: AWS continues to bring new capabilities to market on a regular basis.

Microsoft Azure

Microsoft Azure also offers a deep portfolio of functional services (see Figure 4.2). Again, it also continues to bring new services to market on a regular basis, and also provides SaaS services over Azure, such as Office 365, Skype for Business, Microsoft Dynamics and so on. As of November 2016, there were over 600 Microsoft Azure services in the platform's portfolio.[37]

---

[35] www.openstack.org
[36] https://aws.amazon.com/products
[37] https://azure.microsoft.com/en-us/services

Figure 4.1 Main AWS functional architecture. Adapted from MSV, Janakiram (2011) Designing fault tolerant applications on AWS [Slide deck]. Amazon Webservices. Available from https://www.slideshare.net/AmazonWebServices/designing-fault-tolerant-applications-on-aws [23 November 2017].

EBS: Elastic Block Store; ELB: Elastic Load Balancing; IAM: Identity and Access Management; MFA: Multifactor Authentication; RDS: Relational Database Service; S3: Simple Storage Service; SES: Simple Email Service; SNS: Simple Notification Service; SWF: Simple Workflow Service; VM: Virtual Machine; VPC: Virtual Private Cloud.

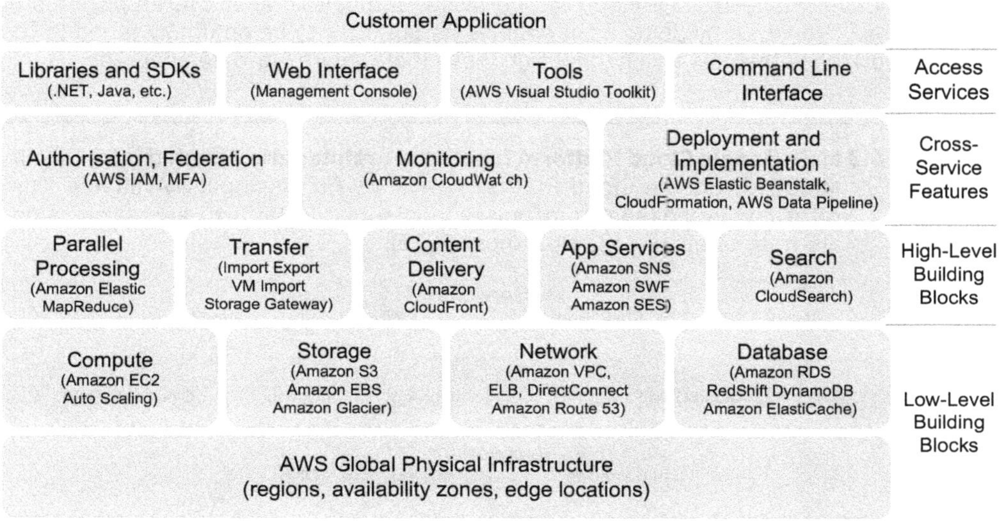

Figure 4.2 Main Microsoft Azure functional architecture Adapted from Niepel, R. (2017) Microsoft Azure overview. Microsoft Azure. Available from http://azureplatform.azurewebsites.net/en-us/ [22 November 2017].

VS: Visual Studio.

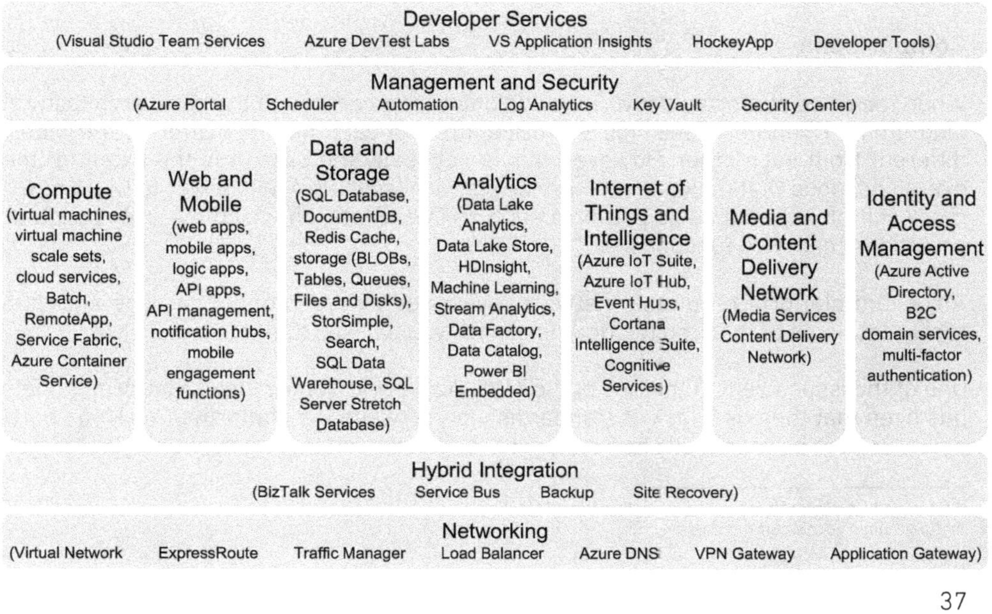

37

Microsoft has also introduced Azure Stack as a private, on-premises version of Azure.[38] Released in September 2017, Azure Stack is available pre-installed on hardware from Dell, HP Enterprise and Lenovo, enabling those wanting a higher level of workload flexibility across a hybrid cloud to achieve this over a more standardised Azure environment.

Google Cloud Platform

Google Cloud Platform (see Figure 4.3) provides a much smaller overall portfolio of functions.[39] However, by doing so, it enables its platform to be optimally tuned to the main workloads that it is trying to attract: those that require big-data analysis.

Figure 4.3 Main Google Cloud Platform functional architecture Adapted from Selcuk, M. (2015) Google Cloud Platform for AWS Professionals. Available from https://www.linkedin.com/pulse/google-cloud-platform-aws-profession-als-murat-selcuk-/ [22 November 2017].

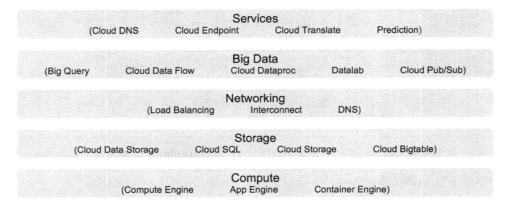

Comparisons

When the three platforms above are additionally compared with the basic architectural diagram for OpenStack (see Figure 4.4), it at first appears that the platforms are widely different from each other. However, this is not really the case: it is the extent of the overall portfolio that makes a full-service platform such as AWS appear to be so much more complex than a basic platform such as OpenStack on which the user builds or provisions their own functions.

Any cloud platform requires a network layer, along with compute, storage and data resources. In all of the architectural diagrams, you will see that this is the case.

One of the issues behind the rise of the AWS, Azure and Google Cloud Platform models has been that there is a lack of standardisation between the platforms. Workload portability used to be essentially non-existent but has been improving over time. OpenStack

---

[38] https://azure.microsoft.com/en-gb/overview/azure-stack
[39] https://cloud.google.com/products

Figure 4.4 Basic OpenStack functional architecture (Source: OpenStack)

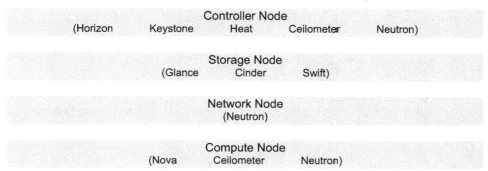

is one attempt to provide a cloud platform that is far more agnostic as to the hardware it can be built on and the workloads that can be run on it. However, another company that has recognised a need for a more standardised approach is Facebook.[40]

OPEN COMPUTE PROJECT

> Facebook was not originally created to be a company. It was built to accomplish a social mission – to make the world more open and connected.
>
> Mark Zuckerberg (founder and CEO of Facebook) in
> S-1 Letter to the SEC, 1 February 2012

In April 2011, Facebook employee Jonathan Heiliger put forward an initiative to openly share design aspects of Facebook's data centres. The idea was that this could be a win–win for Facebook and others looking at hyperscale cloud platforms (platforms built from stripped-down, commodity components that can support millions of concurrent users). Facebook, which had already tried several different approaches to creating a hyperscale cloud, was in the midst of building its new Prineville data centre in Oregon and knew that its design was still not as good as it could be. By sharing some of the basic design principles, Facebook hoped not only to help drive hyperscale cloud computing in other companies but also to gain back ideas as to how to improve what it already had.

Facebook therefore initiated the Open Compute Project (OCP),[41] bringing in Apple, Bank of America, Cisco, Dell Technologies, Ericsson, Fidelity, Goldman Sachs, Google, Intel, Juniper Networks, Lenovo, Microsoft, Nokia, Rackspace and Seagate Technology among others as members of the project since its inception.

OCP has defined several component building blocks for hyperscale clouds, including the following:

---

[40] www.facebook.com/FacebookUK/?brand_redir=20531316728
[41] www.opencompute.org

- Intel and AMD compute nodes.

- Open Vault storage, which was previously code-named Knox.[42] Facebook and Wiwynn introduced a non-volatile memory express (NVMe) JBOF (just a bunch of flash) version of Knox, known as Lightning. Other projects include OpenNVM[43] and Cold Storage. Commercial offerings based around Open Vault include systems from Hyve[44] and SanDisk[45] Fusion-io flash storage cards.

- A mechanical mounting system. Instead of using off-the-shelf 19" racks, OCP has designed and defined racks that take up the same physical space, yet can take wider equipment while improving cooling. This has also led to a new 'OpenU' unit of rack, as opposed to the standard 'U'.

- Better energy designs, including through losing one electrical transformer stage and using 277 VAC (volts alternating current) downstepped to 12.5 VDC (volts direct current) with a 48 VDC backup system.

- There have also been several attempts to standardise on 'OpenSwitch' network hardware, although this has, so far, proved elusive.

OCP operates as a non-profit organisation but has a large and active membership of organisations,[46] although individuals can also become members.[47]

SUMMARY

What have we learned?

- Different major cloud platforms have taken different routes.

- Overall, however, cloud platforms have a common approach to managing resources.

- Cloud functional portfolios, both in private and public spaces, are growing rapidly.

- Cloud service providers and hardware and software vendors are working together to provide higher degrees of standardisation across cloud platforms, both at the hardware and the software levels.

What does this mean?

- As abstraction becomes more standardised, cloud interoperability has improved.

- Cloud workload portability is improving but still has a way to go.

- Organisations must ensure that the overall end platform they are aiming for will not result in a need for wholesale change as a lack of common capabilities bites.

[42] www.opencompute.org/projects/open-vault-storage
[43] http://opennvm.github.io
[44] https://hyvesolutions.com
[45] www.sandisk.com/business/datacenter
[46] http://www.opencompute.org/membership/membership-organizational-directory/
[47] http://www.opencompute.org/community/get-involved/tiered-membership/individual-ocp-community-membership/

5 ALTERNATIVE CLOUD PLATFORMS

You must not blame me if I do talk to the clouds.
> Henry David Thoreau in a letter, 2 March 1842

Alongside the main public cloud providers are a raft of others. Some of these providers have tried to offer (indeed, some still are offering) their own proprietary cloud technology. However, the majority have decided to use a core platform of a more standardised technology, with additional functionality and capabilities as they see fit.

PRIVATE AND PUBLIC CLOUD OFFERINGS

> If you think about the market that we're in, and more broadly just the enterprise software market, the kind of transition that's happening right now from legacy systems to the cloud is literally, by definition, a once-in-a-lifetime opportunity.
> Aaron Levie (co-founder and CEO of Box) in *The New York Times*, 26 August 2012

The major cloud platforms were discussed in Chapter 4, but there are many other choices available to those looking for alternatives. Some aim to be predominantly private cloud platforms, others predominantly public. It is my view that those that are aimed at bridging the gap between the private and public cloud platforms – in other words, becoming hybrid clouds – are the ones that stand the most chance of being successful.

The immaturity of the cloud market has been demonstrated in the dynamics of how the various platforms have emerged, progressed, been acquired, died or been killed off, and many companies have found that the development of proprietary cloud platforms is a quick route to economic ruin. Some platforms have died for purely technical reasons; others for commercial and marketing ones. Some platforms have surprisingly survived due to laser-sharp messaging as to the business value that they offer. This chapter looks at some of the stories behind these platforms.

CloudStack

One such open source cloud platform is CloudStack,[48] originally started by Cloud.com (previously known as VMops). Around 95% of the software that made up CloudStack was released to market under the GNU General Public License version 3 (GPLv3). CloudStack

---

[48] https://cloudstack.apache.org

gained support from a strong vendor when Citrix[49] chose to support it as its main cloud system. However, both Cloud.com and Citrix had also expressed support for OpenStack, and development of the CloudStack platform appeared to be heading towards a convergent OpenStack platform. In July 2011, Cloud.com and the CloudStack software were acquired by Citrix.

Citrix released the whole CloudStack platform under the GPLv3 open source licence system. Citrix also made some advances in the development of the platform, most notably in providing support for Swift,[50] the object storage system that underpins OpenStack. Although CloudStack met with a modicum of success, Citrix donated the software to the Apache Software Foundation[51] in April 2012.

CloudStack became an Apache Incubator product, changed its licence to Apache License v2.0 and became a 'Top-Level Project' in March 2013. It is in use by several organisations (a current list is available on the Apache CloudStack website[52]). However, it is losing out to OpenStack in the overall market.

VMware

VMware[53] released vCloud Air[54] as vCloud Hybrid Service in the commercial public cloud environment in 2013. The idea of this cloud service was to act as an extension of an organisation's existing environment, bridging existing VMware vSphere systems with an elastic IaaS platform that shared common management over a common network system. vCloud Hybrid Service was renamed vCloud Air in August 2014. Subsequently, VMware showed an interest in the use of OpenStack as a cloud platform, but in October 2016 it announced a new technology partnership with AWS, with a VMware Cloud on the AWS platform. The stated aim of VMware Cloud is to provide a common means of developing, provisioning, operating and managing workloads across existing VMware and AWS environments, leveraging existing skills in VMware's product portfolio while gaining the cost benefits and flexibility of the AWS platform.[55] Also in October 2016, VMware announced an agreement with colocation provider Equinix[56] to provide high-speed connectivity between a vCloud Air private cloud user and Equinix's facilities using either Equinix's multi-cloud fast connections (called Cloud Exchange) or Equinix's own PoP capability as an AWS Direct Connect provider; the idea was to enable the more predictable and effective movement of workloads across a hybrid cloud platform. However, in April 2017, VMware divested vCloud Air to French cloud services provider OVH.[57]

---

[49] www.citrix.co.uk
[50] www.swiftstack.com/product/openstack-swift
[51] www.apache.org
[52] https://cloudstack.apache.org/users.html
[53] www.vmware.com
[54] http://vcloud.vmware.com/uk
[55] www.vmware.com/company/news/releases/vmw-newsfeed.VMware-and-AWS-Announce-New-Hybrid-Cloud-Service,-%E2%80%9CVMware-Cloud-on-AWS%E2%80%9D.3188645-manual.html
[56] www.equinix.co.uk
[57] www.ovh.com/us/news/cp2451.ovh_announces_intent_to_acquire_vmware_vcloud_air_business

Dell Technologies

Dell Technologies is another company that has tried a few different approaches to cloud. It initially introduced a proprietary cloud, which was replaced with an OpenStack platform. However, it decided that it could best serve its customers through becoming a cloud aggregator, offering a few fully certified application integrations. Dell would be the main contract holder bearing responsibility for sorting out any issues that became apparent.

However, since acquiring EMC in 2016, the new Dell Technologies has become the owner of several cloud approaches, including VMware's Cloud Foundation, Pivotal Cloud Foundry and Virtustream.[58] Dell is now making Virtustream its main cloud focus going forward, having firmed up on EMC's decision to create Virtustream as a separate division providing cloud services and software.

Virtustream was founded in 2009 and provides a range of cloud services with optimised support not only for cloud-native functions and services but also to enable organisations to host and run non-cloud-native applications. Virtustream does this through a microservices container-based approach, called MicroVM, or μVM. The platform, managed through Virtustream's xStream orchestration, deployment and control services, provides Dell Technologies with a cloud platform that not only is proven in the market but also comes with a collection of good customers, including Diesel Direct,[59] Domino Sugar[60] and the British Transport Police.[61]

IBM Bluemix and SoftLayer

Cloud Foundry also forms part of the IBM Bluemix[62] platform. Bluemix was originally launched as a development testbed where certain IBM services could be tried out and integrated into users' own systems. However, it soon became apparent that Bluemix users wanted to take things further without having to go through a migration path to a run-time cloud, and Bluemix has grown to provide a full-service platform from development through to an operational cloud. Its customers include Wimbledon Lawn Tennis Club,[63] the KLM Golf Open tournament[64] and Citi Bank.[65]

In addition to Bluemix as a development-to-run-time platform, IBM has its main cloud platform, SoftLayer.[66] Founded in 2005, SoftLayer built up a hosting and cloud platform model. By 2013, SoftLayer had grown to have a strong customer base along with an impressive set of capabilities. This caught the eye of IBM, which acquired the company in June 2013. Although formally known as the IBM Cloud Services Division within IBM, SoftLayer has become the accepted name for IBM's main cloud platform. SoftLayer has customers including Jelastic,[67] Coriell Life Sciences[68] and NexGen.[69]

[58] www.virtustream.com
[59] www.virtustream.com/solutions/case-studies/diesel-direct
[60] www.virtustream.com/solutions/case-studies/domino-sugar
[61] www.featuredcustomers.com/media/CustomerCaseStudy.document/BTP_FINAL.pdf
[62] www.ibm.com/cloud-computing/bluemix
[63] www-01.ibm.com/common/ssi/cgi-bin/ssialias?subtype=AB&infotype=PM&htmlid=YTC04041USEN&attachment=YTC04041USEN.PDF
[64] www-01.ibm.com/common/ssi/cgi-bin/ssialias?subtype=PS&infotype=SA&htmltid=MEP03044USEN&attachment=MEP03044USEN.PDF
[65] www.youtube.com/watch?v=VjJ46gJYHoU&feature=youtu.be&t=31m47s
[66] www.softlayer.com
[67] www.softlayer.com/sites/default/files/assets/page/jelastic_softlayer-case-study.pdf
[68] http://cdn.softlayer.com/case-studies/CoriellLife-Case-Study.pdf
[69] http://static.softlayer.com/sites/default/files/assets/page/ss-NexGen-Case-Study.pdf

HP Helion

HP was a relatively early vendor to jump on the cloud bandwagon. HP launched a beta version of HP Public Cloud in May 2012, with a Relational Database Service offering announced at the MySQL User Conference by Brian Aker. HP Public Cloud included an OpenStack technology-based object storage system (HP Cloud Object Storage) and a content delivery network (HP Cloud CDN). In May 2014 HP announced plans to invest over $1 billion across two years in HP Public Cloud, but the decision was later reversed, with HP Public Cloud being shut down in January 2016.

HP then decided that targeting the private cloud via OpenStack was a better option. To bolster its offerings, in July 2015 it acquired ActiveState, through which it gained Stackato, a Cloud Foundry-based application platform that uses Docker containers. Stackato was brought into the HP Helion portfolio. With HP now having split into HP Enterprise and HP Inc, its Helion Cloud portfolio[70] is now offered under the Enterprise (HPE) side of the business. These combined services are now available as the HPE Helion Stackato PaaS platform.[71]

In May 2017, UK-based Micro Focus acquired a large portion of HPE's software business, including the assets from HP's Autonomy, Vertica, Mercury Interactive and Arcsight acquisitions. The loss of some of these assets has left HP Enterprise with a cloud platform but very little else to build on top of it.

HPE also has HPE Helion Eucalyptus,[72] an open source means of creating a hybrid platform where AWS workloads can be more easily moved from AWS to private or other public clouds and vice versa.

HPE Helion has customers including BT,[73] Tiscali[74] and Computacenter.[75]

Oracle

Oracle has been a noticeable latecomer to the cloud party. Although it had put forward a cloud architecture as far back as 2011, this was a highly proprietary Solaris/RISC platform that never really caught the eye of prospective users. A new strategy, built around a more standardised Intel Xeon architecture, was pre-announced with little detail as Oracle Cloud[76] at Oracle World in 2015, with general availability coming through in October 2016. Larry Ellison, Oracle's executive chairman and chief technology officer, stated that Oracle Cloud was capable of 'crushing AWS'.[77] To support this, Oracle has

---

[70] www.hpe.com/uk/en/solutions/cloud.html

[71] www8.hp.com/uk/en/cloud/stackato.html

[72] www8.hp.com/uk/en/cloud/helion-eucalyptus-overview.html

[73] www.hp-cloudstories.com/content/A-Discussion-with-British-Telecom--The-Value-of-HP-Helion-Network?extId=&caid=

[74] www.hp-cloudstories.com/content/Tiscali--Providing-an-End-to-End-Solution?extId=&caid=

[75] www.hp-cloudstories.com/content/Computacenter--HPE-Helion-Partner-Success-Story?extId=&caid=

[76] https://cloud.oracle.com/home

[77] Weinberger M. (19 September 2016) Larry Ellison says Oracle's new cloud will crush Amazon – but the rest of the world isn't so sure. *Business Insider UK*. Available from http://uk.businessinsider.com/larry-ellison-oracle-cloud-amazon-web-services-2016-9.

presented a full portfolio of 'as a service' products: not only I/PaaS and SaaS but also a full cloud marketplace alongside a broad raft of additional services, such as database as a service and a social media cloud service. It has also announced several customers, including M&C Saatchi,[78] Panasonic[79] and Kenya Airways.[80] At its 2017 event, it announced further price cuts with a promise to undercut AWS 'by 50%' and also introduced an autonomous database that could be run in the cloud.

Cisco

Cisco decided that a one-vendor cloud platform would not meet the needs of its customers. It therefore decided to become a cloud aggregator, offering a service that spanned and integrated a range of third-party clouds. This overall platform, to be known as the Intercloud, focused on creating, orchestrating and managing workloads across a fully hybrid cloud. Cisco took an OpenStack-centric approach along with containers to create a standardised platform. Cisco Cloud has customers such as NBC (for its coverage of the 2014 Winter Olympic Games)[81] and the Salvation Army.[82]

In 2016, Cisco announced the planned end of sale of its Intercloud service as of April 2017.[83] It will now focus more on enabling customers to deploy and move workloads between clouds as required. To achieve this, Cisco has introduced a software suite called CloudCentre (based on assets it gained through its acquisition of CliQr) and has partnered with Apprenda[84] to provide a PaaS platform where Cisco can overlay its application-centric infrastructure (ACI). It has also partnered with Pivotal[85] to provide a similarly ACI-powered private cloud platform.

CONTAINER PLATFORMS

> Architecture is basically a container of something. I hope they will enjoy not so much the teacup, but the tea.
>
> Attributed to Yoshio Taniguchi (architect, b. 1937)

A major aspect of cloud computing concerns how the functional services are packaged. In Chapter 19 I take a deep look at the options available, such as VMs and containers. However, there is a need for tooling to be employed to make the use of such packaged systems far easier.

In many cases, these tools will be discrete and layered on top of cloud. However, there are some systems available that are far more capable of being built into the platform, creating a PaaS level of container service. These platforms also bring in various aspects of continuous integration (CI) and continuous delivery (CD) with them (see Chapter 12).

---

[78] http://medianetwork.oracle.com/video/player/4933650747001
[79] http://medianetwork.oracle.com/video/player/4930613824001
[80] http://medianetwork.oracle.com/video/player/4814819740001
[81] https://newsroom.cisco.com/video-content?type=webcontent&articleId=1344037
[82] www.cisco.com/c/en/us/solutions/cloud/featured-case-studies.html
[83] www.cisco.com/c/en/us/products/collateral/cloud-systems-management/interc oud-fabric/eos-eol-notice-c51-738014.html
[84] https://apprenda.com/cisco
[85] https://pivotal.io/cisco

Currently, the main focus of these platforms is around support for Docker containers, but this is expected to change as the container market evolves.

Here are some examples.

Docker's own offerings

Docker has a broad set of its own offerings aimed at managing Docker containers throughout their life.

- Docker Cloud[86] is operated on a platform that is run by Docker itself. However, it allows users to provision and operate their own containers within VMs.
- Docker Datacenter[87] is a means of running containers on the user's premises or on public cloud platforms.
- Docker UCP (Universal Control Plane)[88] adds a management layer over Docker operations, including clusters of containers configured under Docker Swarm.[89]

Cloud Foundry

Cloud Foundry[90] was originally created as a skunkworks project by a small team of Google employees under Derek Collinson as Project B29. The work was then picked up by VMware as part of a cloud PaaS system. Ownership of the Cloud Foundry project was spun out to the Cloud Foundry Foundation in 2014, with EMC, HP, IBM, Rackspace, SAP and VMware as platinum sponsors. Cloud Foundry is available as open source software under the Apache License v2.

Pivotal,[91] a company set up in 2012 as a joint venture between EMC, General Electric and VMware, offers a commercially supported version of the Cloud Foundry platform. As part of the then EMC Federation banner, Pivotal became part of the Dell Technologies company and has now been spun out as a separate company. General Electric also uses Cloud Foundry in its GE Predix[92] platform, as do CenturyLink (in its cloud platform),[93] IBM (within Bluemix)[94] and Swisscom.[95]

Kubernetes

Kubernetes[96] is an open source platform announced by Google in 2014. It uses sets of loosely coupled 'primitives' (building blocks of components) that build into 'services' that group containers together to form a common function. 'Pods' are used as a managed means of grouping containers together. 'Replication controllers' are then used to manage the lifecycle of containers.

---

[86] https://cloud.docker.com
[87] https://blog.docker.com/2016/02/docker-datacenter-caas
[88] https://docs.docker.com/datacenter/ucp/1.1
[89] https://docs.docker.com/swarm
[90] www.Cloud Foundry.org
[91] https://pivotal.io
[92] www.ge.com/digital/predix
[93] https://uk.ctl.io/private-cloud/251w
[94] www.ibm.com/developerworks/cloud/library/cl-bluemixfoundry/index.html
[95] www.swisscom.ch/en/business/enterprise/angebot/cloud-data-center-services/paas/application-cloud.html
[96] https://kubernetes.io

Kubernetes has garnered a great deal of support. It is specifically supported by IBM in its IBM Cloud private product[97] and is used as the base platform by CentOS in Tectonic[98] and by RedHat in its OpenShift[99] product.

OpenShift

OpenShift is, at the time of writing, the predominant commercially supported distribution of Kubernetes. First released by Red Hat in 2011, OpenShift has evolved into a series of products aimed at various needs:

- OpenShift Origin is a freely downloadable open source offering under the Apache License v2.0.

- OpenShift Online is a public cloud development and hosting service offered by Red Hat.

- OpenShift Dedicated is a managed private cluster offering. It can be accessed on AWS and Google Cloud Platform.

- OpenShift Container Platform is a dedicated on-premises version built on Red Hat's own Linux distribution.

Mesos

Mesos[100] is an open source project started in 2009 (as Nexus) and operated under the Apache foundation. Mesos provides a slightly unusual approach, as it operates as a distributed systems kernel that directly abstracts logical resources away from the underlying hardware while providing a set of open APIs that enable application functions (e.g. Elasticsearch, Hadoop, Kafka, Spark) to be enacted. Mesos itself can therefore be used as an application platform.

Mesos also has Marathon, which is its own system for orchestrating and managing containers, along with Chronos, which enables dependencies between jobs to be expressed.

Mesosphere Inc[101] provides a commercially supported product called the DCOS (Datacenter Operating System), which is based on Mesos. In 2015, Microsoft entered into a commercial relationship with Mesosphere to provide container scheduling and orchestration services for Azure.[102]

THE CURRENT CHAOS OF CLOUD

Chaos is inherent in all compounded things. Strive on with diligence.
Gautama Buddha (enlightened ascetic, c. sixth–fourth century BCE)
in the *Mahāparinibbāna Sutta*

---

[97] www.ibm.com/blogs/bluemix/2017/06/ibm-announces-kubernetes-base-ibm-cloud-private-platform/?social_post=9527 37968&fst=Learn&linkId=39144552
[98] https://coreos.com/tectonic
[99] www.openshift.com
[100] http://mesos.apache.org
[101] https://mesosphere.com
[102] https://mesosphere.com/blog/2015/09/29/mesosphere-and-mesos-power-the-microsoft-azure-container-service

Outside the players mentioned above, there are several other cloud platforms available as options. Some of these are aimed at specific markets, others are aimed at offering alternatives to existing platforms and still others are trying to beat the general-purpose cloud platforms at their own game.

An example of an alternative platform is OpenNebula[103], an open source cloud platform and management ecosystem that also has a variant called vOneCloud[104], which purports to be able to replace vCloud as a platform, enabling full portability of vCloud workloads. Another is Jelastic[105], which provides a cloud portfolio to support private and public clouds. Eucalyptus[106] offers an open source capability to build AWS EC2-compatible clouds.

Canonical states that it has the largest market share of OpenStack clouds, which are deployed using its Ubuntu operating system[107]. Canonical offers a full portfolio of tools to help users set up, configure, manage and run an OpenStack cloud environment. Ubuntu is also the most deployed cloud guest operating system (the operating system that the deployed application or service sees), with certified images available for AWS, Google Cloud Platform, IBM SoftLayer, Microsoft Azure, Oracle and Rackspace.

In addition to this variety of cloud platforms, there are a large number of service providers available. Comparing providers is quite difficult, not only because of the hardware, software and services they offer but also because each provider puts forward its own unique selling point. In many cases, this unique selling point is anything but 'unique'; in others, although it is unique, it may have dubious business value. However, many do provide specific services that have discrete value for specific users or types of business.

The following are just a very small sample of the variety of approaches taken by service providers:

- **Alibaba Cloud:**[108] The Chinese cloud computing arm of e-trading company Alibaba.com; effectively, the equivalent of AWS and Amazon for the Chinese and other Asian markets.

- **CenturyLink:**[109] A global provider of cloud, communications and IT business services.

- **CloudSigma:**[110] A broad-scale IaaS and cloud service provider that benefits from a global relationship with Equinix.

- **DigitalOcean:**[111] A global provider of IaaS services aimed at the development community.

- **ElasticHosts:**[112] A global provider focused on developers, systems administrators and engineers.

---

[103] www.nimbusproject.org
[104] http://vonecloud.today
[105] https://jelastic.com
[106] https://github.com/eucalyptus/eucalyptus/wiki
[107] www.ubuntu.com/cloud
[108] https://cn.aliyun.com
[109] www.centurylink.com/business/home
[110] www.cloudsigma.com
[111] www.digitalocean.com
[112] www.elastichosts.co.uk

- **Heroku:**[113] A platform that targets born-in-the-cloud startups and fast-moving companies that believe continuous development and integration are key. Heroku positions itself as a cloud focused on apps.

- **Joyent:**[114] Recently acquired by Samsung, Joyent has to date focused on providing services around Node.js, an object-based storage system called Manta and a 'container as a service' offering called Triton.

- **Nimbus:**[115] A cloud service aimed at scientists, based on an EC2/S3-compatible platform.

- **Rackspace:**[116] A global service provider and the co-founder of OpenStack (with NASA). Rackspace also provides straightforward hosting services alongside its cloud offerings, as well as baremetal servers.

- **Scaleway:**[117] A European IaaS service provider that enables baremetal x86-64 and ARMv7 cloud servers to be provisioned with a pure flash storage back-end storage system.

- **ZettaGrid:**[118] An Australian service provider that offers self-service secure cloud platforms.

Baremetal Cloud Services

Service providers such as Rackspace and Scaleway provide what are called 'baremetal' cloud services. These dedicated servers require the provisioning of a full stack of software from the hypervisor or operating system upward. The concept may seem to be just another form of hosting; however, the idea is that a customer takes several of these baremetal servers and creates a private cloud across them. The service provider supplies all the intra-server interconnects at high speed and the premise is that the customer gets an increase in overall speed as there are no additional software steps between the customer's software stack and the hardware.

Choosing the four or five service providers that should be on an organisation's shortlist is therefore not easy, and many organisations will choose instead to either go for a service provided by their incumbent IT supplier or to go for the 'usual suspects'. However, it is recommended that heavy due diligence is carried out so as to ensure that the service provider is aligned with the organisation's business aims, that it meets agreed security ideals (such as ISO 27001), that it can work with the organisation as a trusted partner and so on.

---

[113] www.heroku.com
[114] www.joyent.com
[115] www.nimbusproject.org
[116] www.rackspace.com/en-gb
[117] www.scaleway.com
[118] www.zettagrid.com

This list of service providers is obviously not complete, but it is provided to offer a glimpse of the variety of approaches that providers are taking to offering cloud services. One company that is trying to help minimise the chaos is Clover, provided by UK-based consultancy Behind every Cloud.[119] Clover is creating a database of cloud providers that enables prospects to input their needs and rapidly identify the service providers that can fulfil those needs. Currently focused on the financial industries, Clover is also looking at other heavily regulated industries and should then be able to reach out into more general markets. However, any attempt to build a like-for-like comparison engine that meets the needs of everyone will be fraught with issues. Not everyone is looking for the same end result from their choice of cloud platform. Trying to deal with each possible need, even for a single market segment, will require a lot of continuous effort in maintaining a database of all service providers' offerings.

The market is also changing on a regular basis. As stated, Joyent has already been acquired by Samsung, and Rackspace was put up for sale a couple of times in recent years before being acquired by private equity firm Apollo Global Management. Alongside these changes in ownership, other aspects of mergers and acquisitions have impacted, and will continue to impact, the cloud service provider market. The overall dynamics in the facility market (e.g. Equinix acquiring Verizon's data centres after also acquiring Telecity) and the consolidation of the cloud market itself (e.g. CenturyLink acquired Level 3, and Canada's ITUtility.net has been acquired by HostedBizz) are likely to continue. Mergers and acquisitions will aim to promote growth in the number of customers being hosted and also in the extra functionalities being offered, so as to try to differentiate service providers in the market.

There is also a vibrant ecosystem of providers of software and cloud-based tools around the whole cloud concept. Although providers such as AWS (with CloudFormation) and VMware (with vRealize Suite) provide a degree of cloud orchestration and management capabilities, there are still many aspects that require third-party software or services to be brought in to provide the required end result. A few of these are:

- **Flexiant:**[120] A provider of cloud orchestration and management software.

- **OnApp:**[121] A company with a portfolio of offerings that help users to manage and orchestrate clouds, mainly focused on service providers. OnApp also offers a 'cloud in a box' service in conjunction with Intel, called Intel Turnkey Private Cloud, to enable service providers to offer quick deployment of cost-effective virtual private clouds to small and medium enterprises.

- **OpenQRM:**[122] Cloud-management and orchestration software provided by German company OpenQRM Enterprise GmbH, which also offers an IaaS cloud service.

- **OpenShift:**[123] A PaaS offering from Red Hat based on Kubernetes and Docker to enable containerised deployment and orchestration in a highly scalable and secure environment.

---

[119] www.cloverindex.com
[120] www.flexiant.com
[121] http://onapp.com
[122] www.openqrm.com
[123] www.openshift.com

- **ServiceNow:**[124] Having acquired ITapp, ServiceNow has a multi-cloud orchestration capability, provided as a SaaS offering.

Again, this list shows only a small selection of the vendors in this space. Around them are all the vendors involved in the end-to-end process of creating, provisioning, monitoring and managing a cloud platform: those in the DevOps space, such as open source Ansible, Chef, Jenkins, Puppet and so on. Other vendors (such as BMC Software, CA Technologies, HP and IBM) provide cloud systems-management capabilities, leveraging their skills built on years of providing tools to manage physical platforms. Then there are vendors that provide cloud platform data centre infrastructure management tools, which have emerged from building information management systems, such as Future Facilities,[125] Nlyte[126] and Vertiv.[127] Others provide systems to monitor software and service usage across a cloud, such as Flexera,[128] Snow Software[129] and RES Software[130] (acquired by Ivanti in July 2017). The list goes on, and its extent creates issues for those investigating just what is required for them to create a cloud platform that does what it is meant to do: facilitate an organisation's needs.

The Rise of DevOps

Historically, IT projects have been run on a waterfall or cascade basis consisting of the coding and introduction of a test version followed by a major release of a working version followed by timed versions of bug fixes and new functionality. The move to Agile project management sped up the capability for IT to get new software functionality into the hands of users. Now, the use of 'DevOps' has appeared, where development and operations teams work far more closely together to ensure that new software is prepared and tested rapidly and is pushed out into the operational environment in the quickest possible time (but still with all the requisite checks and balances in place around software quality). Whereas Agile is a software-focused project-management approach, DevOps covers hardware management as well, although DevOps generally includes Agile constructs in the software side of its processes.

The market is currently a mess. There are far too many low-end small players, and a market reset is due. Creating a complete workable cloud system is like trying to complete a 1,000-piece jigsaw without a picture to work from. Attempting to put together a shopping list for a total cloud-based solution is, in most cases, far too difficult: the market will need to shift much further towards a more complete service model where everything is carried out automatically, from the provision of resources and software to

---

[124] www.servicenow.com/products/orchestration/cloud-management.html
[125] www.futurefacilities.com
[126] www.nlyte.com
[127] www.vertivco.com
[128] www.flexerasoftware.com
[129] www.snowsoftware.com/int
[130] https://res.com

the monitoring and maintaining of performance to the updating and patching of hardware and software. As much of this is actually part and parcel of the original promise of cloud, returning to a focus on that basic definition may be a good idea for many in the market.

The ASP market of the late 1990s collapsed due to a range of business and technical issues. For cloud service providers, what will weed out the poor providers from the strong will be the ability to ensure that prospects' expectations are managed and the ability to deliver continuous improvement in capabilities to meet or better those expectations.

One aspect that is emerging that could help in ameliorating the chaos problem is 'serverless computing'. In this model, also known as function as a service (FaaS) and as compute as a service (CompaaS), the customer does not pay to set up and operate the resources needed to run a service. Instead, the service provider dynamically monitors, provides and manages whatever resources are required and charges for them based on the servicing of the function(s) being run. This removes many of the aspects around the need for orchestration from the end user, but it does mean that the service provider has to get such processes 100% right.

The original concept of serverless computing was based on work carried out around exposing functions via APIs by Zimki in 2006. In 2016, AWS launched its version of serverless computing, which it called Lambda[131] – originally only a means of dealing with Node.js workloads but since extended to include Java and Python as well as other languages, such as Haskell, if Node.js is used as an invocation engine.

Others that have introduced serverless computing capabilities include Google, with its Google Cloud Functions,[132] and IBM, with its Bluemix OpenWhisk[133] service. Microsoft has also announced Azure Functions.[134]

SUMMARY

What have we learned?

- The major cloud platforms do not have the market all to themselves.
- However, many current alternative general cloud platforms are unlikely to survive in the mid- to long term.
- Specialised cloud platforms with discrete capabilities and providing distinct business value services are the most likely smaller cloud providers to survive.
- The ecosystem around cloud computing is both vibrant and confusing. Vendors will need to choose their partners carefully and pick their battles even more carefully to make sure that they are seen as indispensable parts of the overall cloud solution.

---

[131] https://aws.amazon.com/lambda
[132] https://cloud.google.com/functions
[133] www.ibm.com/cloud-computing/bluemix/openwhisk
[134] https://azure.microsoft.com/en-gb/services/functions

- The market will drive a need for less chaotic approaches, including serverless computing.

What does this mean?

- Potential cloud users must be careful in how they choose a cloud provider.
- As an overall cloud platform is likely to involve several different cloud providers, interoperability will be key. Avoid vendor lock-in at all costs.
- The dynamic nature of cloud requires greater degrees of care and due diligence in ensuring the choice of cloud partners that are fit for the future.

6 ALTERNATIVE CLOUD MODELS

Some people don't like change, but you need to embrace change if the alternative is disaster.

Elon Musk (billionaire entrepreneur) in an interview with
The Daily Beast, 25 April 2011

If every workload could be run on the same cloud platform, life would be simple. However, this is not the case. Instead, hybrid cloud is the reality, with workloads running on multiple different clouds. Not every private cloud can provide the services that an organisation requires. Not every public cloud provider fulfils every requirement, either.

Creating an overall platform that enables different workloads to operate together in as seamless a manner as possible requires different types of cloud business models: cloud brokers and cloud aggregators.

CLOUD BROKER

If we as a society do not understand 'the cloud,' in all its aspects – what data it holds, how it works, what the bargains are we make as we engage with it, we'll all be the poorer for it, I believe.

John Battelle (journalist and author) on his blog, 29 August 2012

A cloud broker acts as an intermediary between a customer and several different cloud providers (see Figure 6.1). The idea is that the cloud broker acts as the 'one throat to choke' in the arrangement. Rather than having multiple contracts with multiple cloud providers, the customer has a single overall contract with the broker. Should there be any technical issues, the cloud broker takes the responsibility for identifying where within the mix of cloud service providers the issue lies, and for getting the issue fixed.

Therefore, a cloud broker does not have to own any infrastructure itself. It will need some capability to run its own systems (e.g. for billing and so on) and it may choose to provide portals for its customers to view the overall health of the cloud platforms under its contracts. However, a cloud broker does not have to provide any functional software services in itself.

Examples of cloud brokers include ComputeNext,[135] Skyhigh Networks[136] (which operates as a cloud access security broker), CloudMore[137] and IBM.

---

[135] www.computenext.com/cloud-service-brokerage
[136] www.skyhighnetworks.com/cloud-access-security-broker
[137] www.cloudmore.com

Figure 6.1 Cloud broker

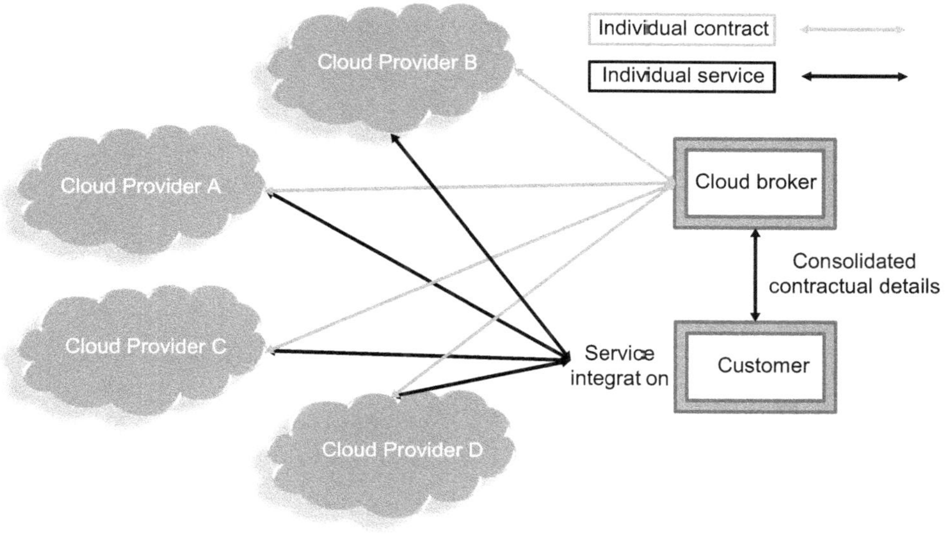

However, most cloud brokers will not take any responsibility for integrating different cloud services together: the customer retains responsibility for this. Whether this is carried out via one of the cloud service provider's platforms or via the customer's own data centre is down to the customer.

To avoid this added complexity and gain access to integrated services, a different entity is required.

CLOUD AGGREGATOR

When people look at clouds they do not see their real shape, which is no shape at all, or every shape, because they are constantly changing. They see whatever it is that their heart yearns for.

José Eduardo Agualusa, *A General Theory of Oblivion*, 2012

A cloud aggregator serves as a value-added cloud broker. As well as acting as the main location of contract negotiations and issue resolution, a cloud aggregator should provide integration services that pull together the various third-party cloud provider services under its contracts to better serve the customer (see Figure 6.2).

Therefore, a cloud aggregator does require a platform of its own. In many cases, this platform will be on one of the third-party cloud providers; in others, it may well be that the cloud aggregator has its own facilities.

Figure 6.2 Cloud aggregator

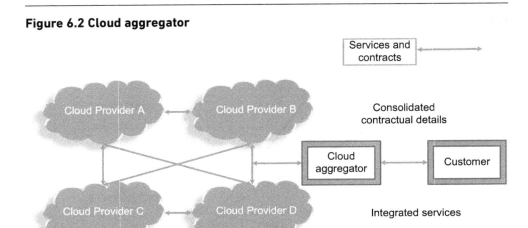

The main problem for cloud aggregators is that they must take ownership of all problems that arise across the multiple systems they have integrated. Therefore, the majority of cloud aggregators actually only offer a subset of services where they can guarantee integrations that they can offer to multiple customers, making it easier to trace problems and to create a cost-effective offer of such services to a customer base.

Where less common applications and services need integrating, it will generally be down to the customer themselves or a third-party systems integrator to provide such services. Cloud aggregators require solid APIs to be in place to ensure that flexible integrations can be carried out and maintained. The use of APIs will be covered in Chapter 11.

Examples of cloud aggregators include Vuzion,[138] Ingram Micro Cloud[139] (which specialises in aggregation services for managed service providers (MSPs) and value-added resellers (VARs)) and Dell Technologies' Boomi.[140]

SUMMARY

What have we learned?

- A hybrid cloud strategy, by its very nature, involves dealing with more than one legal entity.
- Cloud brokers and cloud aggregators can help in simplifying contracts and in dealing with root-cause analysis of issues across multiple platforms.

---

[138] https://vuzion.cloud
[139] www.ingrammicrocloud.com
[140] https://boomi.com

- Cloud aggregators offer additional value through carrying out a degree of integration of services across clouds – at a cost.

What does this mean?

- For organisations that have less capability to negotiate multiple agreements, cloud aggregators and cloud brokers can provide a valuable service.

- For organisations with insufficient in-house skill and/or resources to carry out technical integrations across multiple clouds, a cloud aggregator can help, although in many cases a systems integrator will still be required.

- Cloud aggregators and systems integrators must work with open APIs to provide a flexible, long-term solution. Hard, bespoke coding should only be used as a last possible option.

7 MAIN TYPES OF SaaS CLOUD SERVICES

If someone asks me what cloud computing is, I try not to get bogged down with definitions. I tell them that, simply put, cloud computing is a better way to run your business.

Marc Benioff (CEO of Salesforce.com) in *The Mercury News*, 2009

IaaS and PaaS offer distinct services that appeal to technology-savvy organisations that need greater flexibility around how they provision and manage their software assets. However, not all organisations are capable of dealing with the complexities of such platforms, which is why many look to SaaS as a possible solution. The promise of SaaS is the rapid availability of required functionality with the minimum requirement for technical know-how.

SaaS CLOUD SERVICES

Ultimately, the cloud is the latest example of Schumpeterian creative destruction: creating wealth for those who exploit it; and leading to the demise of those that don't.

Joe Weinman (senior vice president at Telx and author of *Cloudonomics: The Business Value of Cloud Computing*) in *Forbes*, 1 May 2012

Once discussions around IaaS and PaaS have taken place, the use of SaaS tends to remove any arguments around what the underlying stack actually is. For example, Salesforce.com has been successful without having to focus its messaging on the hardware and software technologies it uses. Facebook decided to go its own way and develop its own hardware platform, of which it then released the basics under the OCP project. Both companies' views are that as long as the platform does what their customers require, why should what that platform actually consists of matter?

The same is true of many other players in this area. Many organisations seeking cloud services look at the main SaaS models, which revolve around reasonably self-contained functional blocks that can be used to completely replace specific business processes. Examples of SaaS offerings are Salesforce.com[141] for customer relationship management (CRM), ServiceNow[142] for IT service management (ITSM), SAP Concur[143] for expense management and SageOne[144] for financials. However, other services have also gained popularity.

At the consumer level, these other services include all the social networking sites (such as Facebook, Instagram and Twitter), part of whose appeal is the lure of how they can be used to gain access to the consumer, through whom they can bring applications onto

---

[141] www.salesforce.com/uk
[142] www.servicenow.com
[143] www.concur.co.uk
[144] http://uk.sageone.com

the enterprise's radar via the consumer's role as an employee within the enterprise. LinkedIn has proven itself a survivor in the business space, with individuals and companies using it as a means of sharing information, identifying career opportunities and finding individuals with specific skills.

FILE SHARE AND SYNC

> Many ideas grow better when transplanted into another mind than the one where they sprang up.
>
> Attributed to Oliver Wendell Holmes (former Associate Justice of the US Supreme Court, 1841–1935)

The area where consumer and enterprise have most crossed is in managing the collaboration around information creation. Here, Dropbox was one of the first major movers, providing free cloud storage for individuals to use for their files, whether these were photographs, music, documents or whatever. Box, Microsoft (with OneDrive) and others rapidly followed suit.

Individuals liked what they saw and pulled it into their daily work. Whereas the main means of making a document available across all of an individual's devices had previously been to email it to themselves and then save it to the device, edit it and email it back, centralised cloud-based storage promised a single view of the individual's content.

This meant that the issue of an individual finding that they were working on the wrong version of a document could be avoided. It also cut down on multiple versions being stored across multiple devices and meant that a document would be available from any device that was attached to the public network.

All of this was great for the individual, and the likes of Dropbox and Box became massively popular. Many organisations paid little attention to this growth, some tried to prevent the use of these services and others tried to introduce poorly architected 'enterprise' alternatives. However, the genie was out of the bottle, and the demand for simple and effective file share and synchronisation (FSS) was unstoppable.

However, all this growth came with its own problems, both for individuals and for organisations. For individuals, early versions of FSS did not work when disconnected from the internet; team members often found that they could not work on a document due to it being marked as locked by another user – indeed, in some circumstances, an individual could find that they could not open a document within their own system due to it being locked on another machine they had left turned on elsewhere.

For organisations, the problems were far more pressing, impacting on the very core of organisations' ability to maintain control of their information assets. A major problem was that new silos of information had been created.

IT was more than aware (from its experience with previous platform architectures) of how such disparate stores of data could be a problem. For example, the implementation of a self-contained enterprise resource planning (ERP) package creates a set of data dedicated to that application. The implementation of a CRM package would create a completely different set of (often overlapping) data dedicated to that application. Although organisations needed to have access to the combined data of the two databases, this was not often available out of the box. Instead, extra steps had to be taken to pull the data together.

Various approaches have been tried for integrating the data across these silos. Enterprise application integration, enterprise service buses and master data management all attempt to provide a means of ensuring that different individuals within an organisation can view everything they need through one place, rather than having to run a set of various reports and try to pull them together. However, such approaches tend to be expensive and complex to implement and maintain. On the plus side, though, in this scenario, the IT department knows the data exists and where it is.

The use of FSS creates a slightly different problem. First, the use of Dropbox, Box and other similar offerings is part of shadow IT (see the next section): individuals can sign up to use these systems without IT being aware (indeed, in the majority of cases, without the business being aware). Second, the silos of information that are created in this way are completely outside an organisation's control.

This is bad in several ways. The main reason is that such use of FSS systems means that it is impossible for an organisation to maintain a true audit and governance capability. Files that it believes are being stored and managed within the organisation are also being stored outside the organisation. From that store, the user can accidently (or maliciously) leak the information to a third party, and there is no way that the organisation can know until it is too late.

The second issue is that up-to-date versions of information may not be held in a place that the organisation has access to, meaning that reports run against what is perceived to be the latest information can come up with the wrong analysis. Organisations can find that they are making wrong decisions and can't understand why, until individuals come forward with new information that they have been working on and holding in an external consumer FSS store.

Box, closely followed by Dropbox, recognised the need to meet the requirements of the enterprise as well as the individual. By introducing groups, administration capabilities, advanced security and other capabilities, FSS moved from being focused on the individual into enabling advanced functionality through enterprise file share and synchronisation (EFSS).

Through using EFSS correctly, organisations now have the capability to have centralised data stores that are held in the cloud. They can also use high levels of data control and security and offer highly functional collaboration and communication capabilities across distributed groups that can comprise not only employees but also consultants, suppliers and customers.

Through the use of platform APIs, these cloud-based document stores can be integrated into enterprise applications and other cloud platforms to provide organisations with a powerful base for managing information. That being said, information security still requires a degree of additional thought and design, as will be discussed in Chapter 16.

SHADOW IT

> I believe Shadow IT sprouted from what users perceived as a 'Culture of No' on the part of
> IT organizations. IT was seen as a roadblock to business, so people found a way around it.
> Phil Hagen (SANS certified instructor and course author),
> quoted by Jennifer Yeadon, *Smartfile.com*, 29 April 2016

Shadow IT has also grown to be a major issue for organisations. IT purchases suitable for enterprise use have historically been outside the financial reach of individuals. However, departments have often bought items such as single servers and network attached storage (NAS) boxes as a means of bypassing what they perceived as slow-moving and constraining IT departments and also so as to take what they saw as the most effective steps to deal with their own immediate problems.

This has always had a knock-on impact on the organisation as a whole. Licensing, maintenance and software contracts will have been negotiated based on a certain level of purchase. If shadow purchases are being made outside those contracts, the cost per item could well be extremely high.

The data created and stored on these shadow systems has also not always been made available to the rest of the organisation, making adequate analysis and reporting (and, accordingly, decision making) difficult. Full governance, risk and compliance (GRC) becomes impossible, as completely different data stores, many not even fully visible to IT and the rest of the business, hide the existence of the data.

However, IT can now get to grips with this type of shadow IT using network sniffers, which can identify when a new item of hardware is added to or new software is installed on the corporate network. Software management systems can also carry out audits to identify what existing software is installed and where and to ensure that licensing is managed effectively.

The move towards cheaper, consumer-focused IT that can be easily accessed and used by individuals through their own devices, such as tablets and smartphones, has accelerated and magnified the issues around shadow IT for many organisations. Bring your own device (BYOD) is now the default mode since organisations have failed to apply effective controls around which devices users are allowed to own. As far back as 2014, research carried out by Quocirca showed that around 60% of organisations were either actively or reluctantly embracing BYOD, with most users in organisations that attempted to enforce company devices stating that they paid little to no attention to those rules.[145] Gone are the days of users being grateful for company-supplied laptops as there was no other way of accessing business assets or the network while mobile. Even in the old days of company-supplied mobile phones, many were replaced as individuals found a way of expensing a better-looking phone and just putting the company SIM into it. Now, cheap tablets, mobile phones and wearables are making it impossible for organisations to maintain a hard set of rules around which devices their employees must use.

---

[145] Bamforth, R., Longbottom, C. (2 May 2014) Getting to grips with BYOD. Quocirca. Available from http://quocirca.com/content/getting-grips-byod.

However, BYOD is rife with problems. Each device has its own needs and standards, and each has different security issues. User-downloaded apps can provide back doors into an organisation's network or can be a means for the access of malware. Even where organisations have put in place specific mobile device management (MDM) solutions to try to deal with these problems, it still leaves the biggest problem unsolved: 'bring your own chaos', in which each individual builds up a set of apps that they use on a regular basis and that help them as an individual. Unfortunately, the same tools may not be helping them as part of a team, department, organisation or value chain – and, in many cases, could be opening up the organisation to major security and intellectual property issues.

IT has a responsibility to get to grips with this issue. This must not, however, entail a simple prescriptive approach of 'thou shalt not download apps'. IT must use available MDM tools, such as VMware AirWatch,[146] Citrix XenMobile[147] or ManageEngine Mobile Device Manager Plus.[148] Good MDM tools can provide a means of identifying what individuals are using in their work environment and can provide a secure container on their device where suitable apps can be safely run while minimising the risk of introducing trojans, viruses and other malware into the organisation's main IT environment.

MDM also provides a means of dealing with the risks that follow when devices are mislaid or stolen. Devices can be locked out of the network with one click and can have their contents securely deleted from a central point if deemed necessary.

The ability to identify what is being used by individuals can also be used for the greater good. As IT begins to identify which tools individuals are using during their day-to-day work, it can try to figure out why this is the case and whether the general approach may be of greater use to the organisation.

For example, if IT finds that a large number of individuals are using a consumer-grade FSS app, banning such use will be both difficult and counterproductive. As has long been the case with IT proscription, if something is made difficult by IT, individuals will often find a way to work around the obstacle. However, if the number of people using an FSS app is large, then it may well be that this is demonstrating a real need for an EFSS solution to be put in place.

Therefore, IT needs to talk to users and identify why they are using these apps. IT must then identify an enterprise-class alternative to what the individuals are using (importantly, one that is as easy to use as the consumer-grade app). As the replacement app will be focused on enterprise capabilities as well, it should provide functionality over and above what the individuals have in their existing FSS app. IT must make it clear to the users what this extra functionality is and what value this brings not only to the individual but also to their team, department and organisation. IT must also provide the guidance and help to move existing content from the FSS app to the EFSS one.

Through this approach, IT is seen as being helpful from all sides. It is seen as having accepted the need for a better approach to sharing information, and it has provided a

---

[146] www.air-watch.com/solutions/mobile-device-management
[147] www.citrix.co.uk/products/xenmobile
[148] www.manageengine.com/mobile-device-management

solution that works not only for the individual but also for larger groups around that individual. Finally, in doing so, it has regained control of the data and information, so providing the organisation with greater analytic capabilities, decision support, and audit and GRC capabilities.

The same goes for any other type of app that individuals are using. IT must follow these steps:

1. Identify what software is being used by individuals.
2. Identify why individuals are using the software.
3. Identify whether the software could add value to a broader group (a team, a department or the organisation as a whole).
4. Look at the knock-on impacts through the hierarchy. If it works at the team level, assess whether it would add value at the department and organisation levels.
5. If there is no overall hierarchical value, talk with the individuals concerned to identify what change to their task or process could avoid the issues they are encountering.
6. If there is continuous hierarchical value to be seen, identify whether the software could be used in an enterprise environment.
7. Evaluate possible security issues. Where the security risk is already covered, great. Where there are issues that can be dealt with, take the remedial action that is required. Where the security risk is too high, look for functional equivalents where the security risk is manageable.
8. If the software cannot be implemented to meet the enterprise's needs, identify alternative software that would do so.
9. Ensure that the software meets the needs of all constituents of the hierarchy, from individual to enterprise.
10. Negotiate and implement the required enterprise version of the software.

Following these steps ensures that IT is perceived as being responsive and supportive of end users and the business itself. It helps to change the feeling from users that IT is a department that will always say 'no', shifting instead to the perception that IT is likely to say 'let's take a look'. The end result may still be a 'no', but at least it will be one that is fully backed up with business and technology reasons as to why the user's choice of software is not right for the organisation. These steps also enable IT to be far more rapid in responding to individual and business needs through utilising the rapid time to capability of SaaS-based apps.

Note here the use of 'time to capability'. IT cannot, in itself, provide the business with a faster 'time to market'. Time to market is far more dependent on the organisation's business processes; all that IT can do is to provide the right platform that helps those processes move along more efficiently and effectively, thereby providing the capabilities required by the business itself.

SUMMARY

What have we learned?

- SaaS-based solutions are far less dependent on the user knowing how the platform has been put together than IaaS or PaaS.

- Vendors offering SaaS services cover a broad range of capabilities, from single-function business services (such as expense management) to broad-service functions, such as CRM and ERP.

- FSS has become more important, and the response from the main vendors has moved EFSS into the mainstream.

- Shadow IT has blossomed due to consumer cloud services, and IT must identify and deal with the issues it causes.

What does this mean?

- As part of the hybrid mix of a future platform, SaaS must be considered as a peer alongside any IaaS and PaaS strategies.

- The use of APIs must be high on the priority list to ensure that SaaS can be integrated successfully into the rest of the hybrid platform.

- IT has to identify what individuals are using from the shadow IT space and decide whether it meets with the organisation's needs, and so introduce it properly at an organisational level or find a suitable means of providing alternative but similar capabilities.

8 WHERE SHOULD A CLOUD PLATFORM RESIDE?

If the Internet exists at all in the future, it will be on a much-reduced scale from what we enjoy today, and all the activities of everyday life are not going to reside on it.
James Howard Kunstler (author) in an interview
in *Rolling Stone*, 12 July 2012

It is not a simple matter of deciding that a new cloud platform should be placed *here*. The first decision has to be whether the cloud platform is going to be private, public, mixed or hybrid. The second decision then has to be what form the cloud will take and where all the responsibilities of ownership, management and so on should be.

PRIVATE CLOUDS

There are no rules of architecture for a castle in the clouds..
G. K. Chesterton in *The Everlasting Man*, 1925

Alongside all of the public cloud service providers, there is also the option of building a fully private cloud that supports just the one organisation. This option is not free from the shortcomings of public clouds and also introduces several different issues: with a smaller number of workloads on a smaller volume of compute, storage and network resources, there is still a strong need to ensure that the overall platform is well architected and orchestrated. However, for those organisations that are not yet ready to move fully to public cloud or that have specific workloads that cannot be moved to a public cloud, a private cloud is a good way to make more use of available resources.

This then leads to a discussion on whether the private cloud should be built in a facility owned by the organisation or in a colocation facility owned and operated by a third party.

WHERE SHOULD PRIVATE CLOUDS BE BASED?

In the past, there was hardware, software, and platforms on top of which there were applications. Now they're getting conflated. That is all going to get disrupted by the move to the cloud.
Satya Nadella (CEO of Microsoft) in an interview with *Quartz*, 13 December 2013

Historically, organisations have tended to use privately owned data centres, providing them with full control over not only the IT equipment but also the whole environment, including the facility. Facilities are generally designed to last for 15 to 25 years with occasional updating of power distribution and cooling. The need for IT platform expansion is either planned from the outset; dealt with as data centre extensions; dealt with as incremental, smaller data centre builds; or implemented via a completely new build of a more modern facility.

The effective use of virtualisation and cloud platforms has increased resource utilisation rates. This has resulted in the need for less IT equipment for the same number of workloads, and has also been matched with increasing equipment densities (through more powerful chips, better design and converged architectures). It is therefore more likely at the moment that an owned data centre will shrink than grow in the foreseeable future. Combine this with the incremental movement of workloads from the private to the public cloud platforms and it would be a brave chief information officer who would approach the main board for funding for a brand new, owned data centre facility.

For colocation companies such as Equinix,[149] Interxion[150] and Digital Realty,[151] however, this uncertainty has created a growing market. Organisations that want to have guaranteed high-density power and cooling capabilities along with multi-provider wide area network connectivity and flexible IT space have been looking to move their IT estates into colocation centres.

Many colocation providers have also started to offer value-added services to their customers. By housing many customers in one physical data centre and having dedicated, high-speed managed links between global data centre facilities, colocation providers can offer a marketplace of functional offerings for their customers, many of which will be service providers themselves.

In addition, colocation providers can share the costs of dedicated public cloud connectivity (such as AWS Direct Connect,[152] Microsoft Azure ExpressRoute[153] and Google Direct Peering[154]) as a means of minimising latency in data paths across a hybrid cloud platform.

HYBRID CLOUDS

> Cloud is just emerging but it's high growth.
> Satya Nadella (CEO of Microsoft) in an interview with *Quartz*, 13 December 2013

The concept of a hybrid cloud platform has taken some vendors time to come to terms with. Some existing public cloud providers predicted that all workloads would move over to public cloud. In contrast, many IT vendors with a strong focus on internal data centre equipment sales, such as EMC and VMware, stated that the majority of workloads would remain on the user's premises (or, at worst, in a colocation facility). Even when it has been accepted that the future will entail a mix of workloads on various platforms provided in multiple ways, there have still been strong misunderstandings as to what this means.

---

[149] www.equinix.co.uk
[150] www.interxion.com
[151] www.digitalrealty.co.uk
[152] https://aws.amazon.com/directconnect
[153] https://azure.microsoft.com/en-gb/services/expressroute
[154] https://cloud.google.com/interconnect/direct-peering

The reality is not as shown in Figure 8.1: different workloads on different platforms cannot operate in isolation with different users accessing different platforms. If this approach is used, it is better termed a 'mixed' cloud: separate platforms running defined workloads with little interoperability between the workloads.

Figure 8.1 Disconnected hybrid platform

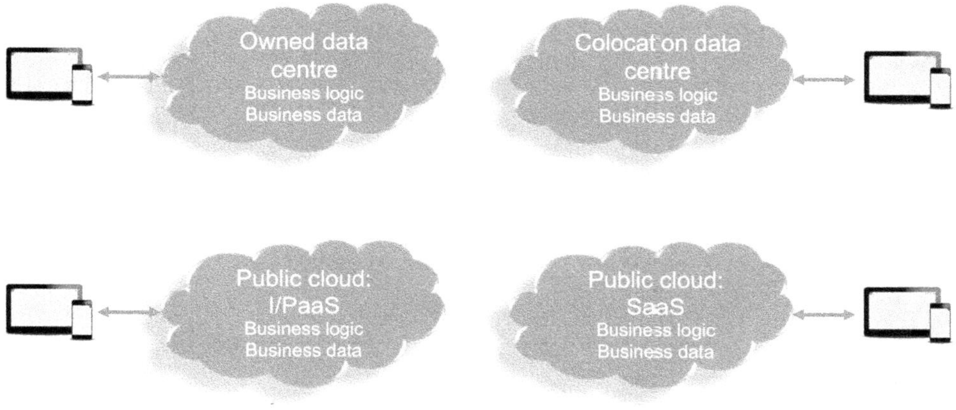

What is needed is shown in Figure 8.2: a mix of methods of functional service provision, all integrated and operating as peers in an overall IT platform, with access to all aspects of the platform provided from the one access device as required.

Figure 8.2 Integrated hybrid platform

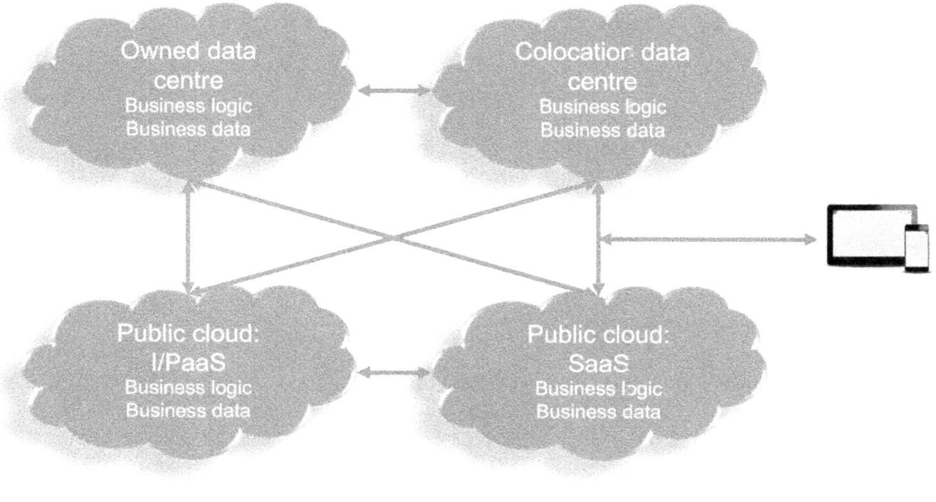

THE ORGANISATIONAL VALUE CHAIN

Though I have no productive worth, I have a certain value as an indestructible quantity.
Alice James in *The Diary of Alice James*, 1934

It is also important to look outside the organisation. Historically, it may have been easy to draw lines around certain groups of people and buildings and say, 'This is our organisation.' However, such concepts are becoming less easy to maintain. A modern organisation will consist of its own employees working alongside self-employed contractors and consultants employed by third-party organisations. It will need to deal in a more integrated manner with its suppliers and customers.

As the need for more streamlined logistics and more reactive responses to customers grows, 'the organisation' (in the sense of the organisation a certain person is involved with) is becoming part of an increasingly complex chain. This chain involves not just direct suppliers and customers (see Figure 8.3) but also the suppliers of the suppliers and the customers of the customers.

Figure 8.3 Simple value chain

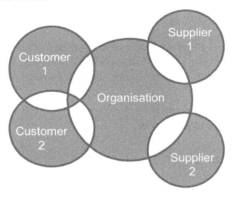

This 'value chain' of interacting and collaborating parties needs to be able to exchange data in an open yet secure manner, with the data accessible 24 hours a day, 7 days a week. However, as shown by the overlaps in Figure 8.3, it is very important to ensure that only the right information is shared with the right value chain constituent at any one time. Suppliers do not want other suppliers to see their confidential price lists. On the other hand, certain details, such as product availability and inventory, need to be shared with multiple customers.

Attempting to provide this via a fully owned facility brings issues to the fore, such as ensuring that enough resources (particularly network bandwidth) are available to provide a good enough end user experience to all parties; ensuring that the systems are fully supported and available 24/7 and ensuring that data security is managed at all times.

The need to manage multiple external identities brings in a need for identity access management (IAM) systems. These are available for use within a private environment from vendors such as CA with its Identity Suite,[155] IBM's Security Access Manager[156] and SailPoint.[157] Many public clouds provide their own IAM systems, such as AWS,[158] Microsoft Azure[159] and Google Cloud Platform.[160] Vendors such as GlobalSign,[161] Okta,[162] Centrify[163] and OneLogin[164] offer cloud-based IAM solutions (IAMaaS or IDaaS) that provide flexibility for users as they move along their cloud journey.

These needs must be met not just on the one organisation's systems but across all of the various platforms that are involved in the value chain. This can become a difficult and expensive issue to deal with.

THE USE OF COLOCATION FACILITIES

Silicon Valley is a mindset, not a location.
Reid Hoffman (founder of LinkedIn) in an interview with the *Financial Times*, 17 March 2012

A move to a private cloud in a colocation facility can help with the provision of a more flexible and highly available technology platform, but the organisation still needs to provide full support for the IT equipment to maintain systems availability, along with a high degree of platform and data security. It also has to manage the complexity of access not only at the data level but also at the physical facility, physical hardware and overall platform levels.

Moving to public cloud starts to lower the bar. As long as a suitable partnership is in place and service levels and key performance indicators have been agreed with suitable underpinnings to ensure they are met, the basic I/P/SaaS platform should have higher levels of availability and base-level security than the majority of private organisations could afford to provide using a dedicated facility.

Again, as an organisation moves through the I/P/SaaS tiers, less (note *less*, not *no*) focus needs to be placed on platform and data security. The 'organisation' can put more emphasis on ensuring that partners along the value chain have secure access to the data they need in order to optimise and streamline the overall business processes. The organisation can work with its main partners to determine how processes can be changed to make them more differentiated in the market.

---

[155] www.ca.com/gb/products/ca-identity-suite.html
[156] www-03.ibm.com/software/products/en/access-mgr
[157] www.sailpoint.com
[158] http://docs.aws.amazon.com/IAM/latest/UserGuide/introduction.html
[159] www.microsoft.com/en-gb/cloud-platform/azure-active-directory
[160] https://cloud.google.com/iam
[161] www.globalsign.com/en/identity-and-access-management
[162] www.okta.com
[163] www.centrify.com
[164] www.onelogin.com

This then brings us back to how colocating services within a single cloud provider's environment can add value through enabling data transfers at data centre speeds, rather than the data having to go through external connectors. Indeed, the awareness of such shared capabilities is growing, although it is still slow. Some colocation providers, such as Equinix and Virtus,[165] already provide self-service portals where their customers can identify what services are available within the same data centre facility, or across the highly managed and high-speed-connected overall environment, and sign up to and use these services in an optimised manner.

Many public cloud providers either only use colocation facilities or use colocation facilities alongside their own data centres to access markets where building their own facility does not make economic sense. By then using specialised connections between their cloud services and the rest of the environment, they can enable better levels of service and connectivity than can be achieved by attempting to connect one data centre facility to another through any other means.

For the value chain, this means that it may be possible to gain additional business value through colocating platforms within the same colocation centre, or by using a public cloud provider that colocates or uses dedicated optimised connectors to that colocation facility.

Similarly, for those constituents of the value chain that are using stand-alone public clouds that are hosted within the cloud providers' own facilities, access to these high-speed dedicated interconnects can provide bridging across the clouds and into other facilities as required.

DATA CENTRE AND CLOUD TIERING

The first wave of the Internet was really about data transport. And we didn't worry much about how much power we were consuming, how much cooling requirements were needed in the data centres, how big the data centre is in terms of real estate. Those were almost afterthoughts.

Padmasree Warrior (former CTO of Cisco) in an interview with
The Mercury News, 9 March 2009

Not all data centres and the cloud platforms built within them are created equally. However, choosing a suitable data centre is made easier through the range of accreditations and standards that have been created so that different facilities can be compared on various levels.

As well as being a strength, though, this can also be a weakness. There are currently several closely linked but differently operated standards around data centre facilities and cloud platforms that can catch out the unwary.

---

[165] https://virtusdatacentres.com

The Uptime Institute

At the data centre-facility level, the Uptime Institute created a data centre tiering model[166] in the mid-1990s. Although there have been some changes, the main backbone of the model has been built around the definition of four tiers. Tier I and Tier II data centre facilities are generally not used for mission-critical services; few colocation and cloud service facilities can survive if they only meet the requirements of these two lower tiers.

Tier III and Tier IV certifications are only provided where the facility owner can demonstrate that the overall facility meets rigorous requirements around uptime, connectivity and the processes in place to implement, maintain and deal with any problems that arise in the data centre. It is also worth noting that, due to the complexities of the tiering criteria, the Uptime Institute requires the design of the facility to be submitted prior to it being built. As of July 2017, the Uptime Institute had awarded 938 tiering certificates across 85 countries.

Aside from its tiering classifications, the Uptime Institute has a 'Managed and Operations (M&O) Stamp of Approval' for existing facilities. To gain this certification, an existing data centre facility must be able to demonstrate that its staff meet a range of requirements, including numbers employed, levels of qualification, maintenance and planning within the data centre, and overall coordination and management. Reassessment is required every two years to maintain the certification.

The Telecommunications Industry Association

The Telecommunications Industry Association (TIA) launched a document in 2005 named 'The Telecommunications Infrastructure Standard for Datacenters', known as TIA-942 or ANSI-942.[167] This document sets out the basic requirements for a data centre to fit within a similar set of four tiers to those set out by the Uptime Institute. Tier 1 data centres are defined as essentially server rooms with little to no systems redundancy or special facilities. A Tier 4 facility will have multiple redundant systems to provide solid business resilience should any part of the facility suffer issues. It will also meet certain security needs, such as the use of biometric entry systems to give access to highly zoned, compartmentalised areas within the facility.

Datacenter Star Audit

Germany has a separate programme, called Datacenter Star Audit (DCSA),[168] that covers five levels of 'gratification' around data centres needs, with certified data centres gaining a star rating. Although a 1- or 2-star rating is theoretically possible, the DCSA issues certificates at a 3-, 4- or 5-star level. Although predominantly used by German data centres, the DCSA rating can be found in other countries, generally for data centres owned and operated by German-headquartered companies. The programme was reviewed in 2013 to update the requirements to a new level (version 3.0), which remains current as of November 2016.

---

[166] Uptime Institute (n.d.) *Tier Classification System*. Uptime Institute. Available from https://uptimeinstitute.com/tiers [1 November 2017].

[167] Telecommunications Industry Association (TIA) (2017) Telecommunications Infrastructure Standard for Data Centers (TIA-942), Revision B. Arlington, VA: Telecommunications Industry Association. Available from www.tiaonline.org.

[168] www.dcaudit.com/about-dcsa.html#1

Leadership in Energy and Environmental Design

The Leadership in Energy and Environmental Design (LEED) programme,[169] developed by the US Green Building Council, assesses the sustainability and green credentials of any building. Originally aimed at homes and public commercial buildings, the programme has been expanded to include data centre facilities. The first LEED-certified data centre was one of the US Federal National Mortgage Association's (Fannie Mae) facilities in 2005. There are three levels to the programme's certification: Silver, Gold and Platinum.

The programme looks not only at direct energy usage but also at areas such as how much water is used in the running of the building. A Platinum LEED facility will need to be able to demonstrate that it has taken steps to use advanced cooling systems to minimise energy usage, that it monitors and acts upon energy usage in real time, that it uses a clean energy backup system, that it uses renewable energy sources, that it has used renewable building resources in the facility's construction and that it has utilised an intelligent design approach to house the IT equipment within it.

The Green Grid and PUE

As well as LEED and energy usage, a common measure that is employed across data centres is 'power usage effectiveness', or PUE. PUE started off in 2006 as a simple means of calculating the relationship between the total power used by a facility and the power used in operating the 'useful' IT equipment it contains. The metric was developed and put forward by the Green Grid.

For example, a data centre that takes 100kW grid power and has IT equipment that uses 50kW would have a PUE of 2 (100 ÷ 50):

$$PUE = \frac{\text{Total Facility Energy}}{\text{IT Equipment Energy}}$$

The idea behind PUE is that the lower the number, the more efficient the whole data centre platform is. A theoretical perfect data centre would score a PUE of 1 (i.e. all energy used goes to powering IT equipment, with none being used for cooling, lighting, auxiliary power systems and so on). However, many providers have been able to quote PUE figures of around 1.1 to 1.2. In 2015, Allied Control claimed a PUE of 1.02 through the use of immersive 3M Novec 7100 fluid cooling.[170] Facebook claims that its overall data centre PUE is running at 1.10.[171]

However, PUE is a very poor way to look at such efficiencies. Assume that you cut down on cooling and other peripheral energy usage. The PUE of the overall platform improves, but there may well be issues with systems crashing due to poor cooling. PUE also takes no account of actual IT equipment utilisation: a system running at 5% resource utilisation is not distinguished from one running at 80% utilisation. Therefore, PUE is too easy

---

[169] www.usgbc.org/leed
[170] http://investors.3m.com/news/press-release-details/2015/3M-Novec-7100-Fluid-Used-in-Worlds-Largest-Two-Phase-Immersion-Cooling-Project/default.aspx
[171] https://sustainability.fb.com/our-footprint

to skew according to the message the service provider wishes to give out. Instead, a more nuanced measure has long been required: an effective PUE, or ePUE.[172]

The Cloud Industry Forum

Cloud platforms themselves can also be certified. The Cloud Industry Forum (CIF) provides a self-certification programme for cloud providers with a code of practice that has been developed and agreed by a group of practitioners n the industry.[173] Originally agreed purely as a self-certified system, CIF later acknowledged that some degree of additional policing would be required for users to maintain a level of trust in the system. Therefore, CIF has introduced a 'CIF Certified +' level, where an independent audit of the service provider has been carried out.

SUMMARY

What have we learned?

- Systems architects must still apply thought around how the application logic and data are situated within the overall platform. Getting this wrong could produce poorly performing systems that are disliked by users.
- It is key to ensure that integration across the hybrid cloud is effectively managed.
- Data centre and cloud tiering and effectiveness measures mean different things to different people. Make sure you understand the various models before talking to possible cloud partners.

What does this mean?

- The overall architecture of the hybrid cloud will remain a core area for organisations to deal with for the foreseeable future. Smaller organisations should minimise the number of cloud service providers they use so as to minimise their integration and architectural problems.
- Comparing different clouds is not easy. Try to create a matrix of capabilities that allows for better comparisons to be made.

---

[172] Longbottom, C. (30 April 2010) PUE? Phooey! Quocirca. Available from http://quocirca.com/article/pue-phooey.
[173] www.cloudindustryforum.org/content/cop-detailed-overview

9 PAYING FOR CLOUD SERVICES

It's not what you pay a man, but what he costs you that counts.
Will Rogers (American humourist) in *Weekly Comments*, 22 March 1925

Whether or not an organisation is moving to cloud services purely for cost reasons, the service will still need to be paid for. Unfortunately, in many ways this is still the black art of cloud. There are few accepted basic ways to compare one cloud service's costs against another's. Plus, as the market is still evolving, prices are changing on a continual basis and new services are being brought to market with different cost models.

THE BATTLE BETWEEN COST LEVELS AND THEIR PREDICTABILITY, AND BUSINESS FLEXIBILITY

Flexibility has become a modern-day value that everyone wants. But flexibility comes with a cost.
Maynard Webb (CEO of LiveOps) in *CCW Digital*, 22 June 2010

One of the main reasons why the original ASP model failed was the inability of ASP companies to come up with a business model that was both attractive to prospects and profitable for the service provider. The same problem has been taxing many new cloud service providers, but the commoditisation of hardware, the increasing use of open source software and a broader acceptance of cloud models by the market have made the problem less severe.

The two major needs of an organisation wanting to use a cloud model are, unfortunately, not completely coherent. The ideal service should be completely predictable in how it meets the user's stated needs while also providing the lowest possible cost. That these two competing areas also have to take into account that customers want as much technical and business flexibility as possible has been at the root of why many cloud cost models are so complex.

For public cloud service providers, this is a problem. The lowest possible cost is better served through having a consumption-based model where the customer only pays for the resources that they use. This, however, is less predictable.

It also can push those responsible for financing services in the customer organisation to look to minimise the usage of a service so as to ensure that the costs are also minimised. This can be counterproductive in that not using a service, while it keeps costs low, also means that the overall advantages of using the service may be minimised. Customers must make sure that they maintain a balance between the value gained from, and the costs of, any services being used.

The simplest model (a per-user, per-month subscription charge) works well with SaaS but is harder to implement in an IaaS or PaaS environment. Therefore, the majority of I/PaaS providers use a resource-based cost model, but this can get complex and confusing.

A further issue for cloud service providers is that they also need a degree of predictable cash flow, both to manage their own growth and to show the financial markets that they are capable of being in the market for the long term. For this reason, completely open contracts, where customers can sign up for a month and leave whenever they want, do not make a good model for many providers. However, tying customers in for 12 months or more can scare them off, as they fear being locked in with the specific provider.

To this end, we can expect to see constant changes not only in the actual price of the services offered but also in the way they are offered.

BASIC COST MODELS

You tell them – you tell them there's a cost ... Every decision we make in life, there's always a cost.

Brad Meltzer, *The Inner Circle*, 2011

The following provides a list of basic cost models seen in the market:

- **Transaction throughput:** Payment is made based on the number of actions being used. For example, a service provider may charge per actual computer transaction or by the number of times a service is called.
- **Storage usage:** Payment is made based on the volume of data that is stored by the provider.
- **Network usage:** Payment is made based on the volume of traffic that passes between the customer and the service provider. This is generally, but not always, based on an equal bi-directional model, where the cost of sending data is the same as the cost of receiving data.
- **Power used:** Payment is made based on how many kilowatt hours of power are used by the service provider in powering the customer's equipment during a billing period.
- **License plus maintenance:** Not used often as there is a move away from such models, but a few cloud providers do still offer a standardised licence plus 'maintenance' (generally the same as a subscription) model for organisations that still prefer to be billed in this way.
- **Per physical core:** A hangover from the days of pure hosting services, this is almost impossible to deal with in a public cloud environment, due to all the physical resources being shared. However, in a private cloud platform, the software provider may charge for the software based on the actual number of

physical cores being used. Some vendors have to add a weighting to different physical CPUs; for example, an UltraSPARC physical core may have a higher cost than an Intel Xeon core.

- **Per virtual core:** A far more common model. Here, the vendor defines a basic 'standard core' that has an identifiable nominal power. It can then use a conversion table to state how many virtual cores a physical CPU is worth, and charge accordingly.

Other aspects that can be brought in on top of the above models include:

- **Commit vs. burst:** An organisation agrees to a basic amount of resource usage that it will commit to paying for no matter what. Anything above that (the burst) is paid for separately.

- **Bulk vs. pay as you go:** An organisation commits to buying an amount of resources up front that it can call off against over time. With pay as you go, all resources are paid for as they are used.

- **Pricing break points:** Resource usage is tiered, generally with an agreed commit tier (the organisation pays that amount per period of time regardless of actual resource usage). If the organisation exceeds the commit tier, they then move into one or more additional payment tiers for the extra resources used.

INCREASING COST MODEL COMPLEXITY

That which costs little is less valued.

Miguel de Cervantes, *Don Quixote*, 1605

As cloud usage has grown, it has become increasingly difficult for public cloud providers to create and hold to a single model, and customers will quite often find themselves faced with a far more complex approach to billing.

An example is AWS Glacier Storage, a low-cost, long-term/archival storage system.[174] Here, there is a set of prices that cover putting the data into an AWS Glacier Vault. These costs vary by region and according to whether the user wants an enhanced-security AWS GovCloud Vault or just a standard vault.

There are similar costs for making requests to retrieve the data from the storage vaults, although 5% of average storage volumes per month can be retrieved free of charge. Data transfers into AWS Glacier Vaults are free, and transfers of data across AWS Glacier within the same region are also free. However, data transfers out of region, or out of AWS Glacier itself, have variable costs depending on the regions and targets involved.

It can be difficult with cost models such as these for users to come up with a predictable price on an ongoing basis. However, it is the only way that AWS can make Glacier work as a low-cost, low-retrieval-volume storage system for both its customers and itself.

---

[174] https://aws.amazon.com/glacier/pricing

As discussed in Chapter 5, a move to serverless computing may provide a means to deal with some of the complexity in dealing with cost models. However, it will still not create completely solid, known costs for the customer on a per-time basis. Most organisations will have to accept that the use of cloud models will result in some degree of variability in cost, yet this is also what they see in many other areas, such as utilities (electricity, gas, water, telephone), employee expenses and so on. The aim, therefore, must be to move from complete predictability to approximate predictability.

COST TIERING

Everything has a cost, October; remember that. It may be a long time before the bill comes due, but everything has a cost.

Seanan McGuire, *One Salt Sea*, 2011

One approach to offering approximate predictability is usage tiering. Rather than a contract being agreed based on actual usage, a contract can be drawn up that covers tiers of usage.

This is demonstrated in Figure 9.1. The first column shows how a fixed event price model would work. The service provider here charges the same amount per event and charges on a per-event basis. The column has been shaded such that comparison can be better made with the alternative tiered contracts (columns two, three and four). In this first column, all events in the bottom portion cost the same as each of those in the top three portions.

Figure 9.1 Tiered costing

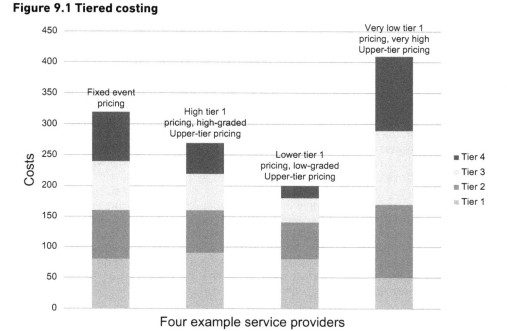

With such a fixed event price provider, the customer pays per actual usage, which is a wholly variable cost. However, the cost is based purely on usage, so a low-use period of time will result in a low-cost invoice, whereas a period of greater use will result in a higher overall charge.

With the tiered providers (columns two, three and four), each column shows four different cost tiers. The customer pays one of four amounts, depending on their overall usage. Tier 1 covers a basic number of events, Tier 2 covers an agreed band of overage events, Tier 3 covers a further band and Tier 4 covers yet another band. The customer pays the agreed tier amount, no matter where in the tier their actual usage lands. There is less variability in costs, but there is greater predictability in what those costs are likely to be.

The fixed event price provider (the first column) has what appears to be a reasonably low cost per action. As long as all action activity levels fall within Tier 1, then the fixed event price provider will prove to be cheaper than the next two examples.

The service provider in the second column has a relatively high base cost per event in its Tier 1. In this case, for the first agreed minimum number of events per period of time, the user organisation agrees to pay a minimum amount to the service provider to cover its usage, even if little actual activity occurs. The cost is predictable: if the user organisation completes a lower number of events than is covered under Tier 1, it will still pay that complete Tier 1 price.

As can be seen, in column two, if the user organisation consistently uses less than its Tier 1 agreement, it will pay more for that usage than it would to the fixed event price provider. However, if the company runs into overage, then it may have agreed a much cheaper cost for the number of events that can be carried out within its Tier 2 agreement, meaning that if the user organisation often runs up to its Tier 2 limit, it will be paying the same to the tiered contract service provider as it would to the fixed-price one. If it consistently exceeds the Tier 2 agreed limits, then it could be saving considerable amounts of money than if it were with the fixed-price provider, due to the increased discount provided in the contract on a tiered basis.

The third column shows how small changes in the contract can make big differences. Here, the service provider has agreed that it will charge the same per-event rate as the fixed event price provider in its Tier 1. Although the customer must pay that whole agreed Tier 1 amount every time period, if it runs into overage, then it starts to benefit from a much greater negotiated discount for Tier 2 than the previous provider allowed. If the customer often has enough events to fall into Tier 4, then it will always be cheaper than the fixed-price or previous tiered provider.

The last column shows how going with a 'loss leader' provider can be a false economy. Here, the provider is offering a very low entry cost: at close to half the fixed event price provider's entry cost, it is trying to attract customers that base their decisions on headline price alone. However, rather than offering a discount on overages, this provider regards such excess usage as a value-added service and charges at an additional rate for such usage. Therefore, for any organisation that exceeds its Tier 1 activities, the costs of such a provider become prohibitive.

At first glance the use of a tiered pricing model may appear to be not so attractive, in that a single event over the base Tier 1 agreement wil. result in a massive extra cost covering the whole of the Tier 2 payment. However, it does have many useful aspects.

First, it provides much greater levels of cost predictability. In its predictions, finance can allow for groupings of known costs, rather than ranges of less definable costs as would be the case in a fixed-price, per-usage cost model. Second, it can enable better overall price negotiation. A service provider must cover its costs, end, if it has little to no fully predictable revenues, then it will have to price its services to manage that risk accordingly. However, if it has a known basic recurring revenue stream, based on the agreed Tier 1 deals with its customers, it can then agree greater discounts on the Tier 1 actions and even greater ones for the tiers above.

Therefore, for organisations that know that they will have relatively large amounts of actions and also know that these may be cyclical or variable, the negotiation of a tiered usage model can be very advantageous. The key here is to try to negotiate the best possible base tier agreement with the best possible discounts in the tier in which you expect your organisation to mainly fall. It is recommended that the negotiations do not try to create a Tier 1 that covers where the organisation will be for the majority of the time: use this as a baseline where it is understood that the organisation will pretty much always have greater activity than the tier allows for.

Through this means, the organisation can start to make use of the discounts that the higher tiers offer. Obviously, the provider will not want a customer consistently getting massive discounts on a very large proportion of its activities, but sensible negotiation should come up with a set of tiers that works for both sides.

Against this is the need for complete transparency. As an organisation using a cloud provider's services, are you going to trust the provider's own monitoring and measuring systems when it comes to the bill? In many cases, cloud providers will present customers with a reasonably detailed breakdown of how they have arrived at the overall charge, and customers must ensure that they check this against expected usage costs. Other providers may present a less detailed summary of usage with only a single-cost line item presented as the charge. This makes it harder for a customer to determine whether the charge seems correct.

However, if it is believed that a provider's calculation contains errors, it will be hard to argue against the provider unless proof is available. Therefore, organisations should ensure that they can monitor key usage statistics in real time themselves and can set alerts, whether they are using a portal provided by the provider or have installed and are operating their own monitoring system. Being able to have alerts sent when certain functional usage levels exceed defined limits, when resources are being overstretched and when extra charges are being applied creates a better foundation for a trusted relationship between the organisation and the cloud provider than trying to argue against costs that have been presented within a monthly or quarterly invoice.

SUMMARY

What have we learned?

- There is no one-size-fits-all approach for how cloud services should be paid for.
- There are probably too many different cost models being used at the moment, and predictability of cost is suffering.
- A tiered usage model can offer the best balance between actual costs and predictability.

What does this mean?

- Ensuring that an organisation gets real value for money from the cloud is important. However, no organisation should lead with cost as an issue.
- Fully understanding what the cloud provider's needs are is just as important as knowing what the organisation's are. Ensuring that neither side is going to lose out on the deal must be the aim.

PART 3
THE VERY NEAR FUTURE
Cloud at a more complex level, as you should be implementing it

10   BUILDING THE RIGHT CLOUD

Eventually, we will have the Intercloud – the cloud of clouds.

Kevin Kelly, *Wired* magazine, 2007

In the early days of cloud computing, there were long and vociferous arguments as to whether the future would be based predominantly around organisations focusing on private cloud platforms or on public ones. Over time, the real answer has become apparent: there will be a mix of both platforms.

However, although some organisations believe that they are looking at implementing and running a hybrid cloud, many of these platforms are still essentially two completely separate platforms, with any mobility of workloads being a manual operation. This is, in reality, a mixed cloud model. The future for most organisations is more based around a logically singular platform that mixes private and public clouds in a seamless manner: a true hybrid cloud.

MIXING CLOUDS

The Internet is the Viagra of big business.

Attributed to Jack Welch (former chairman and CEO of General Electric)

Any of the basic cloud models can be instantiated as either private or public. For the majority of organisations, the resulting platform will spread across both private and public clouds. However, it will also still have some aspects of the old-style distributed computing model, and it may include mainframe and Unix-based systems. It is necessary to ensure that all of the various platforms still being used are included within the overall IT architecture.

'Hybrid' does not just mean having a mix of different workloads across public and private platforms. As touched upon in Chapter 2, these workloads need to interoperate – not just among themselves but increasingly across the value chain. Data created by your organisation's systems will need to be securely ingested and used by others. For example, real-time logistics needs data to be fed directly from the retail web system through to the supplier and/or warehousing, in combination with GPS and other data created within the logistics function. Much of the resulting data may then need to be shared along the value chain to create a straight-through, end-to-end process.

Organisations will be on a cloud journey. For reasons that may be technical or more visceral, certain workloads will not be moved onto a cloud platform as quickly as other workloads. For example, some organisations are still using older systems such as IBM

AS400s, HP-UX or Oracle/Sun Solaris, which are far more physically based systems than cloud based. Although IBM has done a good job in transforming the mainframe into a cloud-capable platform in itself, many mainframe organisations will still be running workloads that cannot easily be moved into the cloud. Embracing such platforms through data connectivity and using SOA principles alongside APIs will enable such systems to participate within the overall cloud environment.

PLANNING FOR WORKLOAD MIGRATIONS

History in its broadest aspect is a record of man's migrations from one environment to another.

Ellsworth Huntington (professor of geography at Yale University) in
The Red Man's Continent: A Chronicle of Aboriginal America, 1919

More can be done as time moves on. As with any journey, planning out the route is an important first step. If the organisation takes a 'cloud-first' strategy, any new business requirements should be considered in the following manner:

1. Can this business need be best met now and for the foreseeable future through existing functionality?
2. If not, can it be best met through using a SaaS system?
3. If not, can it be effectively met through building on a public I/PaaS cloud?
4. If not, can it be effectively met through building on a private cloud?

Only if all of these options are exhausted should any other option, such as a clustered or stand-alone solution, be considered.

With existing workloads (i.e. existing applications, services and functions), the following process should be used:

1. Is the workload fully meeting the business's requirements? If so, carry on using it and plan for a careful migration to the cloud as and when the workload requires major change or fails to meet the business's needs.
2. Is the workload just about meeting the business's needs? If so, plan for a rapid but careful transition to a new workload as and when feasible.
3. Is the workload already acting as a constraint on the business's needs? If so, this is where the highest priority on change needs to be applied. Look at the workload and apply the previous set of planning criteria (as set out in the four steps above) to identify where the workload should be provisioned and run.

In addition, look at your overall workloads as the equivalent of a 3D cartographic map over time. Look at mainframes and dedicated scale-up computers as being the mountains, dedicated servers and clusters as being rolling hills, and a general cloud platform as being the valleys. Now look at how the workloads on these are set out. Is that mainframe carrying out file and print services? If so, erode these services away by washing them down to become simple functions in the private cloud. This then frees up valuable resources on the mainframe to carry out the work where it adds real value, such as online transaction processing (OLTP) services. The same goes for scale-up systems: you do not want the available resources on these systems to be used by functions that can be far more cost-effectively carried out elsewhere.

Do the same with the dedicated servers and clusters. Wash down the simple workloads to where they can be more effectively and efficiently dealt with.

IT'S ALL ABOUT THE PROCESS

Excellence is not by accident. It is a process.
    A. P. J. Abdul Kalam (former president of India) in *Business Standard*, 25 October 2013

When looking at how to best support the business, bear in mind that a business runs on processes. However, a process is too large an item to deal with in one chunk. Each process can be broken down into a set of far more simple, discrete tasks. It is IT's role to facilitate the carrying out of each of these tasks in an efficient and effective manner while ensuring that the overall process meets the needs of the business.

Figure 10.1 Bridging the capability gap

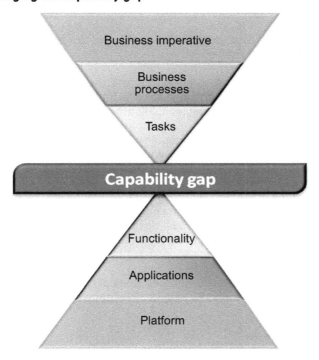

In a 2010 report,[175] Quocirca covered how this works and how it is important within a cloud strategy. Figure 10.1 shows how the business imperative is fulfilled through a series of business processes, each of which is made up of a set of individual tasks. The business imperative is created and set by the organisation's main board, the processes are enacted by groups of people and the tasks are completed by individuals.

IT should be working with the business to identify which tasks are already fulfilling needs and provide the technical capabilities to enable these tasks to operate more efficiently and effectively. As shown in Figure 10.1, a capability gap assessment needs to be carried out, which then brings us back to the need to evaluate how such enablement is best sourced: through existing functionality, SaaS, public I/PaaS or a private cloud platform.

Note here two key words: 'efficiently' and 'effectively'. Many organisations confuse the two terms, assuming them to be pretty much the same. However, they are completely different.

Consider a process. The existing process fails 3 times out of every 10. Aiming for better efficiency would entail aiming to carry out more of the same process. So, instead of managing 100 instances of the process every day, the business could aim to manage 1,000 instances. However, whereas previously 30 processes were failing to provide a suitable outcome per day, now the number of failures is 300. That is *efficiency*.

Instead, the organisation decides to first focus on ironing out the issues in the process that end up with 3 out of 10 instances failing. Through small changes to the process, it manages to reduce the failure rate to 1 out of a 100. This is *effectiveness*.

In more simple terms, efficiency can be seen as output divided by input. Effectiveness can be seen as output divided by effort.

By carrying out an effectiveness programme and then enacting an efficiency programme, an organisation can move from having 30 failures a day based on 100 process runs to having 10 failures a day based on 1,000 process runs. That is transformational.

This is a much better way to approach problems with processes in an organisation. The organisation makes massive gains in its ability to trust that the desired outcomes are occurring as required and on a more frequent and reliable basis.

Figure 10.2 shows how processes within an organisation have different weights. There are 'commodity' processes (e.g. the purchasing of stationery items). Although ensuring that such items are purchased at the best possible price against quality is a requirement, it hardly defines how an organisation operates. Essentially, commodity processes are things that the majority of organisations have to do.

At the next level are 'differentiated' processes: ones that have a direct and measurable positive impact on the bottom line as long as an organisation carries them out better

---

[175] Longbottom, C., Tarzey, B. (6 July 2010) Cloud computing: Taking IT to task. Quocirca. Available from http://quocirca.com/content/cloud-computing-taking-it-task.

Figure 10.2 The process pyramid

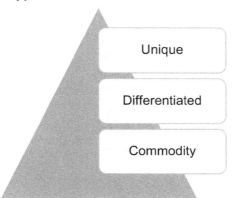

than its competition. This may be in areas such as managing data feeds in accordance with a Food and Drug Administration approval process in pharmaceuticals, or managing the full stream of processes required to achieve a patent within manufacturing.

At the top are the 'unique' processes: the processes that define the organisation as a unique entity in the global market. These may be processes around brand recognition or loyalty, around how new services or products are brought to market, or around how employees are compensated in how they provide innovative input into the organisation.

This then allows for a further level of cloud filtering:

1. If a process or task is commodity, it should be run on the most cost-effective, most commoditised platform. There is little benefit to be gained in running such processes or tasks on a differentiated platform.
2. If a process is differentiated, are all the tasks that comprise that process differentiated? This is unlikely. By breaking the process down into tasks, more of the workload can be washed down onto a commodity cloud environment.
3. This then frees up resources (people, time and money) to focus on the unique processes: the area where, through focusing investment and ensuring effectiveness, the organisation should be making the most profit.

Many of these processes can still be run in the cloud, but it may be that a more special-ised cloud platform is required. It may be that all that is required is a solid, measurable, proactive and shared-risk service level agreement (SLA) between the organisation and the cloud service provider. It could be that a platform that has tiered storage offerings is required. Or there might be a need for dedicated offload engines such as graphics processing units (GPUs) or field programmable gate arrays (FPGAs), or even dedicated server types, e.g. a mainframe fully integrated into the cloud environment.

The power of this approach is that it helps to prioritise the way that an organisation looks at its cloud journey. It also helps to provide certain cost/value criteria around where investments should be made.

SUMMARY

What have we learned?

- 'Hybrid' does not just mean a mix of private and public cloud. It also has to include existing systems where there are workloads that are not yet ready to be moved to the cloud.

- Prioritising which workloads should be reviewed and moved must be carried out in relation to the organisation's needs – not just IT's.

- There is a massive difference between effectiveness and efficiency. Both IT and the business must understand this difference and plan for changes in how processes are reviewed and modified accordingly.

What does this mean?

- By breaking down the organisation's processes into sets of tasks, it becomes far easier to identify where there are functional gaps and how best to plug these with existing or new IT capabilities.

- By putting effectiveness before efficiency, an organisation can gain enormous benefits.

- Running the right function on the right type of cloud will help in ensuring that effectiveness and efficiency are optimised.

11   ISSUES WITH CLOUD COMPUTING

The computer industry is the only industry that is more fashion-driven than women's fashion. Maybe I'm an idiot, but I have no idea what anyone is talking about. What is it? It's complete gibberish. It's insane. When is this idiocy going to stop?
Larry Ellison (Oracle executive chairman) at OracleWorld, 2008

As with all of the platforms that have promised so much before, cloud computing is no silver bullet: there remain many issues in how it is implemented, run and maintained. As a relatively new platform, it is still fighting through many of the growing pains that can be expected. It is also having to fight to educate possible users about what it can – and cannot – do at the moment, while painting the right picture as to what it could possibly do in the future.

The main issues can be summarised as follows:

- system availability;
- data security;
- performance;
- the need for standards and APIs;
- 'noisy neighbours';
- the business issues of highly dynamic cloud-based systems;
- software and usage licensing issues;
- the mirage of self-service;
- the cessation of service by a provider;
- maintaining governance in a hybrid cloud.

Let's look at each of these areas in more detail.

SYSTEM AVAILABILITY

I think that technology – computers and smart phones and 24-hour availability – often leaves me, and others I know, feeling blank and depressed at the end of a day.
Rebecca Traister (writer) in an interview in *ArtsBeat* (*New York Times*), 21 January 2011

In much of Quocirca's research, data and process security have come out as the top concerns for respondents.[176] However, more up-to-date research from May 2017 has

---

[176] Longbottom, C., Tarzey, B. (30 September 2015) Masters of machines II. Quocirca. Available from http://quocirca.com/content/masters-machines-ii-0.

begun to show that systems availability is becoming more of an issue.[177] For cloud providers, a lack of good systems availability is a major issue. For a single-user data centre, a systems failure or service interruption only impacts the one organisation using the facility. For cloud providers, even a small fault can impact multiple customers, and a large outage can impact hundreds or thousands of customers.

AWS, Google Cloud Platform and Microsoft Azure have all had unplanned systems downtime that have impacted some of their customers' critical capabilities. For example, in September 2015[178] AWS had problems at its North Virginia US-EAST-1 site (its oldest running site) that brought down such AWS customers as IMDb, Netflix and Tinder. Quora, Trello and other services were brought down by a failure in AWS's S3 storage system in North America in March 2017.[179] This failure was caused by a systems administrator using a flawed script that was meant to decommission a few servers; unfortunately, the script spread, bringing down a large number of live servers.

In 2012 Google Compute Cloud suffered an outage that brought down services including Dropbox and Tumblr.[180] In April 2016 it experienced a network issue caused by a poorly implemented removal of a block of IP addresses that knocked down access to its Google Compute Engine for all users across all regions.[181] Although this lasted for only 18 minutes, it was the first reported incident of a cloud service from the 'big three' going down for every single user. This followed on from a similar outage resulting in high connection loss in February 2015.[182]

Microsoft Azure has also had multiple failures. In November 2014 it suffered an outage that was traced to operator error.[183] A scheduled update to the binary large object (BLOb) configuration uncovered an existing fault with the BLOb front-ends, which then forced these to go into an infinite loop, preventing them from accepting any new traffic. In September 2016 a DNS problem within Azure led to users losing access to many services.[184]

However, the big three are becoming more responsive in how they deal with such issues. Alongside improved resiliency in their services and better technical process management, their service dashboards try to keep all users aware of the status of any problems.

It must also be borne in mind what the overall levels of availability are across cloud platforms. Organisations such as CloudHarmony, a Gartner company, maintain a running status of cloud uptime.[185] CloudHarmony publishes data for the past month, and many of the cloud platforms manage 100% uptime over this period of time. Indeed, as

[177] Tarzey, B. (25 May 2017) Masters of machines III. Quocirca. Available from http://quocirca.com/content/masters-machines-iii.
[178] Smolaks, M. (21 September 2015). AWS suffers a five-hour outage in the US. DatacenterDynamics. Available from www.datacenterdynamics.com/content-tracks/colo-cloud/aws-suffers-a-five-hour-outage-in-the-us/94841.fullarticle.
[179] Lee, D. (28 February 2017) Amazon data centre fault knocks websites offline temporarily. BBC News. Available from www.bbc.co.uk/news/world-us-canada-39119089?SThisFB.
[180] Magnusson, P. S. (26 October 2012) About today's App Engine outage. Google App Engine Blog. Available from http://googleappengine.blogspot.co.uk/2012/10/about-todays-app-engine-outage.html.
[181] https://status.cloud.google.com/incident/compute/16007
[182] https://status.cloud.google.com/incident/compute/15045
[183] https://azure.microsoft.com/en-us/blog/update-on-azure-storage-service-interruption
[184] Foley, M. J. (15 September 2016) Global DNS outage hits Microsoft Azure customers. ZDNet UK. Available from www.zdnet.com/article/global-dns-outage-hits-microsoft-azure-customers.
[185] https://cloudharmony.com/status

of November 2016, the lowest performing cloud provider being monitored (out of 49 cloud service providers) had an availability of 96.4832%, and this was just for one of its facilities. By using failover to other facilities, the overall availability for the provider would be much higher.

Indeed, many of the technical issues that a cloud provider encounters will have little to no impact on users. Correctly architecting the IT equipment and software along with the facility and connectivity means that high levels of functional redundancy can be built into the platform at a relatively low cost. As this cost is then shared across all customers, these high levels of availability can be reached and maintained in a manner that few single-user platforms can achieve.

DATA SECURITY

> Security depends not so much upon how much you have, as upon how much you can do without.
>   Joseph Wood Krutch (author, critic and naturalist) quoted in *The American Scholar*, 1950

A further concern for users is around data security. Security breaches of a large cloud service provider will hit the news headlines. Security breaches of a single-user facility either will not hit the headlines (if the breach is small enough) or will be viewed from outside as a case of it being down to that one company's lack of security capabilities. The perception has been that security in the cloud is suspect; it is seen as being far better to 'own' the security.

Again, for those running their own data centre and IT platform, the levels of data security that they can put in place will generally be less than those a cloud provider will have. This comes down to a mixture of reasons:

- There is a high cost to employing people with the right skills to be able to implement solid security, which is increasingly beyond the reach of many organisations.

- Keeping these skills up to date is also costly. Even where an organisation funds the necessary learning and qualifications, it is likely that the person will take these enhanced security skills and move on to a better-paying position, generally within one of the public cloud providers.

- Gaining access to enough information on the changing dynamics of the security landscape requires considerable resources. The big public cloud providers will have groups dedicated to ensuring that they are aware of the latest threats, and even the smaller providers will ensure that they have access to sufficient sources to be able to take steps to avoid up-and-coming security issues.

However, it must be borne in mind that a cloud provider is a much more attractive target to a hacker than a single-user data centre. Whereas breaking through the security around a single-user data centre will provide access to one set of data, a successful breach of a cloud provider's security will potentially give access to the data of every customer housed by that data centre. Therefore, most cloud providers take not just data security but also overall security very seriously. Remember, though, that it is not enough to depend on the cloud service provider's security. As an organisation, there is still a responsibility on you to secure your own data. The cloud service provider can make it harder for a hacker to get through the perimeter, but it is down to you to ensure that what is within that perimeter stays secure from both outside and inside attacks.

The issues around cloud computing and data security are covered in more depth in Chapter 16.

PERFORMANCE

Hook enough computers together and what do you get? A new kind of utility that offers supercomputer processing on tap.
M. Mitchell Waldrop (author and journalist) in *MIT Enterprise Technology Review*, May 2002

A further issue lies in the overall performance of a cloud computing environment. In the early days of single-cloud computing systems, the end user experience could be poor. Connections between the user and the cloud were made via a combination of local area network (LAN) links and wide area network (WAN) connections, generally over the public internet. Although the LAN was under the organisation's control and could be reasonably predictable, the public internet was predominantly a 'best efforts' performance environment. It was impossible to provide predictable performance, and when there was heavy traffic on the public internet the user experience could decline rapidly.

Even implementing dedicated connections between the users and the cloud was not always successful. Leased lines and dedicated internet connections were expensive, and gaining sufficient bandwidth to meet the requirements of badly architected cloud workloads was not easy. Even where an organisation could afford its own dedicated connections, if a member of the value chain could not, then it was back to best efforts for the overall end-to-end performance.

Even now, with cloud providers offering quality of service (QoS) over dedicated connections, the user experience may still leave much to be desired. There is a strong need to ensure that workloads are architected and implemented correctly to minimise data paths in the process.

Figure 11.1 shows four different workload architectures. Where two different clouds are being used (top left), one holding the data and the other holding the business logic, the client accesses the business logic over a network connection. This connection will have its own degree of latency. However, this is not a major issue; where the real latency issues come in is between the business logic and the data itself. Every time the business logic needs to access the data, it has to send a call over a WAN connection and wait for the data to respond. Depending on whether any data needs to traverse the WAN link, the latency can be anything from a few milliseconds to many hundreds of milliseconds or more. Performance is likely to be poor, and user acceptance of the system will also suffer.

Figure 11.1 The impact of data latency in different architectures

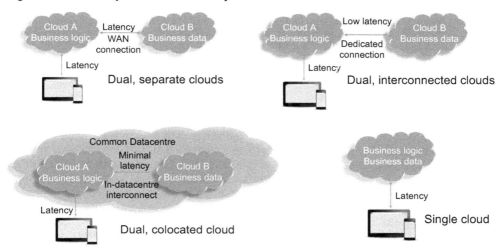

The issue can be somewhat ameliorated through the replacement of the general WAN connections with dedicated links between the two cloud platforms (top right). This can provide streamlined paths with guaranteed quality of service, but it will still be dependent on how well the business logic has been developed to deal with the data. However, with latencies dropping into the low milliseconds, overall performance will be noticeably better for the end user.

However, if the two cloud services are collocated (bottom left), then the connectivity between the services can be operated at data centre, rather than WAN, speeds. Latencies drop into the microseconds, and performance starts to appear as if the application were being run in a dedicated data centre with connectivity over a LAN.

The best performance will be gained where the business logic and the business data are held in the same cloud (bottom right). The user experience is then governed predominantly by the latency between their device and the platform, and by how well the business logic has been written. However, as the hybrid cloud becomes the norm, it will not be possible to go for such an approach across all workloads.

That being said, even where the architecture of the cloud platform has been optimised, there will still remain a need for constant monitoring of end-to-end performance to ensure that there is no unwanted drift that could impact the user experience. Vendors such as Virtual Instruments[186] and CA[187] provide tools that can monitor and report on performance across a hybrid cloud platform, enabling faster identification and remediation of the root cause of problems, and optimisation of decisions based on a better understanding of where workloads should be deployed.

---

[186] www.virtualinstruments.com
[187] www.ca.com/gb/products/ca-application-performance-management.html

THE NEED FOR STANDARDS AND APIs

Flying by the seat of the pants must have been a great experience for the magnificent men in the flying machines of days gone by, but no one would think of taking that risk with the lives of 500 passengers on a modern aircraft. The business managers of a modern enterprise should not have to take that risk either. We must develop standard cloud metrics and [return on investment] models, so that they can have instruments to measure success.

Dr. Chris Harding (director for interoperability and SOA at the Open Group), *The Open Group Blog*, 9 January 2013

To provide the optimum performance and experience within an overall cloud platform, APIs must be used. While this may seem to be a sweeping statement, I believe that it is true. In the past, applications based on single-issue functionality (such as CRM, ERP or human resources) created islands of automation and silos of data that required complex forms of integration to take place. From point-to-point integration through enterprise application integration and enterprise service buses and SOAs, attempts at solving the problem of process and data integration have all met with major problems, particularly where one part of the overall platform changes and has knock-on impacts on the rest of the platform. The emergence of APIs took the best parts of what had gone before but also built on them to provide much greater flexibility and capabilities to deal with the constant change of both technology and the business's processes.

Many commentators are now talking about an 'API economy': an environment where the use of highly standardised, open APIs makes such process and data integrations simple to put in place, to change, to monitor and to audit. That APIs can be used across a complete value chain is also important: the API economy is dependent on processes and data being able to traverse hybrid cloud platforms and travel through to other organisations' platforms. The API economy therefore needs an orchestration layer to ensure that the APIs themselves do not become an issue.

In a highly dynamic, technical environment such as hybrid cloud, it is almost impossible for APIs to be defined and then remain static. Indeed, for an organisation to be able to implement a full DevOps and continuous delivery model, there is a strong need for APIs to be continuously evolving as well. This battle between API stability and the need for continuous evolution further drives that need for effective API orchestration across the whole hybrid cloud platform.

The Cloud Foundry, along with the Cloud Native Computing Foundation,[188] has launched an open source project called the Open Service Broker API.[189] The project is aimed at creating a highly standardised specification to provide an easier means for developers, independent software vendors (ISVs) and SaaS vendors to deliver services to applications running within cloud-native platforms using tooling such as Cloud Foundry, as well as those using other tools such as OpenShift and Kubernetes. It will do this by abstracting a catalogue of 'capabilities' from a service and making them available through a single simple interface. As with all Cloud Foundry projects, this has the backing of multiple technology companies, including Fujitsu, Google, IBM, Pivotal, Red Hat and SAP.

---

[188] www.cncf.io
[189] www.openservicebrokerapi.org

Some public clouds, such as AWS,[190] Google Cloud Platform[191] and Microsoft Azure,[192] provide their own API-management and orchestration capabilities.

For those wanting complete control and the ability to span multiple different clouds, a stand-alone API-management system may be required. Here, vendors such as Akana,[193] Apigee,[194] Mulesoft[195] and Tibco Mashery[196] offer suitable systems.

Other software companies have taken a slightly different approach to the problems of integrating their services into other environments. In the world of online retail, the focus has been on how organisations can integrate capabilities by just dropping a few lines of code into an existing environment. The code then triggers a call to the software vendor's own cloud, where the service's actions are carried out, and the results are then sent back to the calling environment.

As an example, Transversal[197] provides a cognitive system that uses machine intelligence to understand the context of a user's question and provide a guided path through an organisation's website in real time. This approach, based on what Transversal states to be the system's ability to understand the question, anticipate the answer and continuously improve on the answers provided to the user, can drastically improve customer satisfaction and cut down on the need for contact centres to have to deal with customer inquiries. And all of this is done without having to create any code to integrate Transversal's system into the existing environment.

Similarly, although PayPal has its own API,[198] simple code can be created and dropped directly into a website to enable PayPal payments to be taken. Again, this is without the need for a developer to be involved.

'NOISY NEIGHBOURS'

> We want to live, love and build a just and peaceful society. We dedicate ourselves to working with our neighbours day in and day out to create this peaceful society.
> Betty Williams (Nobel Peace Prize winner), acceptance speech, 11 December 1977

In the public cloud, where the underlying resources can be shared between many different customers, issues such as 'noisy neighbours' can arise. Here, the actions of one customer can have a direct impact on the performance of another.

For example, let's say one of a customer's workloads suddenly spikes, hitting the storage resources and network hard. As long as this spike is short and controlled, the rest of the customers will generally not notice much degradation in their own services.

---

[190] https://aws.amazon.com/api-gateway
[191] https://cloud.google.com/endpoints
[192] https://azure.microsoft.com/en-gb/services/api-management
[193] www.akana.com
[194] https://apigee.com/api-management/#/homepage
[195] www.mulesoft.com
[196] www.mashery.com
[197] www.transversal.com
[198] https://developer.paypal.com/docs/api

However, if the spike is prolonged and is due to an uncontrolled fault in coding causing an unplanned flooding of the system, a poorly monitored and managed cloud platform will try to meet the resource requirements of this workload – and start to crowd out other workloads around it. Indeed, in the worst-case scenario, the cloud platform will attempt to meet the needs of all the workloads at the same time based on agreed SLAs, but, finding this to be impossible, will essentially go into a bit of a meltdown.

At best, this kind of problem with a noisy neighbour can slow down other workloads that are using the same resource pools. At other times, the results may look more like a DDoS attack.

It is imperative that a public cloud provider has its own set of tools that monitor for such abnormal events across its estate. It then needs to deal with the events as best it can, rationing the resources being provided to the rogue workload while alerting the workload owner or, in the worst cases, preventing the workload from running at all by stopping new resources being assigned to it. As a good cloud service provider will not, for privacy and data security reasons, have full visibility of the type of workload running on its servers and the types of data traversing its network, it will be difficult for them to apply quality and priority-of-service rules across the whole estate. However, they should have enough visibility and capability to identify where workload and data traffic patterns are beyond normal parameters.

The live feeds from such tools should also be available to all customers, not with full customer and workload details but just so that there are more eyeballs watching what is happening. This will put the provider in a better place to be able to raise early warning signals that something may be going wrong.

Indeed, as the performance of an organisation's workloads and the overall performance of the public cloud itself are key, organisations planning on using a hybrid cloud strategy should be looking to those providers that have their own internal monitoring capabilities that can be made visible to the customer in an anonymised manner. Again, this is where the use of APIs comes in: customers can use the data feeds provided through APIs as a means of aggregating the information into meaningful reports.

Managing a complex hybrid cloud platform – one that includes not only the private and public cloud platforms but also any physical and virtualised platforms that have not yet been embraced within the overall cloud environment – requires tools that can cover a broad gamut of needs. However, attempting to integrate a large mix of best-of-breed tools may not fulfil these needs, as systems-management tools must not only recognise that the physical and logical layers of the platform are different but also that they are inextricably linked in such a way that a change to one can have a direct impact on another. Even where an organisation attempts to minimise the number of tools, there must be a general means of ensuring that the contextual dependencies between the logical and physical resources are understood and managed. For example, using one tool that excels in managing the logical resources presented by a virtual cloud platform and using another to deal with the underlying physical servers, storage and network can lead to a series of back-and-forth attempts to remediate issues. Instead, it is necessary to identify a functional toolset that can cover the physical aspects of an overall platform, alongside clusters, the virtual environment, and private and public clouds.

An example here is Electric Cloud[199] with ElectricFlow. Although nominally aimed at software delivery through DevOps, the toolset has to have a strong knowledge of what is happening across the whole platform in order to carry this out.

Other vendors that provide good general capabilities include specialised cloud-management systems such as those provided by RightScale,[200] Scalr[201] and CliQr[202] (now part of Cisco) and complete hybrid physical/virtual monitoring, management and predictive suites such as those offered by Future Facilities,[203] Nlyte[204] and Vertiv (previously Emerson Network Power) Trellis.[205]

The aim must be to provide a single view of the truth for all people concerned. If a storage specialist sees a problem and then tracks it down to a network issue, the network specialist must be working on the same data, even if they have a different portal through which they see the results. Only through these means can the finger-pointing of 'it wasn't our fault' be avoided and the organisation be fully supported.

THE BUSINESS ISSUES OF HIGHLY DYNAMIC CLOUD-BASED SYSTEMS

> There are no secrets to success. It is the result of preparation, hard work, and learning from failure.
>
> Colin Powell in *The Leadership Secrets of Colin Powell* by Oren Harari, 2003

As more organisations start to use composite rather than monolithic applications, the need to monitor and manage these at a more granular level will tax many. Having flexibility in how technology acts to support dynamic business processes is all well and good. However, should there be a business problem down the line, being able to prove what the process was may be difficult.

For example, in the UK, the main banks have been dealing with mis-selling claims around payment protection insurance (PPI) for several years. The costs to the banks to date exceed £37 billion, with additional amounts having to be set aside every year.

PPI arose even though the processes behind selling such cover were well known and relatively static. Indeed, the banks knew what they were doing in getting people to part with money where the likelihood of the insurance paying out was low. However, when it came to tracking back to show which customers had taken PPI for the right reasons or even asked for it themselves, the banks had no capability to identify what had been done at the time. Therefore, the law has tended to fall on the side of the customer rather than the banks.

There have been similar issues around linking endowments to mortgages and around dealings with small businesses concerning bank loans. In these cases, a set of relatively

---

[199] http://electric-cloud.com
[200] www.rightscale.com
[201] www.scalr.com
[202] www.cliqr.com
[203] www.futurefacilities.com
[204] www.nlyte.com
[205] www.vertivco.com/en-us/products/brands/trellis

rigid processes was identified and became the basis for how banks responded to their customers. The problem in dealing with the resulting customer issues has little to do with the processes involved; these were relatively rigid and easily codified. The problem was that the banks failed to create enough of a record of the processes to be able to fully audit (at a point in the future) what had happened. This lack of effective record keeping has cost customers and financial institutions heavily: yet, just as it is dawning on companies that they must ensure that better records are kept, the landscape is shifting away from them.

With a cloud-based environment using composite applications, the processes underpinning any transaction become far more transient, changing on a regular basis. Figuring out exactly what was offered to a customer at any specific time becomes even more difficult. As well as changes to the tasks and processes, larger changes may have occurred: for example, the company may have changed cloud provider within its hybrid cloud platform since the original sale was made. Therefore, it is incumbent on the organisation to maintain adequate and full records of the manner in which processes were enacted and the results of the processes at all times. This may look like a case of 'store everything forever – just in case', but it need not be.

What is needed is to create and store the metadata around the processes used. It is not necessary to be able to reproduce the exact process with the same applications across the same platforms with the same data, but storing details of the steps taken along with what the outcomes were for each step can provide a full enough description of what was offered to a customer at a specific time.

As an example, consider the offer of a loan to a customer. The customer was offered the loan five years ago. The reality may be that they used a bespoke application on such and such a platform that is now no longer in use. The application had just undergone an upgrade, so it was different from what had been used the day before. Since then, the organisation has moved off the application, has moved from an internal data centre to a cloud-based SaaS solution and has been acquired by another bank. The customer is now complaining that they were mis-sold the loan, as part of the overall process provided misleading information.

Based on traditional thinking, the need is to recreate the exact process – but the application, the platform and even the original organisation are no longer there. Instead, the new organisation can delve into the metadata records and provide something along the following lines:

- The customer applied for a loan.
- The following questions were asked.
- The customer provided the following answers.
- These met the organisation's requirements.
- The customer was presented with the following terms and conditions.
- The customer signed to accept the terms and conditions.
- The organisation requested these items (e.g. proof of ID) to meet with the legislation at the time.

- The customer provided acceptable items.
- The loan was provided along with the following details regarding a cooling-off period.

The technology itself is not relevant here. Instead, the organisation has provided a fully adequate time-stamped list of information that can be used to show the customer or the requisite legal body what the real steps were, rather than just what the customer believes happened. Through the use of non-repudiation technologies, such as proof-of-content cloud email services (e.g. those offered by eEvidence[206]), such information is legally admissible in court, though it will generally be enough to prove to the customer prior to the matter reaching a courtroom that their case has little to no merit anyway.

However, the contrary argument is also true. In those cases where an organisation has mis-sold something, the records will show this. The records will then allow for all those affected to be easily and effectively identified, and so minimise the costs of dealing with the issue.

As the burden of regulation becomes heavier, organisations must plan for such issues. Having a strategy of 'we hope it won't happen' is not enough: being able to reproduce enough of the process to show how an individual customer was dealt with can help to ensure that many aspects of GRC are fulfilled.

SOFTWARE AND USAGE LICENSING ISSUES

> Software is like entropy. It is difficult to grasp, weighs nothing, and obeys the second law of thermodynamics; i.e. it always increases.
>
> Norman Ralph Augustine (former US Under Secretary of the Army)
> in *Augustine's Laws*, 1984

In the 'old' world of computing, the licensing and usage of software were a problem. Many organisations found it difficult to monitor how licences were being used. Moreover, where 'golden' serial numbers (serial numbers that can be used multiple times across an organisation, rather than a list of unique serial numbers having to be maintained) were provided, organisations could often find themselves facing reparations and fines when software audits were carried out by the application vendor themselves or an industry body such as the Federation Against Software Theft.[207]

Companies such as Flexera[208] and Snow Software[209] created software that could identify and manage licensing, creating a market for software asset management (SAM). With additional functionality around areas such as patch and update management, SAM morphed into software asset lifecycle management (SALM).

---

[206] www.eevid.com
[207] www.fast.org
[208] www.flexerasoftware.com
[209] www.snowsoftware.com/int

However, cloud is changing the landscape. Although some cloud services are still provided on a basic licence-plus-maintenance basis, the majority are now provided on more of a usage basis. This is completely true for SaaS services: each user must have their own credentials in order to access the service. For IaaS and PaaS, such licensing depends on which functions, services and applications are being run on top of the platform. For those companies that have moved a standard licenced application to the cloud, the problem of SALM remains; however, for those that have moved to more of a cloud-native application/service approach, the issues will have changed.

Therefore, modern SALM systems must be able to deal with such hybrid systems. They must still be able to deal with standard licence models but must also include various user/role-based models alongside time-, resource- and other unit-based models. No organisation should fall for the perception that moving to cloud removes the need for SAM or SALM; it just changes the way in which they have to be instantiated.

Most SALM vendors have now moved to providing cloud-based systems themselves, negating the need for an organisation to install and manage the software. The systems can monitor usage, flagging when users are over- or under-using cloud-based services, enabling fine-tuning of how cloud services are being paid for. SALM vendors are also bringing in the capability to monitor the use of open source licences. Many organisations believe that open source licensing is just a way to use software without the need to pay licences. However, the open source licence landscape is complex and massive, and has many pitfalls that can trap the unwary organisation.

For example, one of the most widely used open source licences is the GNU General Public License (GPL).[210] Now at version 3, the GPL has the following principles:

- the freedom to use the software for any purpose;
- the freedom to change the software to suit your needs;
- the freedom to share the software with your friends and neighbours;
- the freedom to share the changes you make.

This all sounds great – except when you drill down into the small print. If you take any software that has any code in it that has been created under the GPLv3 licence, then the GPLv3 agreement also applies to that software, even if it is not, in itself, GPLv3 software. If you create your own software and it contains any GPLv3-licensed code snippets, then your software is also covered by GPLv3.

OK, that may still not seem too bad – apart from the fact that if you try to charge for that software, or if you have paid for software that contains GPLv3 code, then you are in violation of the GPLv3 licence. Again, this is in itself no bad thing: companies that purposefully try to use other people's hard work (those writing open source software) for financial gain need to be controlled.

But what if the violation is purely accidental? Let's say the code your developer got was a 'conveyance' (GPLv3's terminology for the way new software based on GPLv3 code is

---

[210] www.gnu.org/licenses/quick-guide-gplv3.en.html

distributed) from a third party: it contained some code stubs that had been conveyed to that third party. Purely by accident, the code from the third party did not mention this: the originator's own webpage may well have stated that the code had been conveyed under GPLv3, but the site where the developer took the code from didn't.

Under the previous GPL (v2), the user would be in immediate contravention of the licence – irrevocably. Under v3, the GPL agreement gives a period of grace in which things can be sorted out. This is fine, but it is far better to deal with the issue right at the start.

The Open Source Initiative body currently lists 80 approved open source licences on its website,[211] of which it states that nine are widely used and supported. It also provides a frequently-asked-question section to help anyone who wants to come up with their own open source licence, though this has led to a proliferation of other licences that could catch out the unwary.

Black Duck Software[212] (now acquired by Synopsis) provides a comprehensive means of scanning through code to identify where different open source licences have been used, and provides advice on what this may mean to an organisation. Some of the SALM vendors have also introduced a degree of capability to manage open source licences.

THE MIRAGE OF SELF-SERVICE

Our knowledge is a receding mirage in an expanding desert of ignorance.
Will Durant (historian and author) in *The Reformation*
(volume 6 of *The Story of Civilisation*), 1957

Cloud computing promises the advent of self-service. Here, users can choose the applications and services that they need and have them provisioned and set up for them in real time.

This works with SaaS: you can go to a SaaS site, pay your money and have direct access to the service on offer. Companies such as Xero[213] (with its accounting software) and InLoox[214] (with its project management system) offer full self-service capabilities, where any individual can go to the site and sign up directly using a credit card. In fact, signing up directly for a service (free or commercial) is what consumers are now used to; it is the way they have signed up for Dropbox, Box, Facebook or other services.

For enterprise systems, it may not be so easy. First, the provider may want to exercise a degree of control over what the customer does. Second, the customer (in this case, the enterprise) will almost definitely want to exercise control over what its own users get up to. Therefore, completely open enterprise self-service should not be an aim of a cloud-based system. Indeed, this was never the purpose of the 'self-service' trait in

---

[211] https://opensource.org/licenses/alphabetical
[212] www.blackducksoftware.com
[213] www.xero.com/uk
[214] www.inloox.com

NIST's cloud service definition,[215] anyway. A better definition of enterprise self-service in the cloud world would be more along the following lines:

> Cloud self-service is the capacity to present a portal to an individual that is based on policies defined by the business and enacted through simple means by the IT department, through which users can then choose and have provisioned services to which they are allowed access as and when they need them.

The aim of enterprise self-service should therefore be to provide users with a means of seeing what pre-approved software and services they are able to access and use. This requires a portal-based system that uses details about the individual's role and position combined with business rules around the various applications and services that are available; using this information, a meaningful and useful catalogue can be presented to the user. Details of the user's role and position should not be in yet another database: many organisations will have such details already available through an enterprise directory such as Microsoft Active Directory (AD), other LDAP (lightweight directory access protocol) services or human resources applications. Again, this is where the power of the API economy comes in: self-service portal software should feed off these existing systems as much as possible.

This is important for several reasons, not least of which is the basic ease of use of having a single central database of users and their roles and responsibilities. However, a larger benefit is in dealing with the access rights of individuals as they move roles or leave the organisation. It is far easier to revoke access in part or completely where there is just the one database than it is to try to work through multiple systems in order to ensure that information security and application access are adequately managed.

In itself, having a self-service portal is not enough. Once the user has chosen an application or service, actions must be kicked off to provision this, and then to log the licensing and usage as required. This then brings us back to the need for a cloud-capable SALM system tied in to a suitable provisioning system.

THE CESSATION OF SERVICE BY A PROVIDER

> Crowley thumped the wheel. Everything had been going so well, he'd had it really under his thumb these few centuries. That's how it goes, you think you're on top of the world, and suddenly they spring Armageddon on you.
> Terry Pratchett and Neil Gaiman, *Good Omens: The Nice and Accurate Prophecies of Agnes Nutter, Witch*, 1990

The nightmare scenario for any user of a public cloud system is when that cloud is not available. Whether this is down to a fault at the provider's facility or some other issue, the impact on the business's capabilities to continue its activities is profound. Some of these issues are of the service provider's own making.

---

[215] Mell P., Grance T. (2011) *The NIST definition of cloud computing.* Special Publication 800-145. National Institute of Standards and Technology. Available from http://nvlpubs.nist.gov/nistpubs/Legacy/SP/nistspecialpublication800-145.pdf.

As an example here, an email and collaboration service provider that was used by my own company suddenly stopped delivering email to all users. It took some time for the core problem to be identified, and even longer for it to be fixed. What had happened was that the provider had installed a storage area network (SAN) that had been running happily for some time. The SAN was fully redundant and could cope with failure. The email servers were similarly redundantly provisioned and managed. However, the fibre channel controller connecting the storage to the servers broke down, and the provider had not allowed for systems redundancy at this level; it only had the one controller. As far as the servers were concerned, there was nowhere to store emails. Therefore, all emails that were sent to all valid addresses managed by the provider were irretrievably lost. As a customer, we should have made sure that all single points of failure had been covered via some level of redundancy, but the provider should also have known this themselves.

Even where a customer chooses a cloud service provider that can demonstrate it has provided full redundancy within its own systems, this does not allow the customer to waive its own responsibilities. The customer still must allow for issues around how its own devices will access the cloud service. In many cases of service failure, it is necessary for the customer to undertake architecting for business continuity: providing mirroring across facilities, using multiple redundant network connections and so on.

But what happens during a major disaster, such as widespread floods, earthquakes and so on? If your own organisation is caught up in one of these natural disasters, then it is likely that there will be plenty more on the minds of workers and management alongside trying to deal with technical platform outages. A full business disaster recovery plan may have to be kicked off, which may focus predominantly on the recovery and saving of physical assets and on ensuring the safety of workers.

Notwithstanding, part of this disaster recovery plan will also be focused on maintaining or providing a degree of technical capability. Mirroring of data and application/functional images across facilities (whether this concerns public-to-public or private-to-public cloud platforms) can provide the needed business continuity. Indeed, with public clouds, many of them provide multiple data centres across multiple regions connected by high-speed interconnects. By using these availability zones, the customer does not have to put too much thought into how the mirror is architected; they just find themselves with an effective failover system providing high levels of technical availability.

However, the organisation will still need to be able to provide capabilities for its employees to access and use the technology if the main site where the disaster hits is the organisation's offices. This may mean operating a limited service to customers via employees working from home, or, as in the case of some large financial organisations, having secondary premises available where teams can go to provide a continuance of service.

However, such disasters are not necessarily the worst ones a business can experience. What happens if a provider decides to remove a service? Google has done this on several occasions with its consumer services, some of which, such as My Tracks,[216] had been integrated into a number of organisations' systems. Google Checkout was merged

---

[216] Pai, A. (1 February 2016) Google to shut down its activity tracking app My Tracks this spring. MobiHealthNews. Available from www.mobihealthnews.com/content/google-shut-down-its-activity-tracking-app-my-tracks-spring.

into Google Wallet,[217] but the change required some reworking for some of the organisations that had integrated the capability into their systems.

When this happens, although there may be no problems with the rest of the systems, such a removal of service will at best result in a loss of capability and at worst will result in the failure of a complete business process. It is therefore best to architect based on the premise that this will happen, and to ensure that external functions are integrated via APIs on a 'plug in, plug out' basis.

Should a service be withdrawn, it should be possible to rapidly identify and implement a different service to plug the gap. It is, however, incumbent on IT to maintain an up-to-date list of alternative services that can be called upon to replace at least those being used for mission-critical processes.

The nightmare to end all nightmares, though, is when the provider itself ceases to exist. Although it is easy to fall for the perception that large companies such as AWS, Google and Microsoft are too big to fail, this is easily disproved through looking at history. Outside of companies being acquired because they have been successful, there are those that have been bought up essentially as the remnants of a fire sale.

Ashton Tate was a company founded in 1980, just in time to grow due to the advent of the distributed computing movement. It rapidly became one of the 'big three' software companies alongside Microsoft and Lotus (now, in itself, acquired by IBM). However, due to an inability to move with the times, by 1991, it was a shadow of its former self and was acquired by Borland (now itself part of Micro Focus, which has in turn merged with Attachmate).

In the hardware space, Compaq grew to what was seen as an unassailable position, with server sales ahead of those of Dell, HP, IBM and everyone else. When it tried to move into advanced services through acquisition, beginning with DEC in 1998, things rapidly started to go wrong. By 2002, Compaq was in deep trouble and was finally acquired by HP.

Outside IT, the world is littered with high-profile failures of companies seen as being too big to fail. The financial crash of 2008 saw the end of Lehman Brothers in the US and Northern Rock in the UK, and has also led to the closure of 465 banks in the US by the Federal Deposit Insurance Corporation.[218]

Even the standard failure rate in companies is high; a Forbes article[219] states that 90% of startups fail. In a market as new and dynamic as cloud, trying to pick those providers that are going to stay the course is not easy, and getting it wrong could prove fatal for your own business.

In the US, cloud storage provider Nirvanix raised over $70 million in investment and created a reasonably successful business. However, on 16 September 2013, Nirvanix sent

[217] Shu, C. (20 May 2013) Google Checkout nixed in favor of Google Wallet. TechCrunch. Available from https://techcrunch.com/2013/05/20/google-checkout-nixed-in-favor-of-google-wallet.
[218] Wikipedia (updated 7 October 2017) List of bank failures in the United States (2008–present). Available from https://en.wikipedia.org/wiki/List_of_bank_failures_in_the_United_States_(2008%E2%80%93present).
[219] Patel, N. (16 January 2015) 90% of startups fail: Here's what you need to know about the 10%. Forbes. Available from www.forbes.com/sites/neilpatel/2015/01/16/90-of-startups-will-fail-heres-what-you-need-to-know-about-the-10/#4da610086679

a message to all its customers giving them notice that they had two weeks in which to retrieve their data and move it to an alternative site or they would lose access to it.[220]

The UK subsidiaries of managed services provider 2e2 Group went into immediate administration in 2013.[221] 2e2 had grown rapidly through acquisition: it had acquired 15 companies, many of them relatively small. However, it also made some larger acquisitions, such as Sun reseller Morse for £70 million. 2e2 started to breach its banking covenants, and this signalled a quick and unseemly end. The incoming administrators rapidly decided that the company could not be sold on or rescued through further external investment: 1,000 employees were made redundant within a matter of just over a week. Customers were then locked out from their data by the administrators, who wanted to charge the customers to access and retrieve the data. With few original staff left in place, accounts were left in the dark with no continuity of messaging: failures in communication and in dealing with customer problems .ed to 2e2 becoming a case study in what can go wrong in such situations. Some customers had made the short-sighted decision that having both live and backup data hosted on 2e2's platform was a cost-effective strategy, but now they were locked out from both sets of data.

It is important to write into contracts clauses that cover the need for access to data should this type of thing happen; however, also bear in mind that any contract may be deemed as no longer operable when administrators are called in. A better approach is to combine off-site data backup with the use of a different provider for long-term data, mirroring data to a separate provider for mission-critical live data and, if the provider will allow you, direct mirroring of your data to an NAS device installed within the provider's site, so enabling LAN-speed data mirroring. Should the worst happen, that NAS device is yours; it is not part of the administrator's inventory, and they should allow you to go to the site and remove the device with all its data and move it to a secondary site.

Not many providers will allow this type of use of an NAS device, but it is always worth asking. After all, an image of an application can be easily taken and held elsewhere, ready to spin up should there be a problem. The sticking point will always be the data: the more approaches that can be taken to ensure that a copy of data to a known time and point is available, the quicker an organisation can be back up and running again.

MAINTAINING GOVERNANCE IN A HYBRID CLOUD

> With proper governance, life will improve for all.
> Benigno Aquino III (former president of the Philippines)
> in his inaugural address, 30 June 2010

Governance of information has become a major issue as networks have opened up, value chains have grown and required the secure and effective movement of data, and

---

[220] Robinson, S. (September 2013) Nirvanix failure: A blow to the cloud storage model? *ComputerWeekly*. Available from www.computerweekly.com/opinion/Nirvanix-failure-a-blow-to-the-cloud-storage-model

[221] Robinson, D. (6 February 2013) 2e2 collapses amid failure to find buyer. *Financial Times*. Available from: www.ft.com/content/2332e418-7077-11e2-a2cf-00144feab49a

governments have increased their requirements for the central reporting of financial and other information data.

The perception has been within organisations that, as long as everything is in a central place, governance is easier than if it is spread across multiple different places, including platforms over which the organisation has less control. However, the world has changed, and such views of a rose-tinted past have little place in a world where the capability to share data and information in an open yet secure manner will define the winners in the markets.

Ensuring that there is sufficient governance of data as it flows across the hybrid environment is a key concern, but one where technologies are emerging that can help to ensure that everything is enacted and managed in a fully traceable and reportable manner. In Chapter 20, there is a full section covering the need for, and how to go about providing, full technical audit of data, information and individual actions across a hybrid cloud platform.

SUMMARY

What have we learned?

- There are many perceived issues with cloud. Many of these are receding as the model evolves.
- Some issues do remain, but these are actually little different from the issues an organisation has with its own internal IT platform.
- The key is to plan accordingly, particularly when it comes to the possible loss of service from a third-party cloud provider.

What does this mean?

- The perceived problems with cloud should no longer be seen as show-stoppers.
- Planning to deal with specific issues may not be as easy for some as for others, but the rapid evolution of cloud platforms will enable those who have created a suitably flexible cloud strategy to embrace the needed changes easily.

12 CLOUD AND THE 'CDs'

Releasing software is too often an art; it should be an engineering discipline.
Jez Humble and David Farley in *Continuous Delivery: Reliable Software Releases through Build, Test, and Deployment Automation*, 2010

An area in which there is a strong congruence between emerging models is between cloud and continuous development, delivery and deployment (CD). These three usages of 'CD' can be defined as:

- **Continuous development:** Here, developers can work on small, discrete elements of functionality that can be pushed out through continuous delivery mechanisms to users on a regular (or near-constant) basis.

- **Continuous delivery:** Sometimes used interchangeably with continuous deployment, continuous delivery should be the movement of the completed and checked functional elements from the continuous development stage, ready to be deployed to the live environment.

- **Continuous deployment:** This should be where all the final checks and balances take place to ensure that continuously developed and delivered elements can be successfully provisioned in the operational environment.

Another allied term is 'continuous integration'. Continuous integration is based on using automated services, such as those provided by Jenkins[222] or Atlassian Bamboo,[223] to ensure that changes in code are safely integrated into the downstream continuous delivery and deployment processes.

For the purposes of this chapter, I will use the term 'CD' to cover the above three processes as a singular item.

WHY USE CD?

Without change there is no innovation, creativity, or incentive for improvement. Those who initiate change will have a better opportunity to manage the change that is inevitable.
Attributed to William Pollard (Quaker writer and minister, 1828–1893)

With CD, the idea is that rather than presenting a new version of a software application in large chunks at planned (often long) time periods, smaller, incremental upgrades to functionality are prepared and provisioned on a far more immediate and continuous

---

[222] https://jenkins.io
[223] www.atlassian.com/software/bamboo

basis. Historically, such an approach has been anathema to an organisation. It was received wisdom that users did not cope well with change; it was deemed to be far better to store up changes and create a major upgrade (along with a set of patches to fix functionality problems) every six months or so. In this way, users and the help desk could be trained on the changes before they happened.

However, consumer technology has changed all of this. Users with smartphones and tablets are now used to seeing small changes in their apps on a regular basis; indeed, they pretty much demand that apps change on a regular basis. The thought of working with the 'static' model of an enterprise application is no longer appealing.

This has driven a move away from waterfall or cascade project development programmes through Agile project management towards a DevOps methodology. In DevOps, those within the development environment can create new functionality and use streamlined automation of testing and provisioning to get the new functionality out into the operational environment. As opposed to Agile, which is aimed primarily at software projects, DevOps must, by its very nature, also look to the underlying logical and physical hardware aspects of a project. However, this is not to say that Agile project management is dead; it provides the bedrock for the software aspects of DevOps and should remain a core part of any modern IT project.

DevOps FLOWS

Life is a series of natural and spontaneous changes. Don't resist them – that only creates sorrow. Let reality be reality. Let things flow naturally forward in whatever way they like.
Often attributed to Laozi (Chinese philosopher) but original source unknown

Figure 12.1 shows a conceptual flow chart of the process that underpins DevOps. Attempting to carry out such an end-to-end process across discrete and essentially disconnected development, test and run-time platforms introduces too many weak links into a complex chain.

Cloud's flexibility helps in making DevOps and CD work; by partitioning the cloud environment successfully, developers can work on their code on the same platform as it is tested – and run. Through the effective use of areas such as database virtualisation (e.g. provided by Delphix[224]) and containerisation (e.g. as from Docker, CentOS, Linux LXC/LXD), testing can be carried out on a snapshot of live data, where any changes made to the data are stored as separate metadata from the original, ensuring that any coding problems do not corrupt the main working database. This also allows for a proportion of users to be able to test the new functionality knowing that the performance they see on the test bed will be comparable to what everyone would see if the change were pushed out into the operational arena.

Containers can allow for the rapid provisioning of new functionality into both the test and operations environments. By having a system that is abstracted away from being a physical application on top of a physical platform and by using containerisation, the

---

[224] www.delphix.com

Figure 12.1 Conceptual flow chart of the DevOps process

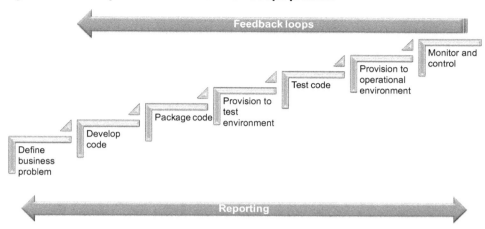

virtual capabilities of cloud enable ideas to be tried out and either pushed out (if successful) or dropped (if they are seen not to work as expected). Other benefits can be accrued through the use of good DevOps and CD orchestration systems, such as easier retro-testing and management of roll-back if needed.

For organisations that are looking to move to a far more constant but controlled rate of new functionality deployment, cloud plus CD is the answer. Within the DevOps environment, the main players have emerged from the open source environment. These include Jenkins,[225] Chef,[226] Puppet[227] and Hudson.[228] Commercial systems that layer over such systems to provide additional functionality come from the likes of CA Automic,[229] CloudBees,[230] EnterpriseWeb[231] and Electric Cloud.[232]

SUMMARY

What have we learned?

- The age of cascade delivery of functionality with large changes at long intervals is over.

- Users expect to have small, incremental changes provided to them at regular intervals.

- Cloud enables a DevOps/CD strategy where development, test and run time are all on the same overall platform.

---

[225] https://jenkins.io
[226] www.chef.io/chef
[227] https://puppet.com
[228] http://hudson-ci.org
[229] https://automic.com
[230] www.cloudbees.com
[231] http://enterpriseweb.com
[232] http://electric-cloud.com

What does this mean?

- Tools need to be chosen to enable a CD strategy.
- This also requires a change in mindset in the development, test and operations communities: there is a much stronger need for all constituents to work together as a single team.

13 CREATING THE BUSINESS CASE FOR THE CLOUD

You don't lead by pointing and telling people some place to go. You lead by going to that place and making a case.

Attributed to Ken Kesey (author of *One Flew Over the Cuckoo's Nest*)

A continuing problem for IT is in gaining the required investment from the business to fund the implementation of new technologies. For many companies, this is down to an ongoing inability for the IT department to put its message across in solid business terms. It may also be linked to the business laying down inappropriate metrics for how a request should be put forward. In the case of cloud, this is made even worse, as the IT team is not only asking for money but also asking for it to be invested in an early-stage concept where the end result is likely to be less control over the underlying aspects of the platform.

The business has generally required a set of arguments based around return on investment (RoI) and total cost of ownership (TCO). Unfortunately, the IT department tends to have little visibility around what the costs of an existing business process are, and the business is also often in the dark too. Trying to visualise accurate costs for what the new process in a cloud environment will be is also fraught with difficulty, due to the complexity of the cost models involved (discussed in Chapter 9).

This leaves IT with the problematic choice of either making up some numbers or requesting that no changes are made to try to solve what could be a pressing issue until it has had the opportunity to create a 'good enough' cost baseline against the existing technology. What is required is a different, more business-focused means of gauging whether a move to cloud makes economic sense for an organisation.

TOTAL VALUE PROPOSITION

Price is what you pay; value is what you get.

Warren Buffet (investor and philanthropist), Chairman's Letter, 2008

To get around such issues, Quocirca has developed an approach that is based around a more holistic, yet overall more simplistic, approach that it calls a total value proposition (TVP). The basic process goes back to 1999 and has been used by Quocirca across most of its interactions with its customers.

TVP is a four-step process that can be used to help check whether a proposed change will lead to appreciable value creation for a business, whether the change is needed for the business purely to survive in the competitive market, or even whether the change is actually not worth carrying out. TVP also provides a basic framework for business-focused messaging to be created to 'sell' the change into the business as a suitable investment. Although it is used here in terms of technology change, TVP can be applied by anyone within an organisation to see whether any change is worthwhile.

Scope, resources and time

The first stage of TVP is based around ensuring that any proposed change fits within the basic known variables of the remit of the project. It looks at whether the change will be possible within the scope of what the business has stated it requires, whether it will fit within the timescales required by the business, and whether there are sufficient resources (people, skills, finance) available to carry out the change (see Figure 13.1).

Figure 13.1 Total value proposition: scope, resources and time

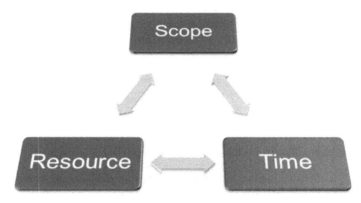

It is important that the person using TVP is honest with themselves at this point. Any problems that are not addressed at this stage will result in a project failure further down the line, or in project overspend or time delays that will only lower the perception of the effectiveness of IT in the eyes of the business.

Asking the right questions at this stage will also help to uncover where extra input is required. For example, if there is a lack of existing skills within the company, what will be the cost and time impacts of acquiring them, and will they make the project less likely to be successful? Will skills need to be brought in full time, or will a consultant or contractor, or even a specialist charging by the hour, better fit the bill?

Value, risk and cost

Once these aspects have been aligned to the satisfaction of the individual, the next stage is to look at the business aspects of the change. Here, any change within a business can only impact three specific variables. These are the risk to the business, the cost to the business and the additional value that is added to the business (see Figure 13.2).

Figure 13.2 Total value proposition: value, risk and cost

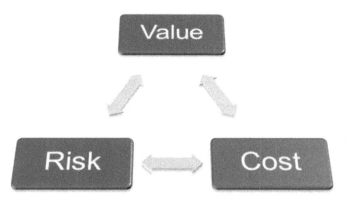

The 'perfect' change would drive down business risk and cost while adding business value. However, this is not a necessity within TVP. If each variable is considered in balance, it is alright to see one variable moving in the wrong direction, as long as the other areas move appreciably in the correct direction.

In the usage of TVP, these three variables can be defined more closely as:

- **Value:** The capability to sell more of an existing service or product at the same or greater margin, or the capability to bring a new service or product to market at an acceptable margin.

- **Cost:** The comparative amount that it will cost the organisation on an ongoing basis to receive the benefits of the change.

- **Risk:** The increased or lowered risks that will have to be carried by the business after the change has been made.

For example, a pharmaceutical company carrying out field trials of a new drug will have grave concerns around any risks associated with people taking the drug. Therefore, the business may well be happy to pay more in order to bring the risks down to an acceptable level.

A heavy manufacturing company running on small margins may take a different view. The business may be willing to carry a little more risk on whether its products are manufactured exactly to design tolerances, as long as the costs are driven down appreciably.

A company in a fast-moving, high-tech market may be willing to invest heavily in a risky environment, provided that the potential business value is perceived to be high enough for this gamble.

This is the most important area for a technical person looking to create the business case for a technological change. It is a waste of time approaching the business with messages based around how a move to cloud will make it easier to keep up with the pace of technological change, how it will make a DevOps strategy easier to manage or how it will bring greater usage of containerisation to the fore. These are essentially meaningless concepts to the business. What the business wants are messages around how the change impacts the business itself. Therefore, it is incumbent on the technical person to take any technical messages and translate them into business terms.

For example, if the technical message is that a move to cloud will make the adoption of DevOps more feasible, then the business message could be around how the move to cloud would enable continuous delivery of incremental change and allow for the demands of the business to be met more quickly. If the message is around keeping up with the pace of technical change, the message can be worded around ensuring that the best and most flexible platform is always in place to support the dynamic needs of the business at all times.

Just bear in mind that the business may still perceive IT as a cost centre: it may be that anything which is perceived by the business as purely an IT cost will be cut if there is something else on the priority list that is seen as more of a business investment. It is incumbent on IT to make sure that the changes it is putting forward are seen as investments, rather than pure costs.

Game theory

However, some changes must be made for other reasons. One of these is where the business runs the risk of falling behind its competitors if the change is not made. To address this point, TVP uses a simple form of game theory (see Figure 13.3).

Figure 13.3 Total value proposition: game theory

Game theory is defined as 'the study of mathematical models of conflict and cooperation between intelligent rational decision-makers'.[233] For the purposes of TVP, it is presumed that the 'intelligent rational decision-makers' are the individual's own organisation and its main competitor. The conflict and cooperation aspects are based around the impact of the proposed change: in this case, the adoption or not of a cloud platform.

---

[233] Myerson, Roger. (1991) *Game theory: Analysis of conflict*. Cambridge, Mass.: Harvard University Press, p. 1.

Creating a graphical representation of likely outcomes in the market should a change be carried out or not enables the cost of not doing something to be seen. The idea here is to compare the organisation with what is perceived as its biggest (not necessarily the largest) competitor in its market. Four simple graphs are constructed:

- **Graph 1: neither carries out the change:** Here, two lines are drawn against a suitable period of time. One covers the expected performance of the individual's own organisation over that time, the other that of the biggest competitor. No real detail is needed; the graph should just be a straight-line extrapolation of easily available information (e.g. from financial reports).

- **Graph 2: the individual's organisation carries out the change:** In this case, it is assumed that the competitor does not make the change. It is to be hoped that the proposed change will positively impact the organisation's performance, in which case its line as drawn in the first graph will become more positively steep. The change may also impact the competitor's line by taking business away from it, making the competitor's line less positively steep or even negative.

- **Graph 3: the competitor carries out the change:** Here, it is assumed that the individual's organisation does not carry out the change but that the competitor carries out something similar to the change. In this case, the competitor's line will grow more positively steep while the individual's organisation's line may become less positively steep or even negative.

- **Graph 4: both the individual's organisation and the competitor carry out the change:** If this were to happen, the worst-case scenario is that both organisations would continue pretty much on the same trajectories. It is possible that both could take market share from other, smaller competitors, but essentially carrying out the change will at least maintain the status quo.

Figure 13.4 Total value proposition: game theory graphs

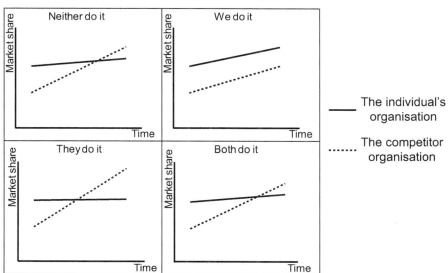

115

A possible outcome from this exercise is shown in Figure 13.4. As can be seen, there is an identifiable cost in not carrying out the change. Even if the competitor does not carry out the change itself, its current performance trajectory shows it overtaking the individual's organisation within the timescale of the graphs. If the competitor carries out the change and the individual's organisation doesn't, that point is accelerated.

However, as long as the individual's organisation does carry out the change, it will either maintain its competitiveness against the competitor or will accelerate away from it. Even if the previous value, risk and cost arguments do not show major overall value to the change, it is possible that the change will need to be carried out just due to the need for the organisation to survive in its market.

Comparative business process costings

The last stage of TVP is the use of comparative business process costings in order to respond to calls from financial people within the organisation for details regarding RoI and TCO. As previously discussed, the likelihood of having enough data to hand to create meaningful calculations will be very low.

However, the question of adopting the change should never be about precise measurement and comparison of costs anyway. Changes in market conditions, in business processes further down the line and even in personnel within the business can make such comparisons meaningless.

What can be helpful is a cost-comparison approach. The first stage is to take the top 5 or 10 processes that are going to be impacted by the change. It is better if the processes chosen are all of around equal weight when it comes to the business itself, but it is not absolutely necessary. Write these down and then score them on a scale of 1 to 5, where:

- 1 indicates that the cost of the process after the change will be a lot less than it is now.
- 2 indicates that the cost of the process after the change will be a little less than it is now.
- 3 indicates that the cost of the process after the change will be about the same as it is now.
- 4 indicates that the cost of the process after the change will be a little more than it is now.
- 5 indicates that the cost of the process after the change will be considerably more than it is now.

Now add up the total of the numbers and then divide them by the number of processes. This will give an indication of how rapid the RoI is likely to be and what the overall TCO is likely to be. For example, if the average comes out as between 1 and 2, then the overall ongoing business costs associated with the change will be considerably lower than they are now, indicating that a low-TCO solution has been chosen that will lead to a rapid RoI.

The other end of the scale is where the score is above 3, indicating that the new solution will lead to more expensive ongoing business costs. This should raise immediate flags to the individual around whether the change is worth carrying out. However, they should also refer back to the game theory graphs to see whether this is an investment for survival, in which case the increased costs may still be appropriate.

An example of this can be seen in Figure 13.5. The proposed change here is aimed at replacing a contact centre sales application with a more direct customer self-service one. This will have five implications.

First, in the new application, data will be input only once and directly by the customer themselves, replacing the error-prone and costly inputting of data by the contact centre agent. Second, the change will introduce the need for automatic aggregation of various data sources, such as using the Experian cloud service to check the customer's financial record, again replacing the need for agents to use a second application to carry out those checks themselves. Third, rather than the customer's product choice being served directly from the existing inventory, it will be passed down to the production line for one-off manufacturing. In this case, it has been deemed to cost more than carrying inventory. Fourth, the move to the cloud is seen as allowing for a more DevOps-type approach, but this is communicated by IT using a more business-oriented message around the use of continuous delivery to ensure that changes in business requirements can be more easily and more rapidly dealt with. Last, the proposed change uses direct, straight-through payment services, as provided by cloud services such as PayPal and Streamline.

Figure 13.5 Calculator for total value proposition, total cost of ownership and return on investment

Existing process	New process	Score
Manual data entry	Automated data entry	1
Multiple data sources for analysis	Automated aggregated data sets	2
Customer delivery from inventory	Customer delivery based on build-to-order	4
Required updated functionality provided on 6-monthly basis	Required updated functionality provided via continuous delivery	3
Payment for goods received by external system	Payment for goods received by straight-through processing	1
		Average = 2.2

The overall score for this very simple calculation is 2.2, showing that the change will result in a system that is appreciably cheaper than the one currently in use, and therefore a reasonably rapid RoI based on that lower TCO.

SUMMARY

What have we learned?

- The business tends to view IT as a cost centre; IT must endeavour to be viewed as an investment centre.
- The business has no interest in technical arguments. To the business, a technical person bringing such arguments to them appears to be a self-interested party just trying to make life easier for themselves.
- A rounded, business-focused set of messages is required. TVP can act as a framework to create the right messages around a suitable change to make the change attractive for investment.

What does this mean?

- Technical messages must be positioned in terms the business understands. This involves using messages that look at impacts on the business's risks, costs and overall value proposition.
- The more aspects of a change that can be messaged, the better the chances of the business investing in the change.
- Using a TVP framework to create a set of messages offers the best chance of a project gaining the right funding.

14 SCALE OUT, SCALE UP AND SCALE THROUGH

In pioneer days, they used oxen for heavy pulling, and when one ox couldn't budge a log, they didn't try to grow a larger ox. We shouldn't be trying for bigger computers, but for more systems of computers.

Rear Admiral Grace Hopper in *OCLC Newsletter*, March/April 1987

Not all workloads are the same, yet many organisations have taken a virtualised or cloud approach that seems to believe that they are. An OLTP workload is different from a big-data workload, which is different from a workload that is focused on video streaming. Therefore, a one-size-fits-all strategy of a single-architecture cloud may not provide the overall benefits that are required. Users must look to a future-state platform that does not constrain them to a 'general' platform: there must also be the capacity for specific workloads to be run on specialised engines within that overall single, logical cloud platform.

BUILDING THE RIGHT CLOUD PLATFORM

When I design buildings, I think of the overall composition, much as the parts of a body would fit together. On top of that, I think about how people will approach the building and experience that space.

Tadao Ando (architect) in an interview with *Architectural Record*, 1 May 2002

Many clouds are built on a standardised platform of Intel/AMD servers with a single type of storage pool connected via standard networking kit. The belief is that if everything is purely about resource availability, the elasticity of resources enabled by cloud provides the answer. Not enough compute power? Just throw more CPUs at the problem. Insufficient storage volume? Just take some from the storage resource pool and allocate it to the workload. More bandwidth required? Just provide a bigger pipe...

However, workloads don't work like this. For example, certain aspects of a workload may require specific compute capabilities, for example through the use of GPUs, IBM Power CPUs, FPGAs or a mainframe engine.

Storage is going through a period of massive change. Whereas a couple of years ago the market was predominantly focused on just how fast and dense magnetic disk drives could become, now solid-state systems have come to the fore, providing a massive leap in base performance. This does not mark the end for magnetic storage, though: it is not yet time to dump the magnetic array and replace everything with flash. Whereas the battle for the past couple of decades has been to find a faster spinning disk that could be deemed to be Tier 1 storage, flash storage has been a game changer. It is apparent that flash will be the new Tier 1, with the magnetic spinning disk being pushed down through the lower tiers as secondary, archive and backup storage. Having a degree of archival material on tape will still be a valid model for some time, particularly for heavily regulated industries where tape is currently mandated as a storage medium. However, even here, cloud-based near-line storage is likely to start to kill off the tape market in the near term.

Such tiering enables different storage workloads to be dealt with in different ways. Across the tiers, though, there will be various types of storage, such as object and block systems. Server-side storage, such as new-generation 3D negative-AND (3D NAND) dual in-line memory modules (DIMMs), NVMe M.2 (a small size of memory card formerly known as NGFF (next generation form factor)) and peripheral component interface express (PCIe) cards are making the storage landscape even more complex. Ensuring that all storage assets can be viewed as a single overall pool while still being intelligently divided into usable, differentiated pools of resources is key. Leading proponents in managing this multitier server-side/networked storage are companies such as Dell EMC and PernixData, which has been acquired by hyperconverged infrastructure vendor Nutanix.[234] Diablo Technologies[235] is taking a slightly different approach, looking to use non-volatile DIMMs (NVDIMMs) as a non-persistent, high-speed intelligent storage tier for those requiring, for example, analysis of massive data sets using approaches such as Spark under Hadoop.

Another vendor, Symbolic IO,[236] is working on the basis of using supercapacitor-backed volatile DRAM (dynamic random-access memory) along with intelligent data volume minimisation software to provide even faster real-time data analysis. Yet another player that came out of stealth mode in March 2017 is Excelero,[237] which provides a software-defined storage (SDS) approach to managing M.2 and PCIe NVMe storage to provide low-latency, high-IOPS (input/output operations per second) storage. Using RDMA (remote direct memory access) connectivity over Ethernet or Infiniband, Excelero misses out many of the weak links in the storage stack and results in microsecond latencies and scalable IOPS for systems certified for its use. This moves the tiering argument from one in which the concern is just to ensure that data is in the best position within a shared array to one where more complex decisions must be made regarding storage and data management systems that are increasingly dedicated to a specific workload.

Within the cloud, such tiering of storage is problematic. All resources are meant to be pooled, but server-side storage is difficult to make available on a logical basis, due to it being firmly linked to a single physical server. However, with a level of intelligent management, server-side storage can provide discrete value-added services to those who want specialised treatment of data within the cloud.

Networks within the cloud have also had to change. It is no longer just about providing high-speed interconnects between the various parts of an IT platform. Now, the network itself has also got to be virtualised – and flattened. Hierarchical network topologies do not work well in the cloud, with too much north–south traffic (i.e. traffic moving into and out of the facility) causing latencies and data collisions that prevent a cloud from operating well. Instead, fabric networks are becoming far more common, with east–west traffic (i.e. traffic moving across servers and racks within the data centre) being prioritised with full quality and priority of service being enabled for different traffic types.

---

[234] https://www.nutanix.com/pernixdata
[235] www.diablo-technologies.com
[236] www.symbolicio.com
[237] www.excelero.com

THE CLOUD AND 'SOFTWARE DEFINED'

Software is a great combination between artistry and engineering.
Bill Gates (philanthropist and founder of Microsoft) in an
interview in *PC Magazine*, February 1982

In 1998, Mark Medovich, a Sun Microsystems employee who had been working on Java, left and set up a company called WebSprocket. Building on work that AT&T had done in attempting to create a software-driven network switch in a project named GeoPlex, Medovich moved from trying to create what GeoPlex had been focusing on as a 'networking middleware' capability to the creation of a full network operating system based on an object-oriented structured run-time model. This led to the release of VMFoundry in 2000 as a structured compiler and of VMServer as the application server itself.

Ericsson[238] then worked with WebSprocket, leading to the first public demonstration of a software-defined network (SDN) system by Ohio State University and the Ohio Academic Resources Network.[239] From this early work, Bob Burke and Zac Carman created an expanded view of SDN and gained two US patents on content delivery control networks. This described the concept of a service preference architecture, from which what we see today as SDN grew.

The University of California at Berkeley and Stanford University worked to progress the idea of abstracting network switch and router hardware capabilities into software. An independent organisation was then set up called the Open Networking Foundation (ONF).[240] The ONF continued work on SDN and created OpenFlow,[241] a standardised means of identifying at the software level the optimum path packets of data should take across a network.

SDN and OpenFlow were widely acknowledged as major steps in moving forward the progress of networking. However, issues were found, particularly by the larger network and cloud service providers. The need for network traffic to be pulled away from the hardware into a software layer for decisions to be made on how it should be dealt with resulted in major latencies being introduced into the system. Therefore, a separate group, called the European Telecommunications Standards Institute,[242] which had already developed standards around such areas as GSM (global system for mobile communications) and DECT (digital enhanced cordless telecommunications), developed an approach to dealing with these sorts of issues. Working with its membership of over 800 organisations, it developed a concept called network function virtualisation (NFV)[243] through a working group known as the Industry Specification Group for NFV.

Even with such *de facto* and *de jure* standards in place, there are still problems in trying to do too much within the software layer. At times, it makes better sense for the data to be dealt with by the device itself, either within dedicated hardware or within firmware.

---

[238] www.ericsson.com
[239] www.oar.net
[240] www.opennetworking.org
[241] www.opennetworking.org/index.phpttps://www.opennetworking.org/sdn-resources/openflow
[242] www.etsi.org
[243] www.etsi.org/technologies-clusters/technologies/nfv

To this end, although software defined has grown in adoption, there is more of a focus on a better hybrid concept of 'hardware-assisted software defined'.

The hardware-assisted, software-defined approach abstracts functions where it makes sense at both a functional and technical level from the hardware to the software layer. However, in some cases data is still better dealt with by intelligence in the switch or router to maintain throughput and overall service response. Which types of data are dealt with by software and which by firmware is highly dependent on usage. The imperative must remain that the end results of any action provide a high level of standardisation in how data is managed across a hybrid platform. It is therefore unlikely that the likes of Cisco IOS[244] or Juniper Junos[245] will go away any time soon, particularly as such network operating systems have evolved to embrace the SDN world as well.

The same sort of thing has happened with storage and compute. As a cloud platform may be highly heterogeneous, there is a core need for as much as possible to be abstracted from the hardware into the software. Virtualisation, through the use of hypervisors such as ESX, Hyper-V and the Kernel-based Virtual Machine (KVM), has provided the basis for creating a software-defined compute (SDC) environment. Much work has been done on creating the same approach for storage; the latest Storage Networking Industry Association (SNIA)[246] work on Swordfish[247] as an abstract means of dealing with mixed storage environments looks promising.

However, a cloud platform is a tightly linked ecosystem: all resources in a cloud context are co-dependent. Having three completely discrete software-defined approaches makes no sense. The SNIA's Swordfish builds on the DMTF's[248] Redfish[249] standard, pulling together two parts of the software-defined message. However, these two standards are at the moment primarily focused on systems management; more is required to create a high-level approach to orchestration and optimisation of a software-defined world.

To this end, the software-defined data centre (SDDC) has been put forward as a model. Misleading in itself, as the name seems to be focused on a single platform within a single facility, the idea behind the SDDC is to create an over-reaching umbrella that understands the contextual requirements between the SDC, SDS and SDN worlds. Changes made to a workload resource that have knock-on impacts on other resources will be flagged as issues that need to be dealt with, or the use of an idempotent model will make sure that changes are made to these resources as well.

THE POWER OF IDEMPOTENCY

If you want to discover just what there is in a man – give him power. It will either make him or wreck him.

Francis Trevelyan Miller in *Portrait Life of Lincoln:
Life of Abraham Lincoln, the Greatest American*, 1910

---

[244] www.cisco.com/c/en/us/products/ios-nx-os-software/ios-technologies/index.html
[245] www.juniper.net/us/en/products-services/nos/junos
[246] www.snia.org
[247] www.snia.org/forums/smi/swordfish
[248] www.dmtf.org
[249] www.dmtf.org/standards/redfish

Idempotency is becoming a new area of focus within the cloud. It is a term used in the context of computing to cover the capabilities of a system to be given a set of instructions and make sure that the outcomes from those instructions are always the same, time after time, irrespective of the underlying platform and the number of times an activity is carried out.

Users of hybrid cloud platforms need a means of defining what is required, and they need the provisioning and implementation of the resulting system to be automated and repeatable. This requires a degree of intelligence: the definition of 'what is right' in resource terms for a workload is becoming difficult for a systems architect to figure out.

Instead, a systems administrator should be able to take a 'best guess' based on information provided through to them as part of the DevOps process. Based on previous implementations, the system should be able to provide advice on what it believes is needed. Once the workload has been provisioned into the operational environment, any rules and policies around agreed service levels for response times and so on need to be looked at by the system and the resources adapted to ensure that the system operates within the agreed levels.

If this is not possible, the system should raise an exception so that the problem can be looked at. It can then be determined whether there is a need for more of an existing resource, or whether there is a need for a new physical resource to be acquired and provisioned, or whether the agreed service levels need to be revisited.

Based on this empirical data, the system should then refresh its internal understanding, creating a capability to better advise up front on what resources would be required for a similar system to be deployed. The system should then also be able to create templates so that the same workload can be deployed again without any issues should the need arise.

Why should the need arise? It could be that an extra instance of an image is required for load balancing or high-availability reasons. It may be that as part of a fast-reaction business-continuity policy, a replacement image needs to be implemented on a remote site within a short time period.

Whatever the reason, the use of an idempotent system means that a workload can be pushed out into a new environment without the need for manual intervention.

CONVERGED AND HYPERCONVERGED SYSTEMS

You can converge a toaster and a refrigerator, but those things are probably not going to be pleasing to the user.

Tim Cook (CEO of Apple) in an interview in *Forbes*, 24 April 2012

Although many public clouds are built on a scale-out platform consisting of commodity server, storage and network components, many organisations have moved to using either converged or hyperconverged systems within their own private cloud environments. These two terms are quite often conflated. However, it is best to ensure that a proper differentiation is made between them, as the focus of the two systems can be markedly different.

A converged system can be viewed as a storage system that also runs a simple set of associated workloads: for example, carrying out data deduplication, compression, encryption and so on. This essentially creates a single system where the SDS aspects are built into the box. As such, IT does not have to purchase, implement and manage third-party software that runs on external systems to achieve the same ends, so saving on time, on complexity and generally on up-front costs as well. However, the main business workloads still need to be run on a separate part of the overall platform, with the converged storage acting as a virtual SAN. Vendors in this space include Dell EMC, HDS, HP, IBM and NetApp.

The logical up-step from this is a hyperconverged infrastructure (HCI) system. Here, compute, storage and network resources are all made available in a single engineered system. Most hyperconverged systems come with full in-built systems management, workload orchestration and in-built virtualisation, with many also including a pre-installed cloud platform. Therefore, HCI systems can pick and choose where software-defined constructs work best for them and where it is best to use hardware instead. This can mean that performance between multiple HCI systems can be impacted, if the systems default to a software-defined model when exchanging data and information between each system.

The idea is that actual business workloads can be run on the system. Such systems can be ideal for those wanting fast time to capability, as all the required resources are in one place. All that is required is to take delivery of the system, plug it in, power it up, add a few variables (such as IP addresses) and then start provisioning workloads against it. Vendors in this space include Cisco (UCS[250]), Dell EMC (Vblock/VxBlock[251] and VxRail[252]/VxRack[253]), HPE (Hyper Converged,[254] Omnistack Solution with HPE Proliant 380[255]) and Scale Computing (HC platforms[256]).

HCI systems can also be offered as a software option. Here, an organisation can choose its own server, storage and network equipment and install an HCI system on the overall platform. This is the epitome of the software-defined model: it only works where the hardware is abstracted as much as possible from the software. However, most vendors offering such an approach, such as Pivot3,[257] Nutanix[258] and HPE SimpliVity,[259] do require that a certified set of hardware components is used. This enables them to hook through from the software to the appropriate hardware capabilities where necessary. To make acquiring the software easier, most of the software-focused HCI vendors also offer a pre-configured hardware option of their own.

---

[250] www.cisco.com/c/en/us/products/servers-unified-computing/index.html
[251] www.emc.com/en-us/converged-infrastructure/converged-systems.htm#collapse=
[252] www.emc.com/en-gb/converged-infrastructure/vxrail/index.htm#collapse=&tab3=0
[253] www.emc.com/en-gb/converged-infrastructure/vxrack-system-1000/index.htm
[254] www.hpe.com/uk/en/integrated-systems/hyper-converged.html
[255] www.simplivity.com/wp-content/uploads/omnistack-with-hpe-proliant-data-sheet-en.pdf
[256] www.scalecomputing.com/products/hardware-platforms
[257] http://pivot3.com
[258] www.nutanix.com
[259] www.simplivity.com

For organisations looking to acquire a software-based HCI platform, the other choices are build-it-yourself or the use of an OEM model where a hardware manufacturer has a strategic agreement with such a software player to provide an overall HCI system, such as with Lenovo (Converged HX system with Nutanix[260]) and Huawei (FusionCube system with HPE SimpliVity[261]).

However, HCI platforms are not quite the silver bullet that they may at first appear. In some cases, scaling out can be a problem. As an example, consider a highly engineered HCI system that comes as a single block. Workloads are applied to it and, at some point, it becomes apparent that extra CPU capacity is required. A well-engineered HCI system should allow for the simple addition of more server nodes to meet this requirement.

Some HCI systems do not allow such scaling, instead requiring a whole new hyperconverged box to be acquired and placed alongside the existing system. Therefore, purchasers can find themselves having to pay for extra storage and network capabilities that are not needed.

For those HCI systems that do allow for incremental hardware to be acquired and implemented, there is a need for advanced monitoring, management and reporting tools to be put in place to ensure that this is managed successfully. All HCI systems come with some built-in tools, and these may be enough to cover one HCI installation. Others may be able to offer some degree of common management across multiple similar HCI systems, enabling, for example, workload portability and real-time movement of workloads across systems.

However, many will find themselves in the age-old position of heterogeneity. Whether this is through choice (not wanting to have all of one's eggs in one basket) or through force (if the original HCI supplier has been acquired by a non-preferred vendor or has gone out of business), it may be deemed best to have the ability to manage a heterogeneous environment through a single pane of glass.

Another issue could be one that is seen in poorly designed and implemented public clouds. The impact of multi-tenancy of different workloads on the one system can have a direct detrimental impact on the performance of some, if not all, of the workloads involved. Those administrating the systems must also look out for 'noisy neighbours', where one workload suddenly spikes in one or more resource usages, crowding out all other workloads from access to the resources (see Chapter 11).

SUMMARY

What have we learned?

- There is a strong movement towards a software-defined world.
- However, software defined is not suitable for every occasion: a better approach is a 'hardware-assisted software-defined' model.

---

[260] http://shop.lenovo.com/us/en/systems/converged-systems/hx_series/?menu-id=lenovo_converged_hx_series
[261] http://e.huawei.com/en/videos/global/2016/201611031114

- The move towards more engineered systems through converged and HCI systems will accelerate the move to software defined. However, such systems have their own shortcomings.

What does this mean?

- Although hardware capabilities are important, organisations need to start to focus on what can and should be moved to the software level for flexibility and standardisation reasons. Hardware acceleration should be used where appropriate, not as a first port of call.

- Choosing converged and HCI systems can cut out a lot of 'grunt-level' work that would otherwise need to be carried out by the IT team and does enable software-defined approaches to be built in at a system level. However, such systems must be chosen carefully.

15 CLOUD AND DATA

The errors which arise from the absence of facts are far more numerous and more durable than those which result from unsound reasoning respecting true data.

Charles Babbage ('the Father of Computing') in
On the Economy of Machinery and Manufactures, 1832

When it comes down to it, organisations are really not bothered about the actual platform (physical, virtual, cloud or hybrid cloud) they use as long as it 'does the job'. This begs the question of what the job of an IT platform actually is. Is it to run applications that are focused on specific business areas, such as CRM, ERP or supply chain management? Hardly: throwing money at CRM software does not mean that a company suddenly becomes a leader in how it deals with its customers. No, the purpose of an IT platform is to ensure that an organisation has the right data/information in the right place at the right time so that informed decisions can be made that support the organisation's aims. And there are other areas around data that need to be considered as well, generally as dictated by a central government or trade body.

Any organisation should ensure that its IT platform provides for needs around:

- data sovereignty;
- data flows;
- database issues;
- distance and latency;
- high availability.

Let's take a look at each of these areas in greater detail

DATA SOVEREIGNTY

We are now physically, politically, and economically one world and nations so interdependent that the absolute national sovereignty of nations is no longer possible.
John Boyd Orr (Nobel Peace Prize winner and first director general of the United Nations Food and Agriculture Organisation) in his Nobel Lecture, 12 December 1949

The very nature of cloud requires data to be shared across organisational and often country boundaries. This has led to issues around data sovereignty – that is, where data must geographically reside in order to meet regulatory needs. In turn, there have arisen broad discussions around how this can be managed, from in-country data hosting to 'embassy storage' (storage systems that are dedicated to holding data from a single country) and so on.

Even where in-country data storage is chosen, this may not meet the complete needs of an organisation. An example here is data being held in Microsoft's data centre in Dublin, Ireland. The US government wanted access to certain emails held in the Dublin data centre. A simple disclosure warrant was issued by a court in the US, demanding that Microsoft hand over the emails under the Stored Communications Act (1986). Microsoft refused to do so, stating that the emails were not in the US and were therefore outside the jurisdiction of the court warrant. The government fought back, stating that this was disclosure based on the same concept of a physical letter and that disclosure of the item was warranted, no matter where the data was. Two lower courts sided with the government; however, Microsoft appealed to the Second Circuit Court, where it had a unanimous finding in its favour. There is still a likelihood, at the time of writing, that the case could be taken to the Supreme Court.

Such data sovereignty issues become more pressing as geopolitical situations change. The rise of more nationalistic policies means that governments are more likely to demand that data resides and is managed within a single jurisdiction: cloud users must be very careful in how they deal with data on a country-by-country basis.

Once data sovereignty has been dealt with, there are then the continuing issues around data and information security. If these can be managed successfully, an organisation can enhance its success through opening up the flows of its information across its value chain.

DATA FLOWS

The Berlin Wall wasn't the only barrier to fall after the collapse of the Soviet Union and the end of the Cold War. Traditional barriers to the flow of money, trade, people and ideas also fell.
Attributed to Fareed Zakaria (journalist, author and TV presenter)

The need for information to flow from suppliers to the organisation and from the organisation to customers and beyond is forcing a change in how organisations are having to view the data under their control. Many IT professionals have been used to working within the principle of maintaining control over data by not letting it move away from a known platform. Now, the approach has got to be around providing secure and effective means of allowing data to be shared with those who need access to it. As governments become more aware of the value of data, they are increasingly enacting laws that aim both to control data and to punish those who do not look after other entities' data in a safe enough manner. The prime example of this is the EU's General Data Protection Regulation, which all member countries will have to have in place in 2018. However, any non-EU-based organisation wishing to interact with EU-based entities will also have to ensure that it is compliant with this regulation.

Cloud helps here: it provides a scalable platform for the storage, analysis and management of data, and a public cloud platform provides high-availability access to anyone who needs to get to the data. This does require high levels of data security, however (discussed in Chapter 16).

Enabling such data flows again means that APIs come to the fore. Rather than forcing each constituent of the value chain to use specific clients to interoperate with server-side applications, APIs allow these constituents to access the data in the way that makes the most sense to them. Even though they are still working with the same data as everyone else, they can use different analysis and reporting systems, and can also deliver their own data into the cloud as standardised streams.

DATABASE ISSUES

> Computing should be taught as a rigorous – but fun – discipline covering topics like programming, database structures, and algorithms. That doesn't have to be boring.
> Geoff Mulgan (CEO of Nesta) in *The Huffington Post*, 11 November 2012

A distribution of data across a single multi-cloud platform is hard enough to manage; one where a number of corporate multi-clouds are involved becomes a major problem. Although this book does not have the scope to cover all the technical aspects of data management in the cloud, the reader should ensure that they have enough of an understanding of the use of such database approaches as atomicity, consistency, isolation and durability (ACID); basically available soft-state with eventual consistency (BASE) for database consistency; and data handling alongside representational state transfer (ReSTful) APIs in dealing with data. A practical starter covering the main areas is Dan McCreary and Ann Kelly's *Making Sense of NoSQL: A Guide for Managers and the Rest of Us*.[262]

Certainly, when looking at how data is used across a complex environment, users must understand the difference between eventual and immediate data consistency. Eventual consistency (otherwise known as 'optimistic replication') works on the basis that over a period of time, any data that has not changed will replicate across a distributed platform so as to be the same across the whole platform, with changes replicating over time. Immediate consistency is just that: all copies of the data will reflect the real state of the data in real time.

Eventual consistency may sound like it has little room for use in a modern organisation. Surely, everyone wants to make sure that the data that they are working with is the one true version? Yes, when that data changes often. However, with data that changes less often, eventual consistency can be far less expensive to implement and will provide a good enough solution to many data (and particularly information) problems, such as many types of information caching and regional serving of such information. For such a solution, BASE will suffice, with changes of the information source being served via metadata and such information being served more slowly from the prime storage system directly to the user.

For data that changes often and is to be distributed across a broad platform, BASE may not be good enough. ACID will provide much faster data consistency – at a cost in terms of resource requirements and complexity of systems.

---

[262] McCreary, D., Kelly, A. (2014) *Making sense of NoSQL: A guide for managers and the rest of us.* Shelter Island, NY: Manning.

DISTANCE AND LATENCY

> Essentially, we're always trying to reduce latency. As you try to reduce the latency of the experience, you can only get it down so far before we start running into the limitations of game engines, computing, the intensity of the experience you're trying to compute.
> Brendan Iribe (founder and former CEO of Oculus VR) in *VentureBeat*, 14 January 2014

There are also issues around how far the data needs to move. Long-distance data synchronisation has been an issue for many years. The more latency there is in a connection, the greater a problem can be if such time delays arise. For example, mirroring data in a data centre at data centre interconnect speeds means that the mirror will be happening in low-millisecond or even microsecond times. Should one side of the mirror stop working, it can pretty much be guaranteed that the other side will be up to date enough to take over immediately.

Now, take this to, say, 6,000 kilometres (approximately the distance from London to New York via connections and undersea cable) over a WAN connection. With a non-dedicated link, there could be anywhere from a third of a second of latency upward. In that time, if one side of the mirror goes down, the other side cannot be sure that it has all of the data that was being sent to it. Without intelligence in place, based around a store-and-forward data bus, some transactions can be lost or left in an unknown state.

Modern interconnects are helping to deal with this problem, as are modern data-handling approaches. Use of, for example, AWS Direct Connect or Microsoft Azure ExpressRoute can provide more predictable, low-latency connections. Global interconnect providers (such as colocation provider Interxion[263] and Equinix, network services provider Colt,[264] and telecoms and general services providers such as BT[265]) will either manage multiple network connections via peering arrangements or act as end points for such connections.

HIGH AVAILABILITY

> The Internet has exceeded our collective expectations as a revolutionary spring of information, news and ideas. It is essential that we keep that spring flowing. We must not thwart the Internet's availability by taxing access to it.
> US Representative Chris Cannon, Speech in the House, September 2003

Storage hardware and data management software vendors have been evolving and maturing their systems to be able to more effectively provide high-availability data services. Rather than depending on RAID (redundant array of inexpensive/independent disks) combined with image-based backup and recovery, vendors are shifting their focus onto other means of providing higher availability of data.

---

[263] www.interxion.com
[264] www.colt.net
[265] www.bt.net/info/peering.shtml

RAID has become problematic as disk sizes have grown. With 10TB drives now having arrived on the scene, the failure of a single disk in a simple five-disk RAID 5 array will result in a disk rebuild time measured in days. During this time, if another disk fails, then all the data can be lost. Also, during this time, a lot of resources that should be ensuring high-performance data services are diverted to carrying out the disk rebuild.

Erasure code has been brought through by some vendors in order to get around this issue. By 'sharding' the data into a number of pieces (where only a proportion of those shards are required to rebuild the data) and then saving the shards in a distributed manner, any single disk failure still leaves a system where further failure is tolerated. RAID generally requires a block-by-block rebuild (i.e. an empty 10TB drive will take as long to rebuild as a full one): erasure code only works on the stored data. Therefore, rebuild times tend to be faster. For cloud providers and for organisations with large disk arrays underpinning their private clouds, erasure code is a far better direction to go than trying to stick with any form of RAID.

With backup and restore, the adoption of snapshots of data, rather than full imaging, means that continuous, asynchronous copies of data can be made where the state of the data is fully understood. This means that the difference between the recovery point objective (RPO: the point of time in the past when the data is known to be valid) and the recovery time objective (RTO: how long it will take to recover the data) is reasonably predictable and the business can plan accordingly.

However, for organisations where the RPO-to-RPO time is too long and the loss of data is too great, extended data mirroring is now available. This tends to be based on moving away from fully synchronous mirroring (which gives an RPC of zero), instead using a fast asynchronous mirror with delayed write. Although this moves the RPO further into the past, modern systems minimise this by using fast writes, particularly when using flash-based storage systems. Examples in this space are IBM with Global Mirror,[266] which extends the capabilities of its Metro Mirror product to distances of beyond 300 kilometres between storage systems, and FlashGrid,[267] with its 0.5 millisecond latency across 100 kilometres mirroring for Oracle-based OLTP workloads.

In addition, stretched clustering can be used to have a load-balanced storage platform across two (or more) locations, provided that they are not too far apart. In the case of VMware's vMSC (Managed Stretched Cluster), latency between the two sites cannot be more than 10 milliseconds, leading to a maximum real-world distance of around 100 kilometres. Dell EMC's VSAN Stretched Cluster HCI system requires even lower latencies of around 2.5 milliseconds.

SUMMARY

What have we learned?

- Cloud computing is not just a case of having a single, global shared storage resource.

---

[266] www.ibm.com/support/knowledgecenter/SSNE44_5.1.0/com.ibm.tpc_V51.doc/frg_c_ct_global_mirror.html
[267] www.flashgrid.io/solutions_stretched_clusters

- Data sovereignty is an increasing issue.
- Managing complex data storage and analytics platforms requires far more than simple tiering.

What does this mean?

- The race for real-time big-data analysis means that there will still be a need for strong skills in architecting the right platform.
- The use of server-side storage will need to be considered, and so will how that impacts on overall data availability.
- The difference between eventual and immediate consistency must be fully understood.

16   CLOUD SECURITY

You could go crazy thinking of how unprivate our lives really are – the omnipresent security cameras, the tracking data on our very smart phones, the porous state of our Internet selves, the trail of electronic crumbs we leave every day.
> Susan Orlean in 'Stay Out of My Dropbox', *The New Yorker*, 18 May 2011

The security of data held in the cloud has long been a source of concern for many organisations that have considered its use. Headlines in the press around breaches of cloud platforms and the leakage of masses of personally identifiable data (PID) and proprietary information have driven a perception that cloud platforms cannot be inherently trusted as secure platforms.

However, those looking to use public cloud should first look to the security present in their own environment. Basic questions such as 'Can we afford world-leading security experts?' and 'Where are the world-leading security experts likely to work?' should be posed before dismissing public clouds as major security weak points.

In this chapter, we look at the various aspects of physical and technical security, and why taking an information-first security approach is better than focusing on hardware or application security.

THE MYTH OF DATA SECURITY IN PRIVATE DATA CENTRES

Science and technology revolutionize our lives, but memory, tradition and myth frame our response.
> Arthur M. Schlesinger, Jr (historian) in *The Cycles of American History*, 1986

It is far better to have total control of the security around your IT platform than to allow someone else to have that responsibility, surely? Not really: this is not (necessarily) true, and in many cases is horrendously and dangerously wrong. There are thousands of breaches of private data centres every year, but few of these will ever get through to the press, as they can be dealt with quietly by the organisation that owns the facility. Even where disclosure of the breach is a legal requirement, it is only likely to hit the news if the organisation that is hit is extremely well known and the data that has been leaked can be shown to pose a problem for customers. However, as an article in CRN showed,[268] during the first half of 2016, the majority of large data breaches were actually through single organisations, and several of these were caused through simple issues such as loss of a laptop or of a set of disk drives.

---

[268] Kuranda, S. (28 July 2016) The 10 biggest data breaches of 2016 (so far). CRN. Available from www.crn.com/slide-shows/security/300081491/the-10-biggest-data-breaches-of-2016-so-far.htm.

With a cloud provider, it is different. A cloud provider will be looking after a lot of different customers – in some cases thousands or tens of thousands of them. Therefore, it is far more attractive for a blackhat (a person with malicious intent and the skills to attempt to carry out that intent) to target the overall security of the platform than to go for just one organisation within in its own data centre. This is not a rule *per se*: if it is a targeted attack where specific intellectual property is being sought, then it makes no difference if that information is being held in a privately owned or a public cloud-based facility. However, for those wanting to uncover PID and use it in other ways (such as phishing expeditions or to use username–password pairs uncovered through such raids in other places for financial benefit), cloud providers can be seen as a better target.

Are cloud providers inherently less secure than a privately owned platform? In the vast majority of cases, no. Cloud providers know that their futures depend on being secure. Providers such as AWS, Azure and IBM have groups of employees dedicated to ensuring that the basic platform is highly secure. ISO 27001:2013[269] provides a basic set of capabilities that any organisation should be able to demonstrate around how it deals with data security, and any organisation looking to use a cloud provider should ensure that the chosen partner has demonstrated ISO 27001:2013 compliance.

Further levels of data security can be provided through compliance with military standards. In March 2016, the US Department of Defense issued its *Cloud Computing Security Requirements Guide*.[270] In the UK, the National Cyber Security Centre has released a series of guidelines called the 'Cloud Security Collection'[271] that lays out 14 cloud security principles that must be adhered to for any cloud service to be considered for government data use. The document on 'Implementing the Cloud Security Principles'[272] is of great value as it lists the principles and why they are important. A quick list of the principles is as follows:

- data in transit protection;
- asset protection and resilience;
- separation between users;
- a governance framework;
- operational security;
- personnel security;
- secure development;
- supply chain security;
- secure user management;
- identity and authentication;

---

[269] www.iso.org/iso/iso27001
[270] Department of Defense cloud computing security requirements guide v1r2. (18 March 2016) Defense Information Systems Agency. Available from http://iasecontent.disa.mil/cloud/Downloads/Cloud_Computing_SRG_v1r2.pdf.
[271] National Cyber Security Centre. (updated 16 August 2016) Guidance: Cloud security collection. GCHQ. Available from www.ncsc.gov.uk/guidance/cloud-security-collection.
[272] National Cyber Security Centre. (updated 21 September 2016) Guidance: Implementing the cloud security principles. GCHQ. Available from www.ncsc.gov.uk/guidance/implementing-cloud-security-principles.

- external interface protection;
- secure service administration;
- audit information for users;
- secure use of the service.

Adherence and proof of compliance with the needs of these areas help to define the types of services provided and the data a cloud provider can hold for government departments. Within the UK government's G-Cloud platform (a cloud platform for providing shared services to central and local government groups), this set of principles has effectively replaced the old Impact Level classifications. By showing the ability to adhere to these principles and by opening up a data centre facility in the UK, Microsoft has managed to get the UK's Ministry of Defence to move its Microsoft Office functions over to Azure.

Such a list of principles forms a good starting point for anyone interested in the basic security of any IT platform they are creating or looking to use.

ASSUME THAT SECURITY IS BREACHED

Once more unto the breach, dear friends, once more.
William Shakespeare, *Henry V*, c.1599

This leads to the crux of the matter when it comes to security: it is best to assume that at some stage the platform itself will be breached. If an alternative approach is taken where the information comes first, far better security can be guaranteed.

The key is that information now has to travel across a broader set of environments than in the past. The complex value chain of suppliers, customers, employees, contractors, consultants, legal and accreditation bodies, and so on means that any security strategy that is predicated on platform security is doomed to failure. Instead, the focus must be on the information itself.

Consider a standard IT stack. The hardware (servers, storage, networking equipment) has to be set up, and various types of security can be applied to it in an attempt to prevent access to the devices themselves through the use of passwords, two-factor authentication (2FA) and so on. The same then has to apply to the users and the devices that they are using. The software stack must also be secured: databases will have to be protected against interference, and applications will need to be secured through extra username–password pairs and 2FA approaches.

Imagine that this is done perfectly. What happens when a report is run against that platform and is sent to an outsider? There is no control or continuous audit trail of activity for that information: once the report (or data, document, whatever) has been sent, it has been moved out of the originating organisation's security capabilities.

Moreover, it is also less than likely that the set-up and security will be implemented perfectly. For example, research carried out by Quocirca on privileged user access[273] in 2009 showed that many organisations allowed systems administrators to share username and passwords. This means that, should a problem occur, it is impossible to identify exactly who caused the problem, even at a system-administrator level. And the same happens with users: they often tend to share username–password pairs so that others can easily access information without having to 'bother' another person.

Platform-based security may be able to pick up patterns of activity that can indicate malicious intent (e.g. through attempted intrusions). However, if an outsider does present a valid username–password pair, then they will be into the heart of the system and will generally have unhindered access to whatever information is allowed via that username–password pair.

This is the case for all IT platforms – the problem is not cloud specific. This is where many have come unstuck: if they store information in the clear (i.e. without any use of encryption to secure the data) in the cloud or have poor security strategies around how that information is secured, then it is more likely to be breached. No matter how solid the cloud provider's security strategy is, it does not replace the onus on the customer to ensure that the information is inherently secure in itself.

Therefore, a holistic information security strategy is required, rather than a mix of hardware, application, database and document security approaches. The first step to creating such an information security strategy is to understand that it must be platform independent and that it needs to reach out well beyond the organisation's core environment. The second step is to understand that it has little to do with data security. After all, data is just a set of ones and zeros; if the person who has access to those ones and zeros cannot make any sense of them (whether it be through a lack of access to the application that understands the data or because the information denoted by the ones and zeros has been protected in some way), then there is no real problem.

DATA CLASSIFICATION

To be beyond any existing classification has always pleased me.
Boyd Rice (aka NON, experimental musician, b. 1956)

The best place to start in dealing with a fully managed information strategy is with information classification. As a simple example, let's assume that all the information an organisation holds can be split into three classifications:

- **Public:** Any information that would pose no threat to the organisation if it were to be in the public domain, such as post-release announcements, catalogues and public financial reports.

---

[273] Longbottom, C., Tarzey, B. (31 October 2009) Privileged user management: It's time to take control. Quocirca. Available from http://quocirca.com/content/privileged-user-management-it%E2%80%99s-time-take-control-0.

- **Commercial in confidence:** Information that could have a financial impact on the organisation if it were to fall into the wrong hands, such as contract details and future product release dates/designs.

- **Secret:** Information that would severely financially and reputationally damage the organisation if it got into the wrong hands, such as customer PID, acquisition/merger information and pre-release financial data.

The number of and the titles for each type of information are immaterial. It is just important that an organisation agrees on a small number of classifications, and what general levels of security it needs to apply to its information. However, it should make sure that it keeps the number of types of information to as few as possible, otherwise the system will be far too complex and unwieldy to operate from the start.

Now we have a simple basis for how such information needs to be dealt with. Templates can be used right from the point of information creation to apply such classifications to reports, documents, messages and so on. Although there is not enough granularity in such a simple classification, the use of dynamic metadata can be brought to bear to build on the basic information types.

Each person involved in the value chain can be provided with a set of roles and responsibilities. For example, the CEO of the organisation can generally be provided with much higher information access capabilities than a general employee. That general employee can be provided with higher capabilities than a general contractor, who may be provided with higher capabilities than a supplier.

An individual working in human resources may have access to personnel records, whereas one working in marketing should not. A supplier may have access to contracts between themselves and the organisation but not to any other contractual details between the organisation and other suppliers.

Combine this with the mode of access. Access to information via a known device (e.g. a desktop PC that is verifiably connected to the LAN) can have better capabilities than a laptop connecting over a VPN from a hotel room, which would have better capabilities than a tablet coming in over a public Wi-Fi access point.

Then bring in behavioural analysis. For example, if an individual has just accessed information from a verified desktop in London, it is unlikely that they can be accessing different information from a laptop in Tokyo 30 minutes later. Look for abnormal usage patterns as well: does a specific individual appear to be suddenly downloading a large amount of information, whereas they generally only download a few files per day? Are there signs that repeated attempts to log into a system are indicative of a hacker, rather than just someone who has lost their password?

In this way, abnormal behaviour can be more easily identified and investigated. This enables certain information problems to be nipped in the bud before they become major issues.

Classification also helps to decide what needs to be encrypted and what can be left in the clear. Data encryption has an overhead impact in terms of the compute resources required to deal with the encryption and decryption algorithms, and also has major impacts on data storage volumes, as encrypted data is far harder to deduplicate and compress. Save encryption for data that needs it: that which is above the level of 'public'. Combine this with data leak/loss prevention (DLP) approaches (see next section) to completely block or redact certain information from the data flows.

THE BADLY PROTECTED WALLED GARDEN

> A garden should make you feel you've entered privileged space – a place not just set apart but reverberant – and it seems to me that, to achieve this, the gardener must put some kind of twist on the existing landscape, turn its prose into something nearer poetry.
> Michael Pollan in *Second Nature: A Gardener's Education*, 1991

Then there are the security problems posed by data outside an organisation's control. Here, the worst problem may well be falling into a 'perception of security': as all the information is now held in a cloud storage system and that has been made secure, surely then everything is OK.

This is a badly protected walled garden, though. Within the information store are all the individuals that the organisation has authorised to be there: employees, partners, contractors, consultants and so on. While they have the right to be there, they can, unless the right controls are in place, extract data to another environment via email or other data transfer means. Without the capability to track the information and take action on it, the organisation has no idea what is happening.

A prime example here can be seen with salespeople. When they leave the organisation, they want to take a full list of existing contacts with them. If this is held centrally within an enterprise CRM or sales force automation system, they can create a data export to an Excel or text file and simply send that across to an external environment.

Behavioural analysis may pick this up, or it may not. Organisations should also look at implementing DLP technology, which can examine data as it passes over certain internal and external perimeters and carry out actions dependent on what it finds. For example, if it sees that certain PID is being passed to an unknown email address, then it can stop that from happening and raise an alert to the sender's line manager. The line manager can then approach the sender and determine whether the message should be sent or whether this is a malicious action.

However, not all information security issues are caused through malevolent action. Many are just accidental issues, such as an employee sending an email to the wrong person. Again, DLP can help here in checking for many different types of content, with the extra value of ensuring compliance with regulatory needs such as data protection, the payment card information regulations of PCI-DSS (Payment Card Industry Data Security Standard) and so on.

Another use for DLP is in redacting certain data from streams. Let's say that there is a need to send certain data to a third party. However, the complete data contains some

PID (such as National Insurance numbers) that it would be illegal to share. The sending company could carry out a complex extraction, transformation and load (ETL) data activity, stripping the PID from the data, or it could use DLP as a means of redacting this information from the stream. With the PCI-DSS example above, DLP redaction can be used to present just enough information to a third party, such as the first and last four digits of a credit card to show that valid details were taken and used, but not enough for the data recipient to be able to use the information themselves.

A further approach that should be considered is digital rights management (DRM). A growing problem as organisations find themselves working within an expanding value chain is the need to shut down information access to certain partners as they leave or are removed from the value chain. An example here could be when a design partner is removed due to a lack of adherence to contractual agreements or when they are suspected of passing on details to a third party. Just shutting down the party's access to existing systems is no use as they will already have copies of data and information on their own systems.

DRM can help in this area. A good DRM system will associate any information with an origination point. That origination point can then create rules around what can and cannot be done as actions against that information. For example, an entity (an individual, role or entire group) may be able to receive emails and attachments but not be able to create copies of or print those attachments. In this way, the originating organisation retains control over the information asset. Obviously, full technical security still does not protect against individuals copying information manually (e.g. via transcription or photography), but this then is far more likely to be with malicious intent and takes more effort. The technical approaches described help to avoid the vast majority of accidental data loss/leakage and to minimise the amount of malicious data theft.

Some DRM systems also provide time-based access. As an example, this can be useful with documents that the originator wants to be visible for only a short period of time. These can be sent to inside or outside parties who will then find that the document either encrypts itself or deletes itself once that time period has passed. This can also be used where offline access to information is required, for example with executives who travel regularly. Information can be downloaded onto their laptops or tablets for them to work on while they are disconnected from the internet. However, the information held upon the device will time out and become encrypted or be deleted once a certain time limit has been passed without the information assets being reverified by the central server, meaning that the data will not be available should the device be lost or stolen.

It is worth planning for the worst, though. Assume that data will, at some time, leak. The organisation must have in place a plan B for how to deal with possible impacts on those affected by the data leak (e.g. customers, partners, suppliers or shareholders) as well as the organisation's brand. Even if the actual data breach is down to poor security standards implemented by a public cloud provider, this is no defence: the organisation chose and used the provider, and the organisation should have carried out sufficient basic due diligence on that cloud provider and should also have implemented its own security around its own data.

THE IMPORTANCE OF MULTI-FACTOR SINGLE SIGN-ON

Responsibilities are given to him on whom trust rests. Responsibility is always a sign of trust.
Attributed to James Cash Penney (founder of J.C. Penney stores, 1875–1971)

The main problems around security tend to concern end users and insecure means of access. Organisations that enforce many changes in challenge-and-response passwords and insist on mixed alphanumeric, upper- and lower-case passwords of long length with additional non-standard characters may believe that they are creating a safer environment where the passwords will be harder for an external person to crack. However, such measures can lead to the following:

- The use of a single password across multiple different applications and services. Therefore, compromising one application compromises all of them.

- All passwords being written down so they don't have to be remembered. This is actually generally fine for desk-bound workers, as the chances of a malevolent person getting hold of the written passwords is quite low. However, for mobile workers, the chances of a device and the password list being lost or stolen are quite high. Even enforcing 100-character passwords with at least three non-standard characters is useless when the passwords are available with the device itself.

- Sharing of passwords. A user forgets their password and, rather than go through the formal helpdesk procedure to get it reset, just asks a colleague whether they can use their username and password to get a task done. When this happens at the task-worker level, GRC is heavily compromised. At systems-administrator or another raised privilege level, it can lead to major issues in tracking who did what and when should anything go wrong.

A far better approach is to go for a secure means of originally logging in to a system followed by the use of a single sign-on (SSO) system. Here, instead of a simple challenge-and-response username–password pair alone, the user must also provide information from something that has to be with them. This may be a one-time code generator, such as an RSA Secure-ID[274] or a Vasco DIGIPASS[275] token, or a code sent through an authenticator app on a smartphone, such as used by Dropbox, Google, Microsoft and others. This use of 2FA means that even if a blackhat manages to use a brute-force attack to crack a username–password pair, they then have to go through another layer of security that changes on a regular basis. This is very hard to do unless the username–password pair and the 2FA device have been stolen together.

Biometrics have long been touted as a means of making sure that the person themselves must be present when logging in. However, there remain problems with this option. Fingerprints are affected by changes in the weather and the oil and water content of the skin. Illness can change the quality of an iris scan or the sound of a voice. Indeed, in the US, there are unverified reports of a scam[276] in which voice details are

---

[274] www.rsa.com/en-us/products/rsa-securid-suite

[275] www.vasco.com/products/two-factor-authenticators/hardware/one-button/index.html

[276] LaCapria, K. (27 January 2017) 'Can you hear me?' scam warning. Snopes.com. Available from www.snopes.com/can-you-hear-me-scam.

harvested over the phone and then used to authorise contracts where voice details are either all or part of how the contract is finalised.

Once 2FA has done as much as possible to verify that the person signing in is who they say they are, then something intelligent at the back end is required. This is where SSO comes in. Some SSO systems are essentially username–password pair vaults. They log all details that are required by applications, sites and so on and replicate them by pushing them into fields on the screen as required. This is useful, in that users no longer need to remember the password that they set. However, users are inherently poor at setting highly secure passwords. In January 2017, the *Daily Telegraph* provided a list of the 25 most used passwords[277] around the globe. The details, provided by password manager Keeper,[278] stated that the most common password was 123456, with 123456789 as the second most common. The data was based on scouring through leaked and stolen lists containing over 10 million passwords available in the public domain.

Indeed, CloudPets, a manufacturer of soft toys where a message can be recorded and sent to the toy via a cloud service, shows how lax security and poor password management can be problematic. The company's database of more than 2 million recorded messages was easily findable, and passwords such as 'cloudpets' were being used by those who had bought the toys.[279] Therefore, the database was easily breachable.

A better option is SSO systems that automatically create complex passwords, such as those provided with Bitium[280] and Evidian.[281] Such systems can be programmed to understand the type of password specific applications and websites require, how often passwords need to be changed and whether other credentials are needed as well. Through the use of such systems, the user is removed from needing to think up any passwords at all, yet still retains the capability to move from app to application to service easily and transparently as needed. Should the user's master 2FA access be compromised, the SSO system can shut down all their accesses in one go, so providing a rapid means of enabling continuing security.

Many modern cloud services are moving away from username–password pairs. As well as 2FA, there is a move to use token-based security, such as OAuth,[282] a project that has been pulled together under the IETF. OAuth provides a federated means of delegating authority for a third party to access certain data held by another party. For example, Facebook uses OAuth when apps require certain data to be shared by a Facebook user, such as their basic profile details. Rather than share the username–password pair, with its obvious security issues, OAuth provides a granular means of securely accessing only the information that needs to be shared – and nothing else. As such, OAuth is an *authorisation* capability, not an *authentication* one.

---

[277] McGoogan, C. (16 January 2017) The world's most common passwords revealed: Are you using them? *The Telegraph*. Available from www.telegraph.co.uk/technology/2017/01/16/worlds-common-passwords-revealed-using.

[278] https://keepersecurity.com/en_GB

[279] BBC Technology. (28 February 2017) Children's messages in CloudPets data breach. BBC News. Available from www.bbc.co.uk/news/technology-39115001.

[280] www.bitium.com/site/password

[281] www.evidian.com/products/enterprise-sso

[282] https://oauth.net

THE EVOLUTION OF CLOUD COMPUTING

Where a more complete SSO-style authentication approach is required, OpenID, a project from the OpenID Foundation,[283] provides a standardised means of cooperating parties (known as 'relying parties') to use a third-party service to enable SSO. Many companies now support OpenID, notably Amazon, Flickr, Google, Sears, Universal Music Group and WordPress.

The Security Assertion Markup Language (SAML), an OASIS project,[284] is another standardised means through which authorisation and authentication details can be exchanged between cooperating parties. However, the last major update to SAML was in 2012, and OpenID Connect is now seen as the more modern approach to web-based SSO.

In addition to SAML and OpenID, there is an XML-based approach to authorisation called the eXtensible Access Control Markup Language (XACML).[285] Again under the auspices of OASIS, the last full version of XACML was released in 2013.

There are many commercial SSO and secure-access products in the market, such as Okta,[286] OneLogin[287] and Centrify.[288]

EDGE SECURITY

We spend our time searching for security and hate it when we get it.
John Steinbeck in *Paradox and Dream/America and Americans*, 1966

Along with the issues of SSO come the issues of ensuring that those attempting to access a system from outside are authorised to do so and are who they purport to be. As discussed in Chapter 8, there is a need for identity access management (IAM) and other systems to be in place.

As well as IAM, there is the need for intrusion detection systems (IDS) and intrusion prevention systems (IPS) to be in place. These often work by using pattern matching and/or behavioural analytics to identify unusual activity and either stop it in its tracks or hive the stream off to a secondary system. Other aspects of outside security issues can be seen through areas such as DDoS attacks. Around all of these systems there is also the need for data to be collected so that forensic analysis can be carried out as required to try to identify the root source of any issue.

Some of these services will be made available via the service provider themselves; others will fall squarely on the shoulders of the customer. Wherever possible, I recommend that customers use a layering approach employing software-defined constructs, as this allows for a high level of flexibility in attempting to keep pace with the changing dynamics of such security risks in the field.

---

[283] http://openid.net/foundation
[284] https://wiki.oasis-open.org/security/FrontPage
[285] http://docs.oasis-open.org/xacml/3.0/xacml-3.0-core-spec-os-en.html
[286] www.okta.com
[287] www.onelogin.com
[288] www.centrify.com/products/identity-service/sso

PHYSICAL SECURITY

If you think technology can solve your security problems, then you don't understand the problems and you don't understand the technology.
Bruce Schneier (CTO of IBM Resilient) in *Secrets & Lies*, 2000

One area that should not be overlooked is the physical security of a facility. This covers many diverse areas, from ensuring that it is difficult for outsiders to enter the facility without being fully identified and checked, through to stopping any attempts to break into the facility via ram-raiding or other means.

Colocation facility providers will generally have rules that mandate that only named people can enter a customer's environment. These environments will also usually be either mesh or fully covered cages that extend from drop floor through to raised ceiling (the actual hard limits of the floor and ceiling, rather than the ones visible to the person standing in the facility) so that no one can use crawl spaces through from one area to another.

Public cloud providers will generally not allow anyone apart from their own staff and cleared supplier engineers on site, and in many cases such engineers will be accompanied by a member of staff all the time they are on the premises. Colocation and cloud service providers will generally also carry out full background checks on their employees to try to weed out any with a dubious background, or ones where the background does not hold true.

If you look at a colocation or service provider facility, you will see that the majority have few windows into the data centre itself: all external walls give access only to outer corridors that are airlocked from the data centre proper. Workrooms will be made available for customers to utilise if necessary, without going into the data centre itself.

Bollards, planters and other physical systems will be in place to stop ram-raiding and other physical means of access by brute force. Full motion-sensing and closed-circuit television systems will be in place to track people's movements. Some facilities will also use near-field communication (NFC) or radio frequency identification (RFID) devices carried by employees and visitors to track movement at a more granular level.

Finally, these companies will also often prevent anyone from carrying any form of non-pre-checked storage device into the data centre, even mobile phones. There will also be a ban on carrying suitcases and other items where equipment could be smuggled in or out of the data centre. In some cases, all incoming equipment has to be unpacked outside the facility with only the signed-off equipment being allowed into the data centre itself.

All of these 'extras' work towards a holistic security capability. However, they also add cost – a cost that those with a large customer base can afford as they share it across their customer base. Such costs are hard for a single organisation to bear on their own.

SUMMARY

What have we learned?

- Data security is a complex and highly dynamic area.
- Multiple security approaches are required: old-style application, database or perimeter security is no longer valid.
- Ensuring that everything works together in a coherent manner will still be tricky for the foreseeable future.
- Do not neglect the complexities or costs of edge and physical security.

What does this mean?

- An 'information-first' security strategy must be taken.
- Granularity is key: there is no one-size-fits-all information security solution.
- Data classification, metadata, DLP, DRM, SSO and encryption are all major tools in the arsenal for overall information security.
- Software-defined IAM, IDS and IPS enable good levels of flexibility in order to deal with the changes in security attack vectors going forward.

17 VIRTUALISATION, SHARABLE RESOURCES AND ELASTICITY

I like to think of it as this new field. Instead of computer science, it's going to be virtual science.

Brendan Iribe (co-founder of Oculus) in an interview with
The Washington Post, 11 September 2014

Many organisations are surprised to find how much resource wastage there is in their existing IT platforms. The promise of a platform where resources are shared and overall utilisation rates are pushed higher has caught the attention not only of IT departments but also of main board members looking for cost savings. However, gaining the cost savings is not just a case of 'doing cloud'; there are still many areas and variables that need to be suitably considered and covered.

In this chapter, I look at how virtualisation on its own has not met with the expectations set by vendors. I also examine how cloud computing could still fail in the same manner unless due care and attention is paid to various areas.

THE LURE OF VIRTUALISATION

We all live every day in virtual environments, defined by our ideas.

Michael Crichton, *Disclosure*, 1994

Previously, we looked at the impact of a variable single workload on a physical platform (see Figure 3.1). It is not only that the need to drive overall resource utilisation rates from low-to-mid-single-percentage figures up to significant double figures has become a nice-to-have; it has also become noticeable to businesses that their organisations are funding massive waste across many areas when it comes to IT platforms.

Virtualisation was the first move towards providing greater efficiencies. The idea was that multiple workloads could be run on the same underlying physical platform. This was good as far as it went, but, as there was little to no capability to dynamically share resources, the overall physical platform had to be architected to take each workload as a separate entity and then as an aggregated environment. This is shown in Figure 17.1.

Figure 17.1 shows seven workloads, each one the same as used in Figure 3.1. This is the sort of combined workload that would be found on a virtual desktop infrastructure (system): peaks caused by login storms and so on. Therefore, we have a base workload as shown by the solid line: the barest minimum required to run the workloads.

The dotted line indicates the average workload. As can be seen, the combined workload is above this line for a considerable amount of time, and so even a virtualised platform will not provide adequate performance during those times.

Figure 17.1 Aggregated virtualised workloads

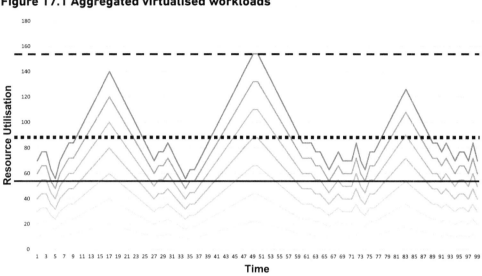

The dashed line shows the peak load. If this is architected for, then the base platform will be able to meet all but the most unpredictable workload spikes, but only by providing around 250% of the base and around 150% of the average resources required. Therefore, this is still a very wasteful option.

THE MOVE TO CLOUD

> I spent my thirties living out of boxes and moving every six months to a year. It was my cloud period: I just wandered like a cloud for ten years, following the food supply. I was a hunter, gatherer, an academic migrant.
>
> Sandra Cisneros in an interview in *AARP*, March 2009

This is where a true cloud comes in. That need for full resource elasticity is where users can gain the most from the available resources.

With a public cloud platform, this elasticity is relatively easy to obtain. As previously mentioned, where there are thousands of workloads being shared across a virtualised, elastic platform, the problems that can result from any one workload spiking can be dealt with by averaging out resource utilisation across the massive total resource pools available. However, in a private cloud, this averaging out is not so easy.

This is best shown by comparing Figure 17.2 with Figure 17.3. Figure 17.2 shows the overall workload on a private cloud with 10 workloads. It shows the cumulative CPU requirements from the 10 workloads, with the bottom workload having a 'bump' in its needs between time points 16 and 38.

The average CPU requirement is just below 150 resource units (shown by the horizontal line). The peak requirement is 182 and occurs at time point 27. This overage of CPU resource requirements (which amounts to 32 units) is more than 20% of the average. Architecting and managing a platform that can experience a 20% variance against the average requires good skills: ones that go well beyond the basic 'architect for what is expected plus 50%, plus a bit for good measure'.

Figure 17.2 Averaging out workloads in a private cloud

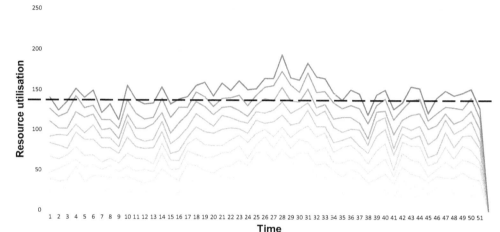

The problem can get worse. It is likely within a private cloud that several workloads will be co-cyclical: quarterly reporting requires multiple workloads to run within a short timescale to provide all the information that is needed to create the necessary reports. Architects end up with a better solution than they would have been able to obtain with a more physical platform, but they do not gain all the benefits of a fully elastic cloud.

Figure 17.3 shows a public cloud platform that is managing 253 workloads. The bottom 10 are the same ones as shown in Figure 17.2. Here, though, the average CPU resource requirement is just over 3,550 units (again, shown by the horizontal line), and the peak requirement (again at time point 27) is 3,717 units. This overage of 67 units is under 2% of the total resources available.

Now ramp this up to the level of the hyperscale public cloud providers, which handle tens or hundreds of thousands of workloads. Sure, there are higher chances of multiple workloads peaking at the same time, but there also higher chances of some workloads being in a trough of requirement. Even where there are many co-cyclical workloads, there are likely to be enough counter-cyclical or non-cyclical workloads that can be used to offset the overall resource requirements. In effect, the combined peaks and troughs of so many workloads are within the realms of the average: there are no noticeable combined workload peaks. Architecting overall resource requirements to provide elasticity to such massive numbers of workloads becomes easier – and far more cost-effective.

Figure 17.3 Averaging out workloads in a public cloud

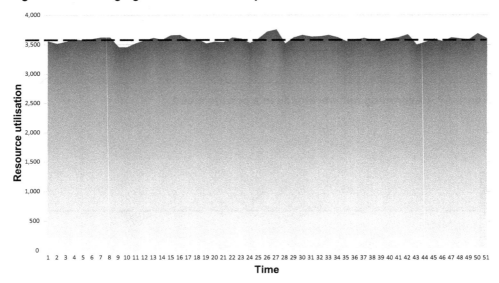

So far, so good. However, each of the above examples only looks at CPU resources. Overall, workloads have a dynamic mix of requirements relating to server, storage and network resources. Again, any attempt to create a physical or simply virtualised platform that can manage in real time the contextual variabilities of these various resources is fraught with issues. Even where a single workload is being considered (e.g. when looking at something like number-crunching on a supercomputer), the amount of skilled architecting that is required is not trivial.

Within a cloud platform, this points to the need for orchestration that doesn't work against each workload separately but instead takes the needs of each workload at the server, storage and networking levels in context with all other workloads using the same resources.

SCALING FOR MASSIVE USE: G-CLOUD

> Dimension regulated the general scale of the work, so that the parts may all tell and be effective.
> Marcus Vitruvius Pollio (Roman author and engineer) in *De Architectura*, first century AD

Some organisations may have the capability to create an environment that, while essentially private, provides the scale benefits of a public cloud. As an example, the public sector is a massive set of disparate groups that are not in competition with each other and share many of the same underlying processes. It therefore makes sense for the public sector to work together to create and use shared cloud platforms where the economies of scale and the economies of shared resources can be best operated.

The UK's Digital Marketplace initiative is an attempt to do this; it runs over a series of framework agreements created by the UK government with various service providers known as the G-Cloud. Although its usage irons out many of the problems of public-sector procurement (e.g. through avoiding the need for individual procurement tenders through a competitive process), the initiative has not met with massive success.

The service started in 2012 and has reached around 1,300 service providers and 15,000 services. However, even with a 'cloud-first' approach being stated as government strategy from February 2014, overall spend since 2012 had only reached £1.7 billion by January 2017, with monthly spend running at around £63 million.[289] A further £103 million has been spent on services through the Digital Services framework. The annual run rate of spend via the G-Cloud and Digital Services framework equates to around 6% of total government IT contract spend.

Why is this the case? Is it that G-Cloud isn't meeting the requirements of those wishing to purchase or those who use the services? Hardly: the main issues revolve around the number of large incumbent IT providers across government that prefer to push their own services rather than advise the use of G-Cloud, along with difficulties in changing the habits of buyers in large departmental groups. It is also noticeable that 77% of G-Cloud expenditure is through completely central government; use in the wider public sector, local government and not-for-profit sectors is not gaining the traction that was hoped for.

What this shows is that a move to cloud is not just about the technology; it also requires a mindset change from those responsible for creating a platform and then using it. Large, complex setups, such as the public sector, have much to gain through using cloud services, but getting there will take a lot of time.

SUMMARY

What have we learned?

- Private cloud carries through many of the problems of a non-shared environment: architecting to provide flexibility will still be problematic.

- Hyperscale cloud providers can even out resource needs far more effectively than a single-organisation private cloud.

- A change in mindset is often required to gain the right buy-in to how and when cloud should be used.

What does this mean?

- Public cloud will increasingly be the choice for those wanting the full experience of a highly flexible, dynamic and elastic platform.

---

[289] https://www.gov.uk/government/collections/digital-marketplace-sales

- Where there are extenuating circumstances, IT and the business must accept that there will be constraints around the capabilities of a private cloud to run those workloads at a highly cost-effective level.

- IT and the business must work with users, groups, departments and incumbent outsourcing providers to ensure that a cloud-first strategy is embraced and works effectively.

18　THE CHANGE IN APPLICATIONS

Cloud computing offers individuals access to data and applications from nearly any point of access to the Internet, offers businesses a whole new way to cut costs for technical infrastructure, and offers big computer companies a potentially giant market for hardware and services.

Jamais Cascio (author and futurist) in *Fast Company*, 21 August 2009

Cloud brings with it a need to rethink the 'application'. The way enterprise applications have worked up until now will be found increasingly unfit for purpose, with the prescriptive and proscriptive nature of in-built process flows and data-handling approaches harming the capability of an organisation to carry out its business. This chapter looks at how the concept of an application will change from a self-contained monolith to a more loosely coupled set of functions instantiated as microservices that are called and used on a near (or actual) real-time basis as the organisation requires them.

THE DEATH OF THE MONOLITH

We need to build change in to our systems and let these systems evolve as circumstances change. Change is inevitable, but we need to do a better job of dealing with it, because when we start building huge gleaming monoliths, I think we start getting into trouble.

Daniel Suarez (technologist and author) in an interview with *The Telegraph*, 20 April 2009

The commonly accepted definition of an application today tends to be what has been known as the 'monolithic' application, such as SAP or Oracle eBusiness Suite. Such applications started off as systems targeted at streamlining and dealing with a specific function. For example, SAP started off as an application that dealt with ERP processes before moving into CRM and other areas. Likewise, Oracle originally focused predominantly on financial management systems before extending its reach both organically and through acquisitions to cover CRM processes, while also having discrete systems for areas such as human resources and product lifecycle management.

As time progressed, extra functions and capabilities were introduced into such applications, making them more capable of dealing with broader processes. For example, as Oracle acquired companies across more areas, it could provide interlinked systems that managed more business-focused processes, such as 'prospect to customer' and 'customer to cash'.

As the functions became more integrated, the enterprise applications became larger and, in many cases, less flexible. However, to achieve the speed and fidelity of throughput of data that organisations at the time were having to deal with, adopting large multipurpose enterprise applications seemed the only way to move forward.

Such monolithic applications come with their problems, however. Incremental functional improvements are hard to implement; in many cases, switching out functionality in the application that is not fit for purpose so as to use a better system is at best difficult and at worst impossible. Often, it seems that the only way to work with some enterprise applications is to change an organisation's processes to fit in with how the application works, rather than attempt to make the application support the business's own processes.

The market downturn after the 2008 financial crash uncovered a raft of problems. Whereas prior to the crash poor business processes that were being run in a bad way were often hidden by the fact that revenues were still looking good and that there were 'good enough' margins, after the crash, the shortcomings of many processes were plain to see.

The need for organisations to be able to react more quickly and effectively to such major changes in the markets became a business imperative. However, even where the business was willing, IT was often the constraint on making things happen. The business may well have decided that it needed a new process to deal with moving prospects along the prospect-to-customer chain; however, if it took IT weeks or months to adapt the existing applications to make this happen, it was not good enough.

IT has had to come to grips with the need to deal with issues that exist *now*. Taking time to deal with them means that IT ends up being seen as a team that deals with issues that are in the past: what may well have been a suitable and elegant solution to the original issue is now too late. The markets have moved on and new issues have arisen instead.

This is where the cloud can help. The cloud offers the capability to move to a new concept: the composite application, in which the application is built from modular components. This is not a new idea and is based on the concept of SOA; however, while SOA failed for many reasons, the only way that cloud will be able to produce on its promise will be to use such an approach.

This does, however, require many changes in the way applications are written and orchestrated. It is not enough to create functional stubs that developers can pull together manually to create a new composite application. All that this does is to create the equivalent of new monoliths: every time a change is required, it must go back to the developers for the function to be moved out from the application and a new function to be integrated back in.

What is going to be needed is a means of having true loose coupling using open and standardised APIs. The service catalogues provided by cloud services must be fully automated and must go beyond the basics of a named and described function.

THE NEED FOR TECHNICAL CONTRACTS

Basically, managing is about influencing action. Managing is about helping organisations and units to get things done, which means action. Sometimes, managers manage actions directly. They fight fires. They manage projects. They negotiate contracts.
Henry Mintzberg (Cleghorn Professor of Management Studies, McGill University) in an interview in *The Wall Street Journal*, 17 August 2009

There is an emerging need for fully defined technical contracts: something that a calling service within a composite application can interrogate on the fly in order to ascertain whether an available responding service meets its needs. As an example, consider a composite application where there is a need for a charging mechanism. Rather than using a developer to write an in-house function that would only replicate what thousands of developers have done before, it is decided to use a third-party, cloud-based service. In the case of simple cloud services with manually created composite applications, the person with the responsibility for the overall application must carry out their research, go to multiple cloud providers, look at their respective service catalogues, choose a suitable charge mechanism function and integrate it into the overall application. If it turns out to be unsuitable for the job, then they have to go back, identify a replacement charge mechanism function and swap it with the previous one.

Now consider this example in the context of a full-service catalogue that supports dynamic technical contracts. The composite application is written in such a way that its various functions work on calling and responding services. Some of these functions may be created in-house; many will be taken from public cloud services. When it comes to the need for a charge mechanism function, the calling service requests details from any responding services that can fulfil a set of prescribed needs. These needs could be along the lines of:

- Do you provide a charging mechanism?
- Can you deal with 100 calls per minute?
- Are your charges below 1 penny/cent per call?
- Can you guarantee latency below 100 milliseconds?
- And so on...

All these requirements can be codified as a standard, such that the calling service can gain responses in real time from functions that can support the stated need. Orchestration and proper audit can then ensure that the function is included in the composite application correctly and that the financial contracts are agreed and logged.

There are obvious problems with this approach.

The first is that it is far too easy for a malicious entity to 'spoof' the system. For example, the entity sets up a public cloud service and sets up responding contracts that state that the services provided do meet the expected requirements of calling services. This could be quite easily done, and the price component of the contract could be set to be marginally lower than anyone else's on the market. However, when the requesting service chooses this service provider and makes its calls, instead of the expected functional responses, it is presented with malware or corrupt data, both of which could adversely impact the business of the calling service's owner.

Therefore, there is a need for agreed directories of available public functions: ones that are either maintained as closed systems by organisations and their value chains or are managed by the user community. These directories could be either more closed or more open in the way that their services are offered and managed.

A closed directory makes sense where the greatest amount of control is required. The closed group maintains its own list of providers who have passed whatever degree of due diligence has been applied. This also maintains the capacity to have contracts negotiated based on minimum usage rates and so on, whereas an open system will tend to be more constrained against list pricing.

A more open system still has to have some controls in place. These can range from the higher end of due diligence (where, for example, independent bodies in discrete verticals can maintain lists of vetted services for use by organisations in their sector) down to full community systems (where any service can be listed but will be rated and commented on as to levels of functionality and adherence to contract levels by individual users).

The second problem with the dynamic approach is that if contractual agreements are required every time a calling service makes the same calls, then latency will be increased massively. In addition, audit will be extremely difficult to maintain as the charge mechanism function changes on what could be a transaction-by-transaction basis. It could also be that the user experience changes from visit to visit as different functions are called as part of the customer process.

Therefore, the technical contract system and the orchestration system must be able to work together to guarantee agreed minimum-time contracts. For example, it may be that once a charge mechanism function has been chosen, the agreement will last for a minimum of, say, three months, unless the function fails to meet the agreed terms of the technical contract. Such time-based agreements can be built into the requesting service's policies and be part of the construction of the codified standards-based technical contract.

The use of such service catalogues alongside dynamic technical contracts and orchestration systems then leads to the possibility of a far more visual capability for business people to define their needs and to gain a composite application that supports these needs. Rather than requiring full systems architects and developers, business people can work with an internal service catalogue that includes lists of available services, and can then work with permissions they have within their own policy profile to create an on-the-fly composite application to support their process needs.

Task workers may not be able to have any choice; they may just be presented with a ready-prepared composite application that enables them to ensure that they carry out the same type of task in a highly defined and reproducible manner, so avoiding any issues in proof of process should something go wrong. However, someone further up in the knowledge worker process may be able to use the service catalogue to pull together sets of functions and to use certain pre-authorised external services to help them in their job. Certain high-value employees may have even greater freedom, being able to use new external functions as they see fit.

As a simple example, consider an employee needing to create a new process for a prospect to choose an item, pay for the item and then input delivery data. Using the visual front end, the user can drag an internal function onto a process diagram. The first one could be something like 'Company Basic Screen Template'. Through simple drag and drop, the user can then add the following functions:

- use internal standard product display modules;
- integrate to internal product catalogue 'xyz';
- use internal shopping-basket module to log order;
- use internal checkout module to deal with shopping basket;
- use pre-authorised external function 'abc' to take payment details and manage transaction;
- use internal payment-reconciliation function to acknowledge payment and log to payment-received system;
- use internal module to take delivery details;
- use external function 'def' to deal with logistics to deliver product as chosen.

Such an approach puts direct control where it is needed: the business has control over how it defines and enacts its processes. It tasks IT with ensuring that the right functions and modules are available through internal and external means, alongside tasking IT with ensuring that it keeps pre-authorised external functions under watch to ensure that they are providing the right levels of functionally at an optimised cost.

Although such systems are not available yet, the move to serverless computing and the strides being made in certain areas of DevOps are beginning to point towards their emergence. IT should start to adapt itself to this new paradigm as soon as possible.

SUMMARY

What have we learned?

- Large, all-in-one applications are ill-suited to the needs of a modern enterprise.
- The growth of microservices and fast orchestration is leading to the emergence of a new, composite application model.
- Cloud provides the ideal platform for operating a microservices model.
- Business users need the tools to enable them to make the most of such an approach.

What does this mean?

- IT must plan for the more distributed computing model of a hybrid cloud, pulling together microservices on a real-time and auditable basis.
- IT must start searching for tools that enable proper service catalogues to be presented to business users.
- IT must also prepare to provide visual systems that enable business users to define the process that needs to be fulfilled and create an automated means to construct the composite application that makes the process possible.
- It will be vital to ensure that audit and reporting are fully covered.

19 APPLICATIONS, VIRTUAL MACHINES AND CONTAINERS

The book is not really the container for the book. The book itself is the narrative. It's the thing that people create.

Jeff Bezos, Founder of Amazon, Interview with *Fortune*, 29 June 2010

Just as applications themselves are evolving, the way that organisations and cloud providers package and deliver applications is also going through change. The need to provision software through full installation via running a batch, an executable file or other approach is passing. The use of specifically packaged, almost-ready-to-run systems based on VMs and containers is quickly taking over. In this chapter, I look at the strengths and weaknesses of the main approaches now coming to the fore.

THE DIFFERENCES BETWEEN VIRTUAL MACHINES AND CONTAINERS

Differences challenge assumptions.

Anne Wilson Schaef in *Meditations for Living in Balance: Daily Solutions for People Who Do Too Much*, 2000

As discussed in Chapter 18, the monolithic application is no longer fit for purpose. A single application that is trying to do many different things just cannot be flexible enough to deal with the changes that organisations face on a daily basis. The need for a new approach that enables processes to be facilitated and completed on an as-needed basis is changing how new applications are viewed.

However, any attempt by outsiders to dictate to an organisation that the only way to move to the cloud is to throw everything out and start again will be (rightly) resisted. Those organisations that depend on existing non-cloud-ready applications may need to start with workloads that are easy to move into a cloud environment and make use of the more dynamic resource capability, so gaining better overall performance on these workloads. Meanwhile, they can then review their situation and plan on a longer-term cloud approach through the replacement of the non-cloud-ready applications with cloud-native composite applications.

Many organisations will already be making some steps towards that future, anyway. For some, the packaging and provisioning of code into the operations environment has been simplified through the use of VMs, while others have started to use containers.

The container world is currently led by Docker.[290] CoreOS[291] has a different container technology created under the Application Container (appc) specification, called rkt.[292]

---

[290] www.docker.com
[291] https://coreos.com
[292] https://coreos.com/rkt

This takes a slightly dissimilar route for app containerisation on Linux platforms, while still maintaining the capability to run Docker containers. In the Linux space itself, LXC and LXD are also available as container approaches.

There are some pretty basic differences between VMs and containers:

- A VM is solely dependent on having a common hypervisor to run on. For example, a VM written for ESX will run on any ESX platform, one for Hyper-V on any Hyper-V platform. There are converters available, such as the Microsoft Virtual Machine Converter, MVMC.[293] However, portability across different hypervisors is not always as easy as it could be.

- A VM contains everything needed for an application to run. This includes the operating system and the rest of the software stack as well as the functional code (see Figure 19.1). The VM also runs its own virtual versions of aspects of the hardware environment. The main benefits of this are that, as well as being fully portable across similar platforms, VMs are fast and can be written in a highly secure manner. As the VM is a self-contained environment, any problems with one VM (whether this is down to it being badly behaved or being compromised by an attacker) remain isolated in that one VM. The downsides are that VMs are pretty large and that they replicate a lot of redundant functionality, so using up resources that could be better used elsewhere.

Figure 19.1 Virtual machines and hypervisors

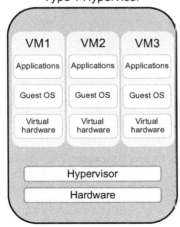

- A container shares a lot of the base resources across the underlying services and hardware. It creates a set of virtual links from the container to the underlying hardware so that services and hardware can be more effectively shared (see Figure 19.2). However, this can introduce performance issues, and it certainly introduces security and availability issues unless the utmost care is taken

---

[293] www.microsoft.com/en-us/download/details.aspx?id=42497

157

when writing the code that goes into the container. Although containers such as Docker can be used securely, a poorly constructed container can introduce issues that not only will hit that container but can also compromise the entire platform beneath it, and so bring all other containers to their knees.

An example here is where a container has code with a privileged level of access in it. That access drills through the container into the physical world underneath it. If a badly written container is compromised, the attacker can then use the privileged access to gain access to the physical resources, and so either infect any other badly written containers or cause problems across the whole estate by creating resource storms (for example) to bring the total platform to a grinding halt.

This has bred a market for container security: vendors such as NeuVector[294] and Aqua Security[295] provide bolt-on tools to enhance and manage container security.

Figure 19.2 Containers

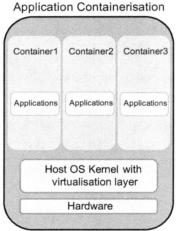

Application Containerisation

- In an attempt to address this, a concept called 'system containerisation' has been touted by Virtuozzo.[296] As can be seen in Figure 19.3, the idea is to take the best of both the VM and the containerised worlds to present a more secure, high-performing environment.

The proxy namespace acts as a means of abstracting the shared platform resources from the applications, apps and/or services within the different containers. Whereas within a simple container environment multiple containers can call on a single physical network port using the same port name, the proxy namespace creates a unique name for that container to use.

---

[294] http://neuvector.com
[295] www.aquasec.com
[296] https://virtuozzo.com

Therefore, if one container is compromised, the attacker has a single port name to use. The proxy namespace ensures that the access is kept separate from all other containers, preventing the failure of one container impacting directly on other containers.

Canonical is also moving to address some of the issues with container security. Although Canonical LXD[297] is primarily aimed at building on the open source LXD[298] successor to Linux LXC[299] containers, it can also support Docker, providing extra levels of granularity and security around how calls between the container and the underlying operating system are dealt with.

Figure 19.3 System containerisation

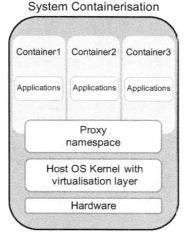

As can be seen, the current situation with containers is a little complex. Provisioning, managing, updating and monitoring containers tends to need a slightly different approach to managing a straightforward cloud stack.

The large cloud service providers have their own systems: AWS has its EC2 Container Service (ECS), Microsoft Azure has Azure Container Services (ACS) and Google Cloud Platform has Google Container Engine (GCE). Cloud Foundry[300] has Diego[301] for those who wish to have a scheduler, provisioner and health-monitoring system.

However, the container companies themselves also have tools. Docker comes with a broad portfolio of (quite technical) tools to enable such management, and CoreOS has a similarly broad capability.

[297] www.ubuntu.com/cloud/lxd
[298] https://linuxcontainers.org/lxd/introduction
[299] https://linuxcontainers.org/lxc/introduction
[300] www.Cloud Foundry.org
[301] www.pivotaltracker.com/n/projects/1003146

For those wanting to manage a containerised environment in a more graphical or simple manner, the use of a third-party tool may be required. Here, Google's open source project Kubernetes[302] is a big player. CoreOS has Tectonic,[303] which offers enhancements to how Kubernetes operates. Similarly, the Apache Mesos[304] project provides functionality for orchestrating containers, with Mesosphere[305] providing enhanced capabilities by pulling together other technologies such as Marathon[306] and Chronos.[307] Commercial offerings are available from vendors such as Cloudify[308] and Flexiant,[309] which both offer agnostic container–cloud orchestration toolsets.

THE FUTURE FOR CONTAINERS

We are made wise not by the recollection of our past, but by the responsibility for our future.
George Bernard Shaw, *Back to Methuselah*, 1921

Containerisation will be a major proof point for cloud computing. Without suitable means of containing code in a manner that enables rapid provisioning, updating and patching, a cloud platform will become too complex and unwieldy to effectively manage. However, even today's container technologies (Docker, rkt, LXC etc.) are nowhere near being able to manage workloads to the ultimate level. For this, a container needs to become a far more low-level concept: one where the container itself becomes a pure metadata holder, bringing together hot and/or cold resources on the fly as necessary.

As discussed in Chapter 18, the promise of cloud can only be realised where the monolithic application is broken down and replaced with a composite approach. This is best served by having discrete functions available as easily provisioned systems that can be called upon in real time.

If each function is still a relatively large VM or container, moving it into the operational environment and making it live will take too much time. Having enough instances of each function already provisioned and running will be a waste of resources and force the costs of public computing up to a point where many will cease to see the overall value of using cloud services.

If metadata containers were to come to the fore instead (see Figure 19.4), then they could use existing hot microservices that are already provisioned alongside very small sub-containerised cold microservices to very rapidly create the required overall functional service with a minimum of latency and wasted resources. Here, the container holds what is essentially a 'recipe' that describes the overall application. It knows which function to call at what time and deals with collecting and handing off the data between the various services and auditing the steps as it goes along.

---

[302] https://kubernetes.io
[303] https://coreos.com/tectonic
[304] http://mesos.apache.org
[305] https://mesosphere.com
[306] https://mesosphere.github.io/marathon
[307] https://mesos.github.io/chronos
[308] http://getcloudify.org
[309] www.flexiant.com

Figure 19.4 Microservice metadata containers

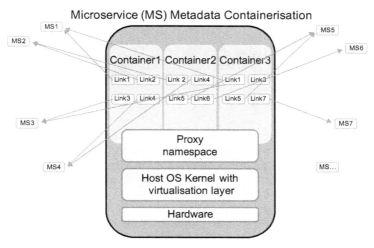

Such an approach may still be some time off, but it will provide the greatest flexibility in gaining the ultimate promise of cloud: massive flexibility that can respond to business needs around changing processes in the shortest possible time.

SUMMARY

What have we learned?

- The move to VMs and containers is rapid.
- Cloud is ideal for containerisation – far more than it is for VMs.
- Current means of 'wrapping' code for deployment have various issues.
- A metadata approach to containerisation could offer a better, faster deployment model.

What does this mean?

- New code should be created in a more abstracted, microservice-based model.
- The use of VMs and containers across a hybrid cloud needs to have strong orchestration.
- A means of auditing process actions is a necessity.

20 FULL AUDIT IS REQUIRED

Technology is dominated by two types of people: those who understand what they do not manage, and those who manage what they do not understand.
Archibald Putt (pseudonym) in *Putt's Law and the Successful Technocrat*, 1981

Every action that is taken across a hybrid cloud environment has to be logged and audited. Parts of the overall platform will not be under the control of the organisation; although some areas (such as in-house private infrastructure) may have full audits, doing this across the whole process becomes more difficult as different colocation, IaaS, PaaS and SaaS platforms are brought into the mix.

However, the increasing impact of legal compliance (in areas such as the EU's General Data Protection Regulation and the US Privacy Shield), combined with internal and other stakeholder requirements around information transparency, means that processes decided some time back and the core data around what was carried out across these processes must be tracked in such a way as to be able to rebuild the basic process at a later date. It is no longer a valid defence to say that the old data is not available; nor is it valid to argue that 'things have changed'.

THE IMPORTANCE OF A FULL AUDIT

I think that all services will have downtime. No matter how much you prepare, have redundant systems, or audit, there will periodically be a black swan event that is completely unlike whatever you've experienced before. It even happens to Google!
Matt Mullenweg (founder of WordPress) in *CNN*, 11 June 2010

From a business perspective, issues around mis-selling, proof of offer, stated terms and conditions, warranty and so on will be raised at some stage. Being able to fully recreate the process of what was done and what was offered is a necessity. In a world of increasing legal requirements around the storage, management and use of data, such capabilities of providing a fully audited process trace must be regarded as a necessity, not just a nice-to-have.

For overall data governance, there are four main types of requirement:

- **Internal:** An organisation will have a set of either implicit or explicit standards to which it operates around information management. Within these standards, it will have certain responsibilities to its employees, customers, suppliers, shareholders and other stakeholders in the business.

- **Vertical:** Many markets will have requirements placed upon them to ensure they meet minimum levels of compliance with stated objectives. Some of these will be advisory standards only, for example in the case of the Fixed Income, Currencies and Commodities Markets Standards Board or the Market Research Society Code of Conduct. Others may carry legal weight alongside their market focus, such as Gas Safe registration for gas engineers in the UK, or the Financial Conduct Authority.

- **Horizontal:** Organisations may find themselves needing to adhere to certain requirements no matter what vertical they operate in. Examples here include such standards as ISO 27001 (for data security) and ISO 9000 (for quality).

- **Legal:** The growing list of requirements here are a mix of the vertical and the horizontal. The Financial Conduct Authority's requirements are an example of the vertical, and the horizontal includes data protection laws such as those issued by the Information Commissioner's Office in the UK and the General Data Protection Regulation from the EU.

It has become increasingly impossible to deal with these requirements through creating a single massive data lake where all of the organisation's data and information are held. Instead, everything is spreading out across the value chain and across the hybrid platforms that are needed to effectively run a business.

This is driving a need for a 'compliance-oriented architecture': one where every action is monitored and audited to create a single view of the truth. Audit needs highly granular reporting capabilities. It needs the ability to report on individual actions carried out against identifiable data and information sources by specific individuals. If any of these cannot be identified, then the audit results will not be trustworthy.

The use of standard document-management systems has been attractive to those in heavily regulated environments for some time. However, with high cost-per-seat licensing and complex needs around setting up and managing underlying databases, even those making the largest use of document management systems (e.g. the pharmaceuticals industry) find that little of their overall information finds its way into their systems.

Indeed, the vast majority of document-management systems are only managing documents that have already passed through several layers of creation and editing before finding their way into the system. Organisations then fall into a perception of control: if a search through the document-management system does not show something, then it can't exist. However, the information may not have gone through the final stages of collaboration and review and may still be there on a simple file share system. The information that could change a business decision just isn't used – and decisions are worse because of it.

The use of such systems also has a major impact where superusers or other users with raised privileges are concerned. Any user who has raised privileges, particularly where they are in a position such as IT administrator and so have access to data and information sources that should nominally be hidden from them, means that they could be breaking any of the governance requirements outlined above. In most cases, such raised privileges can be avoided, only giving the person access to what they are allowed to see. Making sure that no user has direct access to all files in a document-management system or to a file server will help to save the organisation from potential problems. No individual can be trusted implicitly: there is just as much likelihood of a superuser becoming unhappy as there is of any other user. Any mass access to information provides users with the capability to copy it and sell it to the highest bidder or to make it public to undermine the position of the organisation.

Where the provision of raised privileges is unavoidable, other areas also need to be covered. In research carried out by Quocirca,[310] over 40% of respondents stated that administrator account details were shared between multiple users. Upon an issue being identified and traced back to the superuser account, the organisation would be only a little better off – they would still be left trying to identify which individual caused the issue. Therefore, ensure that all accounts with raised privileges include a second factor of authentication: a one-time token that is sent to a personal device, such as a mobile phone or a code generated by an authentication device, so as to provide greater capabilities to identify users at an individual level.

However, monitoring and managing which actions are taken is no simple thing either. An evolving area that is helping in this space uses a combination of metadata and object-based storage.

Metadata can be defined as 'data that describes (or provides information on) other data'.[311] An example here is a Microsoft Office document. Office creates a wrapper around the actual document contents, and the wrapper contains certain information that helps to describe what the document is about. First, it states whether it is a Word, PowerPoint or Excel document. It then provides details of the author, the time and date the document was created and when it was last edited, along with other information such as total time spent editing the document, the document's physical size, and the number of words and pages. An example can be seen in Figure 20.1, which shows the metadata of this document at this point of editing. This data can be accessed and used by external systems, for example for Explorer to list all documents in date or document-type order. However, such metadata is not secure and can easily be changed by other individuals or programs. What is required is a system that creates immutable metadata records.

Object-based storage has been around for a long time and is now in extensive use in cloud platforms such as AWS's S3 and Microsoft Azure's BLOb Store. For those looking to implement their own object-based storage systems, Hitachi Data Systems[312] and HGST[313] have been providing such arrays for some time; others, such as Cloudian[314] and Scality,[315] offer software services to provide a suitable storage environment. Open source alternatives, such as Minio,[316] Ceph[317] and SwiftStack,[318] are also available.

---

[310] Longbottom, C., Tarzey, B. (31 October 2009) Privileged user management: It's time to take control. Quocirca. Available from http://quocirca.com/content/privileged-user-management-it%E2%80%99s-time-take-control-0.

[311] Goff, S. A. et al. (25 July 2011) The iPlant Collaborative: Cyberinfrastructure for plant biology. *Front Plant Sci.* 2 (34).

[312] www.hds.com/en-us/home.html

[313] www.hgst.com

[314] https://cloudian.com

[315] www.scality.com

[316] https://minio.io

[317] https://ceph.com

[318] www.swiftstack.com

Figure 20.1 Microsoft Word metadata

Simple object-based storage treats data as full objects: whereas block and file storage deal with the placement and recovery of ones and zeros onto the storage substrate, object-based storage deals with files as complete items. Through the use of a global namespace, each item has a unique identifier, and actions can be associated with that unique identifier through the use of metadata.

As an example, take a Microsoft Office Word document. If stored against a file storage system, it is ones and zeros held in a hierarchical structure. Someone can come along and change those ones and zeros, but as long as the file is not corrupted, it will still be retrieved by the operating system or application as if it were the original document. Therefore, there is no real guarantee that what was written is what is retrieved, which is a major issue when it comes to GRC.

Now, if object-based storage is used, the file is assigned a unique identifier and is written to disk along with its immutable metadata. At a minimum level, this generally includes a cyclic redundancy check (CRC) figure. If any changes are made to the ones and zeros at the storage substrate level, the CRC of the retrieved file will not agree with the CRC of the saved file, indicating either corruption of the file or malicious activity.

Other metadata can include details such as document type, author, last time edited and so on, enabling searches to be carried out against any metadata field. Add in monitoring of end user actions, such as whether a file has been printed, copied, deleted or whatever, and it becomes apparent that object-based storage provides a platform for highly compliant GRC.

Even when a legal disclosure is needed, object-based storage can help. An issue with legal disclosure is that over-disclosure can happen, which can break laws that the legal disclosure has nothing to do with. For example, consider that a finance company finds itself with a demand for disclosure of details of all documents between itself and a group of named people. Without a means of adequately and efficiently searching and sorting through all its documents, the company may just choose to copy its file servers and make them available to the body making the legal request. However, this also involves providing details of other, completely innocent customers who are outside the legal disclosure requirement.

Through the use of object-based storage and a full text index of the documents, all documents created by, sent by or sent to named people around a specific subject can be quickly and effectively identified no matter where they are, as long as they are registered via their unique identifier in the global namespace and have the right metadata in place.

For many that are still using file or block-based storage systems, there is still a need to build information management as a separate layer on top. This may be through the use of database-style BLOb enterprise content management tools such as Documentum or OpenText (both now owned by OpenText[319]). Increasingly, there is a move to metadata-driven information management. Here, vendors such as Druva,[320] and Commvault[321] with its Simpana[322] product, can provide capabilities to create metadata against information streams as it gets stored. Others, such as M-Files,[323] provide enterprise information management systems that work against complex metadata systems to provide broad-scale information management.

SUMMARY

What have we learned?

- In an increasingly regulated world, full audit is required.
- Across a complex platform such as a hybrid cloud, it is difficult to ensure compliance without having adequate systems in place.
- Object-based storage provides a good basis to maintain adequate GRC.
- The use of a global namespace allows objects to be monitored and controlled across owned, shared and interoperating clouds.

What does this mean?

- The use of uncontrolled file stores can no longer be an option, and archetypical document-management systems are too expensive and complex for the job.
- Metadata held in an immutable manner alongside file details via a global namespace in object-based storage creates a great platform for information management and control across a cloud platform.

---

[319] www.opentext.com
[320] www.druva.com
[321] www.commvault.com
[322] http://documentation.commvault.com/commvault/v10/article?p=whats_new/c_main_overview.htm
[323] www.m-files.com/en

21 MONITORING, MEASURING AND MANAGING THE CLOUD

Anticipate the difficult by managing the easy.

Laozi (Chinese philosopher), 6th century BCE

Any cloud is a complicated environment, due to it having multiple mixed workloads each needing the flexibility of elastic resources. However, a fully hybrid environment is massively more complex, and it will only become more complicated as areas such as DevOps, containers and portability of workloads come to the fore.

Therefore, old-style systems-management tools are no longer fit for purpose; best-of-breed systems can rapidly become unwieldy and issues can fall between the capabilities of the various tools being used. However, complete sets of cloud-management tools have not really matured sufficiently to cover every need. Therefore, it is far more likely that cloud users will need to work with a main management platform with point tools (i.e. tools that are focused specifically on a single task) to cover the weak areas.

In this chapter, I look at how a modern cloud environment requires a distinct set of tools in order to monitor, measure and manage it.

MODERN LEVELS OF STANDARDISATION AND ABSTRACTION

So the universe is constantly moving in the direction of higher evolutionary impulses, creativity, abstraction, and meaning.

Deepak Chopra in an interview with *Beliefnet*, c.2005

Modern systems are far more standardised in the way that information can be exchanged than old systems used to be. As well as existing SNMP (simple network management protocol) traps and other standardised data systems, such as management information bases (MIBs), the majority of systems, devices and software can now offer up detailed information via XML, or at least in a form that can be normalised to an XML stream.

This does mean that many point tools can be 'plugged in' to the main management system, still allowing a single pane of glass to be used to monitor all that is going on across a hybrid cloud environment.

This is becoming increasingly important in a world where individuals can easily build up their own sets of tools. Whereas purchasing quality tools was beyond the pockets of most individuals in the past, the rise of open source has meant that free (or very low-cost) tools are now available to anyone who cares to download them. This means that even within a single organisation, there may be multiple tools being used that fulfil the same functions, or that heavily overlap in functionality.

Clamping down and becoming prescriptive or proscriptive in stating which tools can or cannot be used tends to be counterproductive. The developers, systems administrators and operations staff tasked with monitoring and maintaining the complex hybrid cloud platform want to ensure that they have the best tools that help them – as individuals. They also want to have the flexibility to change their tools as the leap-frog of functional advances continues.

CHOOSING AN OVER-ARCHING SYSTEM TO MANAGE CHAOS

Chaos was the law of nature; Order was the dream of man.
Henry Adams (historian and author) in *The Education of Henry Adams*, 1907

It is important for the IT department as a whole to look for open over-arching tools that can provide an enterprise level of functionality that embraces the use of multiple underlying tools. For example, CA Automic[324] and HashiCorp[325] Terraform provide automation and workflows that can work with open source DevOps tools such as Chef, Puppet and Jenkins and with containers and container-management systems such as Docker, Mesos and Kubernetes.

Since Jenkins 2 was launched in 2016, this tool has become easier to use and more functional, with a curated set of plugins enabling interoperability with a large set of other tools. This is further enhanced through the commercial supported distribution provided via CloudBees.[326] CloudBees has added a more enterprise-like scalable version of Jenkins that distributes the underlying capabilities across a platform. This removes the single points of failure on a single node-based Jenkins installation and lends itself strongly to a distributed, hybrid cloud platform.

Through the use of such tools, a full audit of actions that are taken across DevOps processes can be built up, enabling better and faster root-cause analysis (RCA) and solving of issues. Collaboration flows can be better managed, and roll-back of code can be carried out where major issues occur.

Tools that encompass as wide an environment as possible can help (through integrations of other, more point-focused tools) in identifying all live and dormant images (VMs or containers) across the development, test and operational environments. They can monitor the usage of these systems and shut down and decommission those that are no longer in use and can ensure that licence requirements are fully managed to ensure compliance with contracts.

---

[324] https://automic.com
[325] www.hashicorp.com
[326] www.cloudbees.com

AUTOMATE FOR EFFECTIVENESS AND EFFICIENCY

The first rule of any technology used in a business is that automation applied to an efficient operation will magnify the efficiency. The second is that automation applied to an inefficient operation will magnify the inefficiency.

Bill Gates (philanthropist and founder of Microsoft) quoted in Stephen Manes and Paul Andrews, *Gates: How Microsoft's Mogul Reinvented an Industry*, 1994

The chosen toolset must be focused around automation: the complexity of a hybrid cloud is too much for manual intervention to be used beyond emergency situations. Even where such emergency situations do arise, all actions must be captured and logged to ensure that there is continuity in the understanding of how the platform has been changed.

As part of the overall need to have visibility across the complete platform, access to public cloud-monitoring tools should be seen as a high priority. Although full access to all details will generally be a red line for any third-party cloud provider, many do offer a degree of insight into anonymised data, enabling better root-cause analysis of any problems. As previously described, this is important where issues may be caused by noisy neighbours (see Chapter 11) or public cloud DDoS attacks (see Chapter 3). Being able to see enough information to narrow down the issue to such areas means that the right people can be contacted to fix the issue as rapidly as possible.

Another use of automation is around any need for self-remediation when things do go wrong. Let's say the reporting systems show that there is a problem with a public-facing website, and that website is hosted on cloud provider A's platform. The reporting systems show that the problem is down to a lack of bandwidth to support the number of people attempting to connect to the site. Through the use of automation, the entire image of the website can be relocated to another part of the overall platform (either to another third-party provider or back onto the user's premises) where sufficient bandwidth is available. Another example would be where a workload becomes corrupted in some way, or where an update has gone wrong. Automation can revert systems back to the last known good point, and through the use of containerisation can do this in very short time periods.

In addition, automated load balancing can help in providing better systems availability and overall performance. For example, assume that a DDoS attack is identified on a certain part of the overall platform. Part of the network can be load balanced and prioritised, enabling known 'good' traffic to use one part of the load-balanced system while the possibly 'bad' traffic can be further analysed in relation to the existing connections, and shut down as the bad connections are identified.

SUMMARY

What have we learned?

- A hybrid cloud platform is too complex to depend on manual operations.

- A complex mix of tools to monitor and report on the health of a hybrid cloud is probably little better.
- A single database of activity combined with a single-pane-of-glass reporting system is required.
- Automation of as many activities as possible is the aim.

What does this mean?

- Aim for a main 'engine' for the basic tasks.
- Layer on tools that are required for more advanced tasks, but ensure that these integrate strongly with the main engine.
- Ensure that public cloud services are also integrated as closely as possible.

PART 4
THE FUTURE OF CLOUD
Cloud as you should be planning for it in the further-out future

22 THE ULTIMATE FUTURE

The future cannot be predicted, but futures can be invented.
Dennis Gabor (inventor of holography, Nobel Prize winner and author)
in *Inventing the Future*, 1963

Nothing ever stays the same: cloud computing is an evolution of grid computing, which was a logical evolution of SOA. Cloud will continue to evolve; different underlying technologies will continuously need to be embraced; different global and regional laws will always need to be dealt with.

Indeed, if you are reading this book a few years after it was written, you may be wondering what all the fuss was about. Some 'new' approach with a catchy name will have come through that will need to have a similar book written about it.

However, whatever does come through in the near-term future is unlikely to be as disruptive as cloud is currently being. Cloud is enabling an increasingly abstracted concept around how technology is provided. Whether this is just in how an organisation acquires, provisions and maintains hardware, or whether it is around how the overall business functionality is used and paid for, cloud computing is having major impacts. Combine this with a greater capability to flexibly adjust how resources are applied and it becomes difficult to see how another 'Next Great Thing' will come along that is as great a game changer as cloud has been and continues to be.

THE EVOLUTION OF THE CLOUD

There are no shortcuts in evolution.
Louis D. Brandeis (former Associate Justice of the US Supreme Court,
1856–1941) in a speech to the Boston Typothetae, 22 April 1904

Denser servers, storage and networks; hyperconverged systems; server-side storage; you name it – all of these will have some impact on how the cloud evolves. However, they are unlikely to change the general concept of a platform that enables an organisation to more easily tap into the right mix of resources for a specific workload.

Sure, advances in computing models (such as artificial or augmented intelligence (AI), virtual reality and machine learning) along with possible changes in how computers operate (such as through quantum computing) will all have some impact on the way that technology is provided, but the way that it is used at the business end will still probably maintain a strong relationship with what has been discussed in this book. Such changes are unlikely to fundamentally change how a cloud needs to be viewed at a high-level architectural and operational level. By ensuring that the right approach is taken to putting in place an all-embracing cloud strategy now, organisations can help to provide the business with a long-term platform that supports the business's needs far more closely than IT has managed to do so far.

What else could – and may need to – change? Workload portability is still limited. This is stalling moves to a full multi-cloud model, where workloads can be moved and run where it makes the most sense, at will. A move to more of a metadata-driven container model could help this. Further improvements in WAN data speeds could certainly extend the way that an overall hybrid platform works. This may be helped through the use of things like cloud-optimised packet sizes and priority of service. Increasing investments in general internet speeds and availability may also help, particularly in the accessibility of high-speed wireless through the introduction of 5G services. If more consumers move to wireless models, a degree of load could be taken away from the wired environment, as long as wireless backhaul is attuned directly to the wireless networks and not just used as part of the general internet.

At the business level, changes in global political positions and demographics could have major impacts on how private and public cloud service providers maintain and report data. However, this is something that any company looking at any move to cloud computing should be dealing with now through the implementation of a compliance-oriented architecture. The increasing need for organisations to operate at a global level across a broad group of suppliers and customers while still working within the constraints of more local legislation makes such an approach an imperative.

SUMMARY

What have we learned?

- Overall, cloud is likely to be a long-term approach to how IT platforms are provided.
- A good cloud strategy must allow for new technologies to be embraced as they come along.
- Areas outside IT's control (particularly around legal and political matters) must be allowed for in how the overall cloud platform is enacted.

What does this mean?

- IT must not go for highly specialised, 'of-the-moment' technologies, unless there are strong tactical reasons where measurable business benefits can be identified.
- Improvements in how cloud interconnects and generally in how the internet operates around intercloud traffic are required – and will be coming.
- An information-first approach to how the overall hybrid cloud platform is built will help to safeguard against political and legal changes in how data must be managed.

23 IN CONCLUSION

A conclusion is the place where you get tired of thinking.

Martin H. Fischer as quoted in Smith Dent (ed.), *Encore:*
A Continuing Anthology, March 1945

This book has attempted to cover a broad field. It started by examining the background as to how the world has moved from time-shared access to mainframe computers to shared-resource cloud models. It covered the various models through which cloud can be instantiated, and also covered how the various cloud service providers are presenting themselves in the market in an attempt to differentiate themselves from everyone else.

The book has also provided guidance on the various aspects of implementing, running and managing a cloud platform, whether a single private cloud, a hybrid private–public cloud or a hybrid multi-cloud platform. It has also presented ideas on how to 'sell' cloud into the business, along with discussions around what could still be problems in the short to medium term for the approach.

Additionally, the book has discussed various aspects of the future of cloud, from the need for data and information security through the maturation of containers to what could possibly be the next generation of a cloud platform.

What is clear is that cloud computing has caught the imaginations of user organisations, vendors, service providers and commentators alike. This wide embrace means that your organisation will increasingly be using cloud as at least a part of its technical platform going forward.

Doing so in an *ad hoc* manner is likely to cause negative business impact as projects have to be changed to meet with the needs of other projects, have to be stopped and re-planned due to changes in the market, or have to have technical 'glue' put in place to pull together multiple data and information stores. Key to getting this right is to sit down and review where your organisation is now and where it wants to go, and then carry out a gap analysis as to what IT already has available within its existing portfolio to provide the means of supporting the business's aims and what needs to be provided through other means.

Whether the new functionality is provided through building systems on existing hardware, through new hardware configured as a virtualised cluster or a private cloud, or via public cloud using an infrastructure-, platform- or software-as-a-service model, cloud is where the future lies. Get this right and your organisation will be fully enabled to meet the future.

Get it wrong, and your organisation could be destined to fail.

INDEX

2e2 Group 105
2FA 135, 140–1
5G services 174

abstraction 167–8
access
  mode of 137
  privileged user 136, 158, 163–4
  time-based 139
ACI 45
ACID 129
AD 102
Agile 51, 108
AI 173
Akana 95
Alibaba Cloud 48
Allied Control 72
Amazon 32–3
Amazon Web Services see AWS
Apache Mesos 47, 160, 168
Apache Software Foundation 42
API economy 94
Apigee 95
APIs 29, 129
  management systems 95
  need for 94–5
  open and standardised 152
  in performance management 96
  platform 60
application service providers (ASPs) 11
applications
  change in 151–5
  composite 9, 28–9, 98, 152–5, 156

definition 151
  monolithic 151–2
apps, steps IT must follow 63
Aqua Security 158
architecture of cloud 36–9
  and data latency 92–3
ARPANET 7
Ashton Tate 104
Atlassian Bamboo 107
audit 162–6
authenticator apps 140
authorisation 141
automation 169
AWS 33–5, 36, 42, 159
  functional architecture 36, 37
  systems downtime 90
  see also EC2 Container Service; Lambda; S3
AWS Direct Connect 130
AWS Glacier 76
Azure ExpressRoute 35
Azure Stack 38

banks 97–9, 104
baremetal cloud services 49
BASE 129
behavioural analysis 137, 138
Berners-Lee, Tim 7
biometrics 140–1
Bitium 141
Black, Benjamin 32
Black Duck Software 101
blackhats 134, 140
BLOb configuration 90
Bluemix 43
BOINC 9

Boomi 56
Borland 104
'born-in-the-cloud' companies 34
Box 59, 60, 101
BS ISO/IEC 17788:2014 19, 20
BS ISO/IEC 17789:2014 19
BT 130
bulk, pay as you go vs. 76
burst, commit vs. 76
business case for cloud 111–18
business flexibility, cost levels vs. 74–5
business issues, with highly dynamic cloud-based systems 97–9
BYOD 61–2

CA, performance tools 93
CA Automic 168
CaaS 19, 20
Canonical 48, 159
Canonical LXD 159
capability gap 85–6
CD 107–10
CenturyLink 48
Ceph 164
cessation of service 102–5
charging mechanisms 153–4
Chef 109, 168
Chronos 47, 160
CIF 73
CISC/RISC systems 4
Cisco 45
Citrix 42
Citrix XenMobile 62
client–server computing 6–7
CliQr 97

cloud aggregators 55–6

cloud brokers 54–5

cloud capability types 20

cloud computing, definition 16

cloud computing roles 20–1

Cloud Foundry 46, 94, 159

Cloud Industry Forum (CIF) 73

cloud-management systems 97

cloud models 16, 19, 54–7

Cloud Native Computing Foundation 94

cloud platforms

    alternative 41–53

    basic 32–40

    building the right 119–20

cloud tiering 70–3

CloudBees 168

CloudCentre 45

Cloud.com 41–2

CloudHarmony 90

Cloudian 164

Cloudify 160

Cloudmore 54

CloudPets 141

CloudStack 41–2

CloudSigma 48

Clover 50

cold images 30

collaboration 19, 59, 60, 103, 168

colocation facilities 65, 66, 69–70, 143

Colt 130

commercial in confidence information 137

commit, burst vs. 76

community cloud 18

Commvault 166

CompaaS 19, 20, 52

company failures 104–5

Compaq 104

comparative business process costings 116–17

compliance-oriented architecture 163, 174

composite applications 9, 28–9, 98, 152–5, 156

ComputeNext 54

contact centres 95, 117

container platforms 45–7

containers 108–9, 156–61

    future for 160–1

    metadata 160–1

security 157–9

    virtual machines vs. 156–60

continuous delivery (CD) 45, 94, 107–10

continuous deployment (CD) 107–10

continuous development (CD) 107–10

continuous integration (CI) 45, 107

converged systems 123–5

CoreOS 156, 159, 160

cost 26–8

    levels vs. business flexibility 74–5

    in TVP 112–14

cost models 75–6

    increasing complexity 76–7

cost tiering 77–9

CRC 164

CRM 60, 138, 151

cyclic redundancy check (CRC) 164

data centre tiering 70–3

data centres 70–3

data classification 136–8

data consistency 129

data encryption 137–8, 139

data flows 128–9

data latency 92–3, 130, 154

data leak/loss prevention (DLP) 138–9

data mirroring 31, 103, 105, 130

    extended 131

data protection 128, 138, 162, 163

data security 91–2, 133–44

    assuming breached 135–6

    guidelines 134

    principles 134–5

    in private data centres 133

    see also information security

data sovereignty 127–8

database issues 129

Datacenter Star Audit (DCSA) 71

DCOS (Datacenter Operating System) 47

DCSA 71

DDoS attacks 30, 142, 169

DEC 104

Dell EMC 120, 131

Dell Technologies 43, 46

    see also Boomi

deployment models 17–18

DevOps 51, 94, 97, 108–9, 155, 168

Diablo Technologies 120

Diego 159

Digital Marketplace 149

Digital Reality 66

digital rights management (DRM) 139

Digital Services framework 149

DigitalOcean 48

DIMMs 120

Direct Connect 35

disaster recovery 103

distance, and latency 130

DLP 138–9

Docker 156–7, 158, 159, 168

Docker Cloud 46

Docker Datacenter 46

Docker UCP 46

document-management systems 163–4

Documentum 166

DRM 139

Dropbox 59, 60, 101

Druva 166

DSaaS 19, 20

due diligence 154

EC2 Container Service (ECS) 159

edge security 142

effectiveness 86, 169

efficiency 86, 169

EFSS 60, 62

ElasticHosts 48

elasticity, resource 17, 146

Electric Cloud 97

ElectricFlow 97

email services 103

'embassy storage' 127

ENIAC 3

enterprise application integration 60

enterprise self-service 101–2

enterprise service buses 60

Equinix 42, 66, 70, 130

erasure code 131

ERP processes 60, 151

ETL 139

Eucalyptus 48
European Telecommunications Standards Institute 121
eventual consistency 129
Evidian 141
Excelero 120

FaaS *see* serverless computing
fabric networks 120
Facebook 39, 58, 72, 101, 141
facilities 65–6
failover systems 103
Federation Against Software Theft 99
Ferranti Mark 1 4
field programmable gate arrays (FPGAs) 87
file share and sync *see* FSS
Financial Conduct Authority 163
financial crash (2008) 152
fingerprints 140
flash storage 119
FlashGrid 131
Flexera 99
Flexiant 50, 161
Foster, Ian 9–10
FPGAs 87
FSS 59–60, 62
future
    further-out 173–4
    meeting needs of 28–9
Future Facilities 97

G-Cloud 135, 149
game theory 114–16
gap analysis 175
Gates, Bill 5
General Data Protection Regulation 128, 162, 163
GeoPlex 121
Global Mirror 131
GNU General Public License (GPL) 100–1
Google
    as public cloud provider 35
    see also Kubernetes
Google Checkout 103–4
Google Cloud Platform 33
    functional architecture 38
    Google Container Engine (GCE) 159
    systems downtime 90

Google Compute Cloud 90
Google My Tracks 103
Google Wallet 104
governance
    maintenance in hybrid cloud 105–6
    types of requirement 162–3
GPL 100–1
GPUs 87
graphical processing units (GPUs) 87
GRC 61, 63, 99, 140, 165
Green Grid 72
grid computing 9–10, 11, 21

hardware-assisted software defined 122
HashiCorp TerraForm 168
HCI systems 124–5
Heroku 49
heterogeneity 5, 125
HGST 164
high availability 31, 130–1
Hitachi Data Systems 164
home computers, first 4–5
horizontal governance requirements 163
hot images 30
HP 104
HP Helion 44
HP Public Cloud 44
HPE Helion 44
Huawei 125
Hudson 109
hybrid clouds 18, 66–7, 83
    disconnected hybrid platform 67
    governance maintenance 105–6
    integrated hybrid platform 67
    systems-management 96–7
'hybrid multi-cloud' 18
hyperconverged systems 123–5
hyperscale clouds 39–40
hypervisors 157

IaaS 16–17, 19, 20
    costs 28
    licensing 100
IAM 69, 142
IBM
    as cloud broker 54

as cloud provider 35, 43
and grid computing 9–10
mainframes 4, 84
PC 5
see also Global Mirror; Security Access Manager
idempotency 122–3
identity access management (IAM) 69, 142
Identity Suite 69
IDS 142
IETF 10, 141
immediate consistency 129
information classification 136–8
Information Commissioner's Office 163
information security 60, 135–6
    see also data security
Ingram Micro Cloud 56
InLoox 101
integration approaches 8
Intercloud 45
internal governance requirements 162
internet, birth 7
Interxion 66, 130
intrusion detection systems (IDS) 142
intrusion prevention systems (IPS) 142
iris scans 140
ISO 27001:2013 134
issues with cloud computing 89–106
    business 97–9
    cessation of service 102–5
    data security 91–2
    governance maintenance in hybrid cloud 105–6
    need for standards and APIs 94–5
    noisy neighbours 95–7, 169
    performance 92–3
    self-service mirage 101–2
    software and usage licensing 99–101
    system availability 89–91, 157–8

Jelastic 48
Jenkins 107, 109, 168
Joyent 49, 50

178

Keeper 141
'keeping the lights on' 27–8
Kubernetes 46–7, 94, 160, 168

Lambda 52
LAN 92, 93
latency 92–3, 130, 154
LDAP services 102
Leadership in Energy and Environmental Design (LEED) 72
LEED 72
legal disclosure 165–6
legal requirements 163
Lehman Brothers 104
Lenovo 125
license plus maintenance cost model 75
LinkedIn 59
load balancing, automated 169
loans 97–9
Lotus 104
LXC 157, 159
LXD 157, 159

M-Files 166
machine learning 173
mainframes 4, 83, 84–5
Managed and Operations (M&O) Stamp of Approval 71
ManageEngine Mobile Device Manager Plus 62
Marathon 47, 160
master data management 60
MDM 62
Medovich, Mark 121
Mesos 47, 160, 168
Mesosphere 47, 160
metadata 164, 165, 166
metadata containers 160–1
MIBs 167
microservices 28–9, 43, 155, 160–1
Microsoft
    as 'big three' software company 104
    Dublin data centre 128
    as public cloud provider 35
    see also OneDrive
Microsoft Activity Directory (AD) 102

Microsoft Azure 33, 36, 47, 135
    Azure Container Services (ACS) 159
    BLOb Store 164
    Express Route 130
    functional architecture 36, 37
    systems downtime 90
Microsoft Office 164
    Word document 165
MicroVM 43
midicomputers 4
Minio 164
mixed clouds 67, 83–4
mobile device management (MDM) 62
Morse 105
MS-DOS 6
Mulesoft 95
multi-tenancy 20
MVMC 157

NaaS 19, 20
NAS devices 85, 105
Netflix 34
network sniffers 61
network usage cost model 75
networks, fabric 120
NeuVector 158
NFV 121
Nimbus 49
Nirvanix 104–5
NIST 15–16
Nlyte 97
'noisy neighbours' 95–7, 169
non-repudiation technologies 99
Northern Rock 104
NVDIMMs 120
NVMe M.2 120

OASIS 10, 142
OAuth 141
object-based storage 164–6
OCP 39–40, 58
offload engines 87
on-demand self-service 17
on-premises model 16–17
OnApp 50
one-time code generators 140
OneDrive 59
online retail 95

Open Compute Project (OCP) 39–40, 58
Open Networking Foundation (ONF) 121
Open Service Broker API 94
Open Source Initiative 101
Open Vault storage 40
OpenFlow 121
OpenID 142
OpenNebula 48
OpenQRM 50
OpenStack 42
    functional architecture 38–9
OpenShift 47, 50, 94
OpenText 166
optimistic replication 129
Oracle 44–5, 151
Oracle Cloud 44–5
Oracle eBusiness Suite 151
orchestration systems 154
organisational value chain 68–9
over-arching system, choosing 168

PaaS 16–17, 19, 20
    costs 28
    licensing 100
passwords
    challenge-and-response 140
    shared 136, 140
pay as you go, bulk vs. 76
payment card regulations 138
payment protection insurance (PPI) 97
PayPal 95
PC, rise of 5–6
PCI-DSS 138–9
PCIe cards 120
per physical core cost model 75–6
per virtual core cost model 75–6
performance 92–3
PernixData 120
physical security 143
PID 133, 134, 138–9
Pinkham, Chris 32–3
Pivotal 46
platform security 135–6
point tools 167
power used cost model 75
PPI 97

pricing break points 76
private clouds 17
  averaging out workloads 146–7
  costs 26, 28
  offerings 41–5
  where based 65–6
privileged user access 136, 158, 163–4
processes 85–7
  commodity 86, 87
  differentiated 86–7
  records of 98
  unique 87
proof-of-content cloud email services 99
proxy namespace 158–9
public clouds 18
  averaging out workloads 146, 147–8
  costs 26, 28
  offerings 41–5
public functions, directories of 153–4
public information 136–7
public sector 9, 25, 148–9
PUE 72–3
Puppet 109, 168

quality of service (QoS) 92
quantum computing 173

Rackspace 35, 49, 50
RAID 130–1
recovery point objective (RPO) 131
recovery time objective (RTO) 131
Red Hat 47
Redfish 122
redundancy 103
relying parties 142
resource pooling 17, 146–7
resources
  in TVP 112
  utilisation 23–5, 66
ReSTful 129
return on investment (RoI) 111, 116–17
RightScale 97
risk, in TVP 112–14
rkt 156
RoI 111, 116–17

roll-back of code 168
root-cause analysis (RCA) 168, 169
RPO 131
RSA Secure-ID 140
RTO 131

S3 164
SaaS 16–17, 20
  costs 28
  licensing 100
  types 58–64
SageOne 58
SailPoint 69
Salesforce.com 58
salespeople 138
SALM 99–100, 101, 102
SAM 99–100
SAML 142
SANs 103
SAP 151
SAP Concur 58
scale-up systems 84–5
Scaleway 49
scaling for massive use 148–9
Scality 164
Scalr 97
scope, in TVP 112
SDC environment 122
SDDC 122
SDN 121–2
SDS 120, 124
secret information 137
security
  container 157–9
  data see data security
  edge 142
  information 60, 135–6
  perception of 138
  physical 143
  platform 135–6
  token-based 141
Security Access Manager 69
self-remediation 169
self-service 101–2
  customer 117
  on-demand 17
serverless computing 19, 52, 77, 155
service catalogues 154

service level agreements (SLAs) 87, 96
service-oriented architecture (SOA) 9, 11, 84, 152
service-provision characteristics 16–17
ServiceNow 51, 58
shadow IT 60, 61–3
Simpana 166
single sign-on (SSO) 140–2
Skyhigh Networks 54
SLAs 87, 96
Small Scale Experimental Machine 1 3
SNIA 122
SNMP 167
Snow Software 99
SOA 9, 11, 84, 152
social networking sites 58–9
Softlayer 35, 43
software asset lifecycle management (SALM) 99–100, 101, 102
software asset management (SAM) 99–100
software licensing issues 99–101
software management systems 61
software-defined data centre (SDDC) 122
software-defined model 121–2, 124
SSO 140–2
standardisation 167–8
standards
  around cloud computing 19
  need for 94–5
  role 10–11
storage
  changes in 119–20
  flash 119
  server-side 120
  Tier 1 119
  tiered 87, 119–20
storage area networks (SANs) 103
storage usage cost model 75
stretched clustering 131
Swift 42
SwiftStack 164
Swordfish 122
Symbolic IO 120

system containerisation 158–9

systems availability 27, 28, 69, 89–91, 157–8, 169

tape 120

TCO 111, 116–17

technical contracts, need for 152–5

Tectonic 160

Telecommunications Industry Association (TIA) 71

'three-second rule' 25

Tibco Mashery 95

tiered storage 87, 119–20

time, in TVP 112

time-based access 139

time to capability 63

time to market 63

token-based security 141

tools 167–70

total cost of ownership (TCO) 111, 116–17

total value proposition (TVP) 111–17

transaction throughput cost model 75

Transversal 95

TVP 111–17

two-factor authorisation (2FA) 135, 140–1

Ubuntu 48

Unix-based systems 83

Uptime Institute 71

US Privacy Shield 162

usage licensing issues 99–101

usage tiering 77–9

username–password pair vaults 141

usernames, shared 136

value, in TVP 112–14

value chain
organisational 68–9
simple 68

variable workload model 24

Vasco DIGIPASS 140

vCloud Air 42

vertical governance requirements 163

Vertiv Trellis 97

Virtual Instruments 93

virtual machines, containers vs. 156–60

virtual reality 173

virtualisation 4, 8–9, 25, 66, 108
lure of 145–6

Virtuozzo 158

Virtus 70

Virtustream 43

VMFoundry 121

vMSC 131

VMServer 121

VMware 42, 46

VMware Airwatch 62

VMware Cloud 42

voice recognition 140–1

VSAN Stretched Cluster HCI system 131

Vuzion 56

walled garden, badly protected 138–9

WAN 92–3, 174

warm images 30

web computing 7–8

WebSprocket 121

WIMP system 5

wireless models 174

workload migrations, planning for 84–5

workload portability 29–30, 174

World Wide Web Consortium (W3C) 7

XACML 142

Xero 101

XML 167

ZettaGrid 49